Guide to

Colorado
State Wildlife Areas

Text and photography by Dennis McKinney

WESTCLIFFE PUBLISHERS

www.westcliffepublishers.com

International Standard Book Number: 1-56579-425-7

Text and photography copyright: Dennis McKinney, 2001. All rights reserved.

Editor: Margaret J. Tremper
Designer: Carol Pando
Production Manager: Craig Keyzer

Published by:
Westcliffe Publishers, Inc.
P.O. Box 1261
Englewood, CO 80150
www.westcliffepublishers.com

Printed in Hong Kong through World Print, Ltd.

Library of Congress Cataloging-in-Publication Data:

McKinney, Dennis, 1947-
    Guide to Colorado state wildlife areas / by Dennis McKinney.
        p. cm.
    Includes index.
    ISBN 1-56579-425-7
    1. Wildlife management areas--Colorado--Guidebooks. 2. Colorado--Guidebooks. I.
Title.

SK375 .M35 2001
333.78'2'09788--dc21

                                                                2001026738

*For more information about other fine books and calendars from Westcliffe Publishers,
please contact your local bookstore, call us at 1-800-523-3692, write for our free
color catalog, or visit us on the Web at* **www.westcliffepublishers.com**.

Please Note: Risk is always a factor in backcountry and high-mountain travel. Many of the
activities described in this book can be dangerous, especially when weather is adverse or
unpredictable, and when unforeseen events or conditions create a hazardous situation. The
author has done his best to provide the reader with accurate information about backcountry
travel, as well as to point out some of its potential hazards. It is the responsibility of the
users of this guide to learn the necessary skills for safe backcountry travel, and to exercise
caution in potentially hazardous areas, especially on glaciers and avalanche-prone terrain.
The author and publisher disclaim any liability for injury or other damage caused by
backcountry traveling or performing any other activity described in this book.

Cover Photo: North Platte River running through Verner SWA
Upper Inset: Trophy-sized bighorn sheep, Terrace Reservoir SWA
Lower Inset: Trophy-sized rainbow trout

Previous Page: Woods Lake SWA with Lizard Head Wilderness in the distance

Acknowledgments

For their help—whether in assistance with facts and figures, generous encouragement, wise counsel, or in patience—I am grateful to friends, biologists, wildlife technicians, fellow sportsmen and sportswomen, and the publisher. I am especially grateful to Patricia Trahey, editor of *Colorado Outdoors*, for her insight into the project and for her unwavering support. Thanks also to all of the Division of Wildlife personnel, for without their help this book would not have been possible.

I owe special thanks to my wife, Jan, for her organizational skills, attention to detail, sense of humor, and her willingness to live on the road with me and a hunting dog for the better part of a year.

The author prepares to release a trophy-class Snake River cutthroat trout at Spinney Mountain Reservoir SWA.

Table of Contents

Opposite: *Dolores River and Lone Dome SWA*

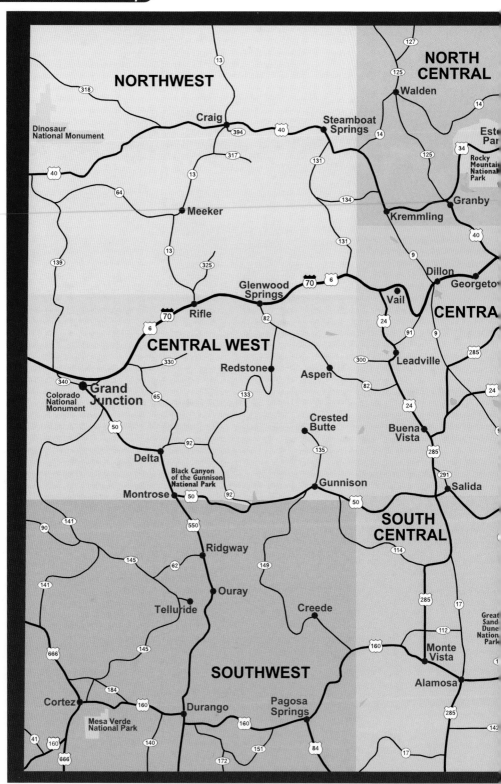

Foreword

Colorado hunters, anglers, hikers, and wildlife watchers owe Dennis McKinney a huge debt of gratitude for exploring and photographing the state's wildlife areas and writing this guidebook. In an age when development is ravaging our wildlands and the human population seems to be spiraling out of control, space for fish and wildlife comes at a premium. And that space is all the more valuable when it provides public access. Over the years, the Colorado Division of Wildlife has done a superb job of preserving open-space treasures through deeds, leases, and easements. But for more than a century the agency has been hiding its light under a bushel. Instead of showcasing the State Wildlife Areas that sportsmen and women paid for when they bought hunting and fishing licenses, it allowed all but a few of the most popular areas to fade into obscure, almost mysterious, hideaways.

The properties needed a private investigator, and at last they have found one who is precisely suited for the job. This is the first guide ever to the state's 240-plus wildlife areas, and I don't doubt that my friend and outdoor writing colleague, Dennis McKinney, is the first person to have visited all but a few of them. Until now, the properties were mentioned only in a brief directory tucked away in the fishing regulation booklet. Many of the directions in that booklet are dead wrong. Some wildlife areas aren't even included in the little directory.

For half a year, Dennis, his wife, Jan, and their golden retriever, Curley, slept in a camper and traveled hundreds of miles unraveling the mysteries of our State Wildlife Areas. Everyone who has ever hankered to set foot on wild lands replete with fish and wildlife will benefit from their exhaustive pilgrimage and Dennis's talented labors to compile so much information. Thanks to his fine reporting, writing, and photography, we can now find our way to these state wildlife areas, enjoy their natural bounty and solitude, and see for ourselves that our wildlife is in good hands on good lands.

—Ed Dentry
Rocky Mountain News

Terrace Reservoir SWA, the "prettiest dead body of water in Colorado"

Preface

The Bodo State Wildlife Area south of Durango, Colorado, provides habitat for big- and small-game species. The property includes a large basinlike area among the features on its 7,500-plus acres. A while back, the Colorado Division of Wildlife (DOW) received a request from a local resident to use that property. It seems that the citizen wanted to erect big, big signs in that basin in hopes that they would be seen by passing UFOs.

The DOW receives a litany of requests from the public to use State Wildlife Areas (SWAs) every year. The Coller SWA provided the setting for "rubber ducky" races for years. The makers of the Billy Crystal movie *City Slickers* tried to get access to Perins Peak SWA, also near Durango, to film there in the middle of the state's hunting seasons. Then there was the proposal to build a five-star restaurant on top of Smelter Mountain in Bodo SWA. A federal agency proposed to build a tower at one SWA, but couldn't tell the state what the tower would be used for. And so on.

Most of the public requests to use SWAs are legitimate and more mainstream than the examples cited above, but many are inconsistent with the state's original intent in purchasing these properties.

Originally, Colorado's State Wildlife Areas were acquired to conserve extraordinary examples of wildlife and wildlife habitat. Like people, wildlife need food, water, and shelter to survive. And that's what the state meant to provide when it created SWAs. In a sense, they were an original attempt to protect habitat from human growth.

Unlike U.S. Forest Service and other public properties, SWAs were not purchased to provide multiple recreational uses. In fact, as late as the 1970s, DOW managers were reluctant to publicize the locations of state properties even among hunters and anglers, whose license fees paid for both the purchase and maintenance of those properties. The goal was conservation, not recreation.

All that has changed over time. Today, Colorado's wildlife managers must try to balance wildlife areas' role in protecting habitat against demands from hundreds of thousands of different users annually.

Each property itself is unique, and the Colorado Wildlife Commission and the DOW annually regulate the uses of those individual properties. When wildlife managers conclude that a proposed use is incompatible with an SWA's wildlife and wildlife recreation purposes, they need to be able to deny or regulate that usage.

The same public that demands use of SWAs can make a difference, however. Hunters, anglers, or citizens struck with the natural beauty of a wildlife area need to remember that Colorado's state wildlife areas were acquired primarily to protect the places that wild things need to live. Other uses of those areas are secondary.

The conservationist Aldo Leopold may have offered users the best advice: "We abuse land because we regard it as a commodity belonging to us. When we see land as community to which we belong, we may begin to use it with love and respect. There is no other way for land to survive the impact of mechanized man...."

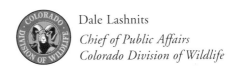

Dale Lashnits
Chief of Public Affairs
Colorado Division of Wildlife

Introduction

This book is written from a sportsman's point of view. I have tried to write what I believe is a comprehensive guide to hunting, fishing, and camping in Colorado's 241 State Wildlife Areas (SWAs). I have included a few fishing tips and some tidbits about watchable wildlife. I hope this guide will give you an idea of what to expect at each of the sites. I have taken great care not to embellish, glorify, or unjustly degrade any of them. What you read is what I found.

In research, I traveled to all but five of the locations and interviewed dozens of people along the way. There were aquatic biologists, terrestrial biologists, habitat biologists, district wildlife managers, area wildlife managers, wildlife technicians, and other Division of Wildlife (DOW) personnel. And there were scores of anglers and hunters like you. I hunted and fished as many of the SWAs as time allowed and write from personal experience whenever possible. Statistics and numbers quoted in this guide come from Colorado DOW publications and from its employees working with each wildlife area. Directions, road names, and the names of the SWAs are correct and come from personal observation and the DOW.

SWAs come under the control of the DOW through fee title ownership, wildlife easements, and short- and long-term leases. The money comes from the sale of hunting and fishing licenses, the Colorado Lottery (Great Outdoors Colorado), and federal taxes on the sale of hunting and fishing equipment. Our money buys the wildlife areas, and the DOW protects them. Although it is our money that buys and maintains the SWAs, the DOW's primary objective is protecting habitat for wildlife.

Therefore, many of the areas are closed to public access during critical times of the year. Wetlands are closed in spring for nesting waterfowl, and mountain pastures are closed for wintering herds of elk and deer. Other properties may be closed year-round to protect struggling populations of endangered species. In short, the DOW works hard for the good of wildlife, and we get to enjoy the fruits of their labors. Through bold, meaningful acquisitions of land, habitat is preserved for wildlife, and hunting and fishing opportunities are created for the public.

Aside from the obvious hope of making a few bucks, I had another selfish reason for writing this guide. I knew that each of the SWAs was acquired for a specific purpose, and I wanted to know how I could use that purpose to my advantage. I suspected that treasures in trout fishing and duck hunting opportunities were hiding within the Wildlife Property Directory's sterile descriptions of the properties. (The directory is part of "2001 [current year] Colorado Fishing Season Information & Wildlife Property Directory," a pamphlet distributed by DOW.) I knew from personal experience that "cold-water stream" in the directory could mean either the best trout fishing in the state, or the worst. My suspicions were confirmed. I found treasures in out-of-the-way places where sportsmen and women can enjoy quality hunting, fishing, and primitive camping in relative solitude on public lands.

I admit that I was tempted to leave a few special wildlife areas out of the book, especially those small streams that have great fishing. I was torn between good and evil, and felt like the old cartoon character, tormented by a devil whispering into one ear and an angel whispering into the other. In the end, I took the higher ground and put everything into the book. Now I put my faith in you to respect these special places.

—Dennis McKinney

Opposite: Horse corrals at Service Creek SWA

Northwest Colorado

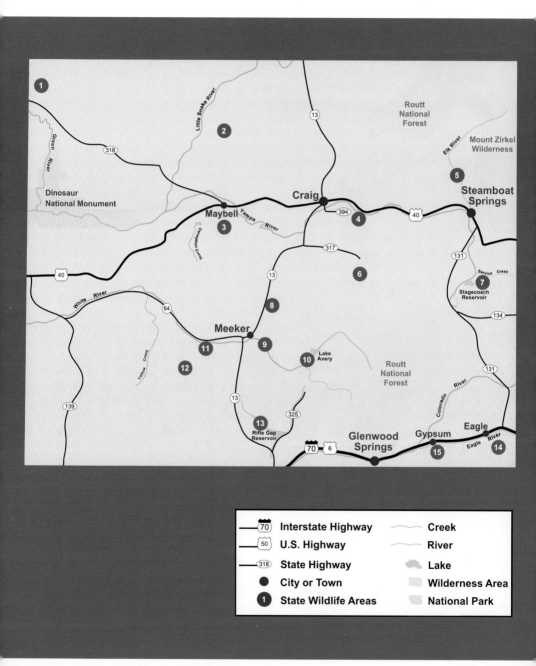

Legend:

- Interstate Highway
- U.S. Highway
- State Highway
- City or Town
- State Wildlife Areas
- Creek
- River
- Lake
- Wilderness Area
- National Park

The lands north of Rifle and west of Steamboat Springs are best known for big-game hunting. Brown's Park is well-known for trophy elk hunting, but the region also has many opportunities for hunting small game such as blue grouse and sage grouse. Some of the locations, such as **Christina SWA** on the Elk River and **Indian Run SWA** south of Craig, play important roles in providing access points to lands in the National Forest. Other wildlife areas such as **Jensen**, **Oak Ridge**, and **Piceance** offer quality hunting within their own boundaries.

Fishing in the northwest region in highlighted by outstanding pike fishing on the Yampa River. **Yampa River SWA** provides put-in and take-out access point for boaters. Trout fishing in the region is found mainly on the White River.

Wildlife Areas in Northwest Colorado

1. Brown's Park SWA

Primary Use: Big-game hunting

Location: Moffat County, north of the Green River

Size: 2,000 acres total

Elevation : 6,000–8,700 feet

Division of Wildlife: Area office in Meeker, 970-878-4493

Directions: **Beaver Creek Unit:** From Maybell, go 59 miles northwest on Highway 318. The property is located just north and west of the Brown's Park National Refuge Headquarters.

Wiggins Unit: From Maybell, go 41 miles northwest on Highway 318 to County Road 10, then 17 miles north (right) to County Road 72, and then 15 miles west (left) to the unit. Continue straight on the dirt road when County Road 72 makes a sharp right turn.

Cold Spring Mountain Unit: From Maybell, go 41 miles northwest on Highway 318 to County Road 10, then 17 miles north (right) to County Road 72, and then 8 miles west (left) to a dirt road that forks to the left and heads south (left) up the ridge.

In earlier times, this lonely country north of the Green River in the northwestern corner of Colorado served as wintering grounds for bands of Ute and Shoshone Indians, and later as a haven for the likes of outlaw Butch Cassidy and outlaw/bounty hunter Tom Horn.

Today, this country serves as wintering grounds for herds of elk and deer, and as a haven for many species of wildlife. The climate is semiarid, with an annual rainfall of less than 10 inches. The terrain is gentle, with rolling mountains carved by dozens of seasonal creeks, washes, and sage-filled basins. The rounded mountains are capped with aspen and pine.

Brown's Park SWA is composed of three separate tracts of land, all lying in the hills north of the Brown's Park National Wildlife Refuge.

Beaver Creek Unit adjoins the northwest corner of Brown's Park National Wildlife Refuge, less than a mile from the Utah border. The creek flows south through the wildlife area to its confluence with the Green River. The habitat is mostly riparian, with cottonwood trees, wet meadows, marshes, and beaver ponds. A hiking trail from the parking area provides fishing and hunting access to the creek and the canyon above.

Wiggins Unit sits on a hillside at the edge of a broad basin in the upper Beaver Creek watershed. This property is located only a mile from both the Wyoming and Utah state lines.

Cold Spring Mountain Unit is a long strip of land stretching across the top of Cold Spring Mountain. The adjacent Cold Spring Mountain State Trust lands offer more than 26,000 additional acres of hunting access.

Fishing

Beaver Creek is a small stream with a string of beaver ponds that have good fishing for brook trout. The upper portion of the stream harbors a near-pure strain of native Colorado River cutthroat trout. All cutthroat trout must be returned to the water immediately.

Hunting

Big-game hunting in this area is managed for a quality hunting experience, and the area is legendary for its trophy-sized elk and deer. All big-game hunting is by limited-license only. It takes several preference points to draw a license, especially in Unit 201. Traditionally, only bull elk licenses are issued for the muzzle-loader and rifle seasons. This area is in Game Management Units 1, 2, and 201.

Other hunting opportunities at the SWA include sage grouse, antelope, waterfowl, and small game. Waterfowl hunting on the Green River in Brown's Park National Wildlife Refuge can be exceptional.

Watchable Wildlife

Same as hunting

Camping and Facilities

Primitive camping is permitted except at the Beaver Creek Unit. There are no facilities.

General Restrictions

See Hunting and Fishing.

2. Little Snake SWA

Primary Use:	Deer and antelope hunting
Location:	Moffat County, 17 miles north of Maybell
Size:	5,000 acres
Elevation :	6,000 feet
Division of Wildlife:	Area office in Meeker, 970-878-4493
Directions:	From Maybell, go 17 miles north on County Road 19 to the DOW sign at the south entrance to the property.

The topography of the Little Snake watershed north of Maybell is generally flat and featureless, yet there is something strangely exhilarating in the vastness of the open landscape. The ecosystem is semiarid desert marked by sagebrush, rabbitbrush, dry gulches, washes, and seasonal creeks. The annual precipitation averages about 10 inches.

Fishing

None

Hunting

This area is in Game Management Unit 3.

Watchable Wildlife

Golden eagles

Camping and Facilities

Camping is prohibited except in self-contained units, and prohibited by all methods for three days before the beginning of regular big-game seasons, through three days after the end of the seasons.

General Restrictions

Discharging firearms or bows is prohibited December 1–June 30.

3. Bitter Brush SWA

Primary Use:	Big-game hunting
Location:	Moffat County, 6 miles south of Maybell
Size:	5,700 acres
Elevation :	6,000 feet
Division of Wildlife:	Area office in Meeker, 970-878-4493
Directions:	From Craig, go 27 miles west on U.S. 40 to County Road 57, then 1 mile south (left) to the first parking area.

Bitter Brush was a Ranching for Wildlife property until purchased by the DOW in 1999. It was acquired to protect critical elk wintering range and to provide public hunting opportunities. The landscape is open rolling hills blanketed in prairie grasses and sagebrush. Deception Creek flows north through the property on its way to the Yampa River.

Fishing

None

Hunting

Elk, deer, and antelope are the attraction here. This area is in Game Management Unit 11.

Watchable Wildlife

Same as hunting

Camping and Facilities

Overnight camping is prohibited and there are no facilities in the SWA. Excellent camping and facilities are found only 6 miles away in the hunter-friendly town of Maybell. The town square is used as a campground for hunters. It has restrooms, showers, and drinking water.

General Restrictions

1. Public access is prohibited January 15–April 30 to protect wintering game.
2. Vehicle access into the property is limited to County Roads 59 and 143.

4. Yampa River SWA

Primary Use:	Northern pike fishing and waterfowl hunting
Location:	Routt County, Yampa River, 7 miles east of Craig
Size:	860 acres
Elevation :	6,200 feet
Division of Wildlife:	Area office in Steamboat Springs, 970-870-2197
Directions:	From Craig, go 7 miles east on U.S. 40 to the access road over the railroad tracks, and then 1 mile south (right) to the parking area. Another access is located 1 mile east on U.S. 40. Both access roads are marked by DOW signs.

Public access is hard to come by on the Yampa River. Land along the river is jealously guarded by private landowners. However, this wildlife area opens up a stretch of the river and its lush bottomlands and riparian habitat for public hunting, fishing, and wildlife viewing.

Fishing

Trout fishing on the Yampa River is rated as fair, but northern pike fishing is fantastic. The SWA is a handy place for launching a drift boat and floating to Craig. This 10-mile stretch of water is loaded with weedy backwater sloughs and eddies where pike lie in ambush.

Note: In an effort to protect endangered native fish in the Yampa River, the DOW is currently removing pike from the river and relocating them to **Rio Blanco Lake SWA** (see p. 27).

Hunting

Waterfowl hunting can be outstanding in the Yampa Valley. At the SWA, wet meadows, flooded fields, and marshes in the river bottom attract good numbers of local and migrating ducks.

Watchable Wildlife

Bald eagles winter in the Yampa Valley. Other watchable wildlife includes great blue herons, sandhill cranes, and a variety of ducks.

Camping and Facilities

None

General Restrictions

Fires are prohibited.

5. Christina SWA

Primary Use:	Access to Routt National Forest and Mount Zirkel Wilderness
Location:	Routt County, Elk River, 7 miles north of Steamboat Springs
Size:	1½ miles of fishing access on the Elk River
Elevation :	7,000 feet
Division of Wildlife:	Area office in Steamboat Springs, 970-870-2197
Directions:	From Steamboat Springs, go 7 miles north on County Road 129 (Elk River Road) to the property.

Without this strategically located little wildlife area on the Elk River, there would be no place to park for the Mad Creek Trail that leads into the Routt National Forest and the Mount Zirkel Wilderness.

Fishing

There is marginal trout fishing on this stretch of the Elk River.

Hunting

Hunting is prohibited.

Watchable Wildlife

Ouzels (dippers) and deer

Camping and Facilities

Overnight camping is prohibited, except during big-game hunting seasons from September 1 to December 31. There are no facilities.

6. Indian Run SWA

Primary Use:	Access to Routt National Forest
Location:	Routt County, 20 miles south of Craig
Size:	2,000 acres
Elevation :	6,700–7,500 feet
Division of Wildlife:	Area office in Steamboat Springs, 970-870-2197
Directions:	From Craig, go 1 mile west on U.S. 40 to Highway 13, then 10 miles south (left) to Hamilton, then 12 miles east (left) on Highway 317 to County Road 67, and then 6 miles south (right) to the property.

This wildlife area provides an access point and parking area for big-game hunters headed into the Beaver Flat Tops region of Routt National Forest. It is popular with outfitters and out-of-state hunters, and receives a considerable amount of use during big-game hunting seasons. Elk and deer winter in the valley just east of the parking area.

Fishing

Beaver and Indian Run Creeks have marginal fishing for small trout.

Hunting

Elk, deer, black bear, and small-game hunting are available in the area. This is in Game Management Unit 12.

Watchable Wildlife

Same as hunting

Camping and Facilities

Primitive camping and vault toilets are available at the parking area.

7. Service Creek SWA

Primary Use:	Trout fishing
Location:	Routt County, Yampa River, 12 miles south of Steamboat Springs
Size:	300 acres
Elevation :	7,000 feet
Division of Wildlife:	Area office in Steamboat Springs, 970-870-2197
Directions:	From Steamboat Springs, go 3 miles south on U.S. 40 to Highway 131, then 3½ miles west and south to County Road 18, and then 7 miles south (left), to the property.

Service is key at this wildlife area conveniently located at the confluence of Service Creek and the Yampa River, and adjacent to the National Forest. The property has access to the river for fishermen, and parking for Forest Trail 1105, which heads southeast into Routt National Forest. It receives heavy use year-round, as Steamboat Springs creeps closer and development continues to fill the Yampa Valley.

Fishing

Trout fishing is rated fair on the Yampa River below Stagecoach Reservoir, and marginal on Service Creek. Fishing on the Yampa in the SWA is restricted to artificial flies and lures and there is a two trout limit. Upstream of the SWA, fishing on the Yampa River is restricted to catch and release.

Hunting

Hunting for deer, elk, and small game is allowed on the property, but success is questionable because of heavy use from hikers and fishermen.

Watchable Wildlife

Same as hunting

Camping and Facilities

Camping is prohibited except three days before the beginning of regular big-game seasons through three days after the end of the seasons. Facilities include a toilet and horse corrals.

General Restrictions

See Fishing.

8. Jensen SWA

Primary Use:	Big-game hunting
Location:	Rio Blanco County, 10 miles north of Meeker
Size:	6,000 acres
Elevation :	7,500–8,200 feet
Division of Wildlife:	Area office in Meeker, 970-878-4493
Directions:	From Meeker, go 9 miles north on Highway 13 to County Road 30 and then east (right) into the property. The entrance is well-marked by signs and an information kiosk.

Helen Jensen's family homesteaded this property in the 1800s and ran cattle and sheep here until the DOW purchased it in 1982. Historically, this area is critical traditional winter range and calving and fawning grounds for elk and deer. The ecosystem here is ideal for big game, small game, and nongame species. Vegetation is a mixture of dense oak brush, mountain mahogany, and other deciduous shrubs interspersed with ponderosa pines, aspen, and grass-filled open meadows.

Fishing

None

Hunting

The region in general, and this property in particular, is highly rated among deer and elk hunters. The wildlife area lies within the range of the 30,000 head of elk in the White River herd. Many deer also winter here. Hunting far from the roads dramatically improves the chance for success, especially during the later seasons. This is in Game Management Unit 12.

Watchable Wildlife

Same as hunting

Camping and Facilities

Camping is available at three designated areas located on County Road 30, which runs through the southern half of the property. There are horse corrals but no other facilities.

General Restrictions

1. Public access is prohibited December 1–July 15.
2. Motorized traffic is restricted to County Road 30.

9. Meeker Pasture SWA

From Meeker, go 2 miles northeast on Highway 13 to County Road 8, and then 8 miles east (right) to the property. Park in the Nelson-Prather parking area.

This small wildlife area straddling the White River 10 miles east of Meeker opens up a ¼-mile stretch of the river for fishing and duck hunting. Fishing is good on the White River for trout, but better for mountain whitefish. There is no camping or facilities.

10. Oak Ridge SWA

Primary Use:	Big-game hunting and trout fishing
Location:	Rio Blanco County, 20 miles southeast of Meeker
Size:	Four units totaling 9,000 acres
Elevation :	6,000–7,500 feet
Division of Wildlife:	Area office in Meeker, 970-878-4493
Directions:	**Oak Ridge Unit:** From Meeker, go 6.3 miles east on County Road 8 and look for the DOW sign on the left. A dirt road leads into the western end of the property.
	Lake Avery Unit: From Meeker, go 20 miles east on County Road 8 to an unmarked, but obvious, gravel road on the left.
	Belaire Unit: From Meeker, go 21 miles east on County Road 8 to County Road 17 at Buford, and then 1 mile south (right) to the access road on the right. The access road is on the north side of the South Fork of the White River.
	Sleepy Cat Ponds Unit: From Meeker, go 16 miles east on County Road 8 to the parking area on the right by the river.
	Sleepy Cat Fishing Easement: Located at Sleepy Cat Guest Ranch directly upstream from the Sleepy Cat Ponds Unit.

This expansive wildlife area provides a wealth of fishing and hunting opportunities. Trout fishing is good at Lake Avery and on the White River. And there is excellent hunting for deer and elk on Oak Ridge, the long ridge dividing the White River and Beaver Creek drainages. Habitat on the ridge is a blend of grasses, oak brush, and piñon-juniper.

Fishing

Lake Avery has a nice camping area, shaded picnic spots, toilets, and a boat ramp. The lake has marginal fishing for stocked trout. However, the White River has good fishing year-round for brown and cutthroat trout, and mountain whitefish.

Hunting

This wildlife area is known for its exceptional deer and elk hunting. The best hunting usually occurs during later seasons when the elk and deer move down from higher elevations. Good hunting opportunities also exist for black bear, blue grouse, and band-tailed pigeon. Hunting is prohibited, except by archery, south of County Road 8, west of County Road 17, and north and east of County Road 10.

Watchable Wildlife

Same as hunting

Camping and Facilities

Camping is prohibited except in designated areas. Toilets are located at the Lake Avery, Sleepy Cat, and Belaire Units.

General Restrictions

1. Public access is prohibited on Sleepy Cat Ponds Unit and Sleepy Cat Fishing Easement, except for fishing.
2. Public access is prohibited December 1–July 15 at the Oak Ridge Unit.

Mountain whitefish are native to the White River.

11. Rio Blanco Lake SWA

To access this property from Meeker, go 20 miles west on Highway 64 to the reservoir. Located 20 miles west of Meeker on the White River, Rio Blanco is a 383-acre lake at 6,000 feet that is managed as a warm-water fishery. Largemouth and smallmouth bass less than 15 inches must be released. Only one northern pike longer than 34 inches may be kept per day. The lake is noted for its trophy-sized northern pike. Waterfowl hunting is allowed. Camping is allowed in designated areas, and facilities include toilets and a boat ramp.

12. Piceance SWA

Primary Use:	Big-game hunting
Location:	Rio Blanco County, 20–40 miles southwest of Meeker
Size:	Undetermined, but large
Elevation :	6,200–7,500 feet
Division of Wildlife:	Area office in Meeker, 970-878-4493
Directions:	**Little Hills Unit:** From Meeker, go 20 miles west on Highway 64 to County Road 5 (Piceance Creek Road), then 7 miles south (left) to the Dry Fork turnoff, and then 3 miles east (left) to the site.

Piceance Creek/Yellow Creek Unit: From Meeker, go 20 miles west on Highway 64 to County Road 5 (Piceance Creek Road), then 6 miles south (left) to County Road 20 at the Piceance Creek Unit, and then 5 miles west (right) to Yellow Creek Unit.

Square S Summer Range Unit: From County Road 5, go 20 miles west on County Road 26 to the property.

The remaining small parcels of land are located west of County Road 5 in **Yellow Creek** (Road 20), **Duck Creek** (Road 20), **Box Elder Gulch** (Road 24), and **Stake Springs Draw** (Road 91).

Maps are available at the DOW office located at the intersection of Highways 64 and 13 in Meeker.

This wildlife area consists of a complicated array of small and large parcels of land scattered like bomb fragments across the beguiling landscape of the Piceance Plateau. The main body of land is the Little Hills Experimental Station Tract, located just south of the White River. The station is a center for mule deer research. The next largest tract is the Square S Ranch Summer Range Tract, 20 miles southwest, near Brush Mountain. Scattered in between are eight smaller parcels of land lying along various creeks and gulches.

The landscape is raked with dozens of creeks, gulches, and washes that run from the top of the plateau down to Piceance Creek. The ridges between the creeks are covered in piñon, sage, and rabbitbrush, and the basins are awash in tall sage. Access into this country is via dirt roads that turn to gumbo when wet, making four-wheel-drive vehicles a necessity.

Fishing

None

Hunting

Big-game and blue grouse hunting is best at the Square S Summer Range Unit. Big-game hunting is generally slow at the lower units until heavy snows or hunting pressure pushes the animals out of the high country. Yellow Creek and Duck Creek have surprisingly good duck hunting. Other species found on the plateau include sage grouse, mountain lion, and rabbit.

Watchable Wildlife

Same as hunting

Camping and Facilities

Primitive campsites can be found on the properties and on the surrounding BLM lands. There are no facilities in the remote units.

General Restrictions

DOW employees reside in the houses at Little Hills Experimental Station, so please respect their privacy.

13. West Rifle Creek SWA

Primary Use:	Hunting
Location:	Garfield County, 8 miles north of Rifle, above Rifle Gap Reservoir
Size:	490 acres
Elevation :	7,700 feet
Division of Wildlife:	Area office in Glenwood Springs, 970-947-2920
Directions:	From Rifle, go 4 miles north on Highway 13 to Highway 325, then continue north (right) 6 miles to County Road 252, at the reservoir, and then 1½ miles northwest to the southern end of the property. There are several more parking areas north on Road 252.

Straddling several miles of the West Fork and the Middle Fork of Rifle Creek, this wildlife area protects a good portion of the drainages from encroaching development. The creek bottoms also provide winter range for elk and deer. The habitat is riparian bottomlands, and hillsides heavily vegetated with oak brush, mountain mahogany, and other low shrubs.

Fishing

None

Hunting

Although the actual SWA is marginal for big-game hunting, it has a rapidly expanding population of wild turkeys. The property provides access to neighboring BLM lands.

Watchable Wildlife

Same as hunting

Camping and Facilities

A fantastic campsite is located on the north end of the property, but it's open only during the big-game hunting seasons. Facilities include toilets, picnic tables, and drinking water.

General Restrictions

Camping is prohibited, except from the day after Labor Day to December 31.

14. Eagle River SWA

Starting about a mile east of Eagle on U.S. 6, this string of leases provides 5 miles of fishing access on the Eagle River. These stretches of the river are leased for fishing access only and no other activities are allowed. Dogs are prohibited and access is allowed only from designated parking areas.

The Eagle River has a struggling population of brown trout and a few rainbows. Heavy flows of silt entering the river from upstream tributaries suppress the production of aquatic insects necessary to support a healthy trout population. There are marginal hatches of caddis and midges in summer. The rock outcroppings on Bellyache Ridge to the east are a nice backdrop to the scenic river.

15. Gypsum Ponds SWA

Primary Use:	Trout fishing
Location:	Eagle County, town of Gypsum
Size:	90 acres
Elevation :	6,490 feet
Division of Wildlife:	Area office in Glenwood Springs, 970-947-2920
Directions:	From Interstate 70 at Gypsum (Exit 140), go east on the south frontage road (bear left on the gravel road at the mobile home park) to the property.

These small ponds located beside the river east of town are highly regarded by the citizens of Gypsum as a means of teaching their children to enjoy the outdoors. Ponds like this are uncommon in the Eagle River Valley. The ponds were created during the construction of Interstate 70.

Fishing

Because the ponds are located in the Colorado River watershed and sit below 6,500 feet in elevation, federal laws protecting endangered species in the river prohibit the introduction of warm-water species such as bass and perch. In 2001, unwanted fish will be removed and the ponds restocked with rainbow and Snake River cutthroat trout.

Hunting

Waterfowl and deer

Watchable Wildlife

Same as hunting

Camping and Facilities

Camping is prohibited. There are no facilities.

General Restrictions

1. Boat launching and takeouts are prohibited on the Eagle River.
2. Dogs are prohibited March 15–June 15 to protect nesting waterfowl.
3. Fires are prohibited.

Rainbow trout

Central West Colorado

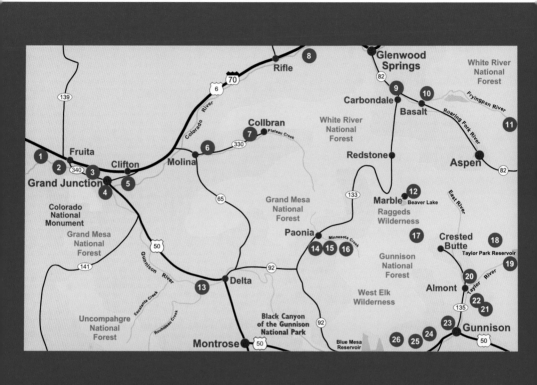

🛣 70	Interstate Highway	〰	Creek
〰 50	U.S. Highway	〰	River
〰 318	State Highway	🟦	Lake
●	City or Town	🟦	Wilderness Area
①	State Wildlife Areas	🟦	National Park

The central west region includes the Gunnison River drainage from Crested Butte to Grand Junction, and the lower Colorado River from Rifle to Utah. State Wildlife Areas in the region vary from beautiful high-country places such as **Beaver Reservoir SWA (Minnesota Creek)** by the West Elk Wilderness, to the beguiling red rock canyons at **Escalante SWA**, and the expansive rolling hills at **Sapinero SWA**, north of Blue Mesa Reservoir.

Hunting opportunities for deer and elk abound on most of the SWAs in the region. The wildlife areas located in the Gunnison Basin alone provide more than 14,000 acres of prime elk hunting, and access to thousands more acres in the Gunnison National Forest.

The huge trout at **Taylor River SWA** and the superb brown trout fishing on the Gunnison River highlight trout fishing in this region.

Wildlife Areas in Central West Colorado

1. Loma Boat Launch SWA

To reach this property from Fruita, go 5 miles west on Interstate 70 to the Loma exit (Exit 15), and then 1 mile south (left) to the frontage road, and ½ mile southeast to the parking area. Camping is prohibited. There is a toilet at the parking area.

Located on the Colorado River west of Grand Junction, this property provides drift boat launching and parking for rafters heading down the Colorado to BLM campsites in Horsethief Canyon and Ruby Canyon.

Many SWAs in the Central West region offer great fishing for brown trout.

2. Horsethief Canyon SWA

Primary Use:	Waterfowl hunting
Location:	Mesa County, Colorado River, west of Fruita
Size:	1,200 acres
Elevation:	4,600 feet
Division of Wildlife:	Area office in Grand Junction, 970-255-6100
Directions:	From Interstate 70 at Fruita (Exit 19), go 1 mile south on Highway 340 to the entrance. This is one of the newer properties and it is well-marked with signs.

Despite a long list of regulations to comply with, and a gauntlet of hoops to jump through, waterfowl hunting in this popular wildlife area is worth the effort. Canada geese and a variety of ducks are common in the area. There are nice views of the Colorado River from parking areas located on bluffs overlooking the river.

Fishing

Fishing is fair for catfish in the Colorado River.

Hunting

Although the property is managed primarily for waterfowl hunting, additional hunting opportunities exist for rabbits, mourning doves, and pheasant. Waterfowl hunting is tightly controlled through a check station where hunters choose from a list of established blinds. There are 15 blinds located by the river and around the sloughs and ponds. The blinds are assigned on a first-come, first-served basis. Hunters must hunt from the blinds. Walking the river banks is prohibited.

1. Hunting is prohibited on Saturdays except for youths and their mentors, but is open to all hunters on the opening days of waterfowl and small-game seasons.
2. Waterfowl hunting is prohibited from Wednesday through Friday each week, except on Thanksgiving, Christmas, and New Year's Days.
3. Hunting is restricted to shotguns, handheld bows, and muzzle-loading rifles. All center-fire rifles are prohibited!

Watchable Wildlife

Excellent for ducks and geese

Camping and Facilities

Camping is prohibited. Facilities include toilets, picnic tables, and an interpretive trail.

General Restrictions

1. All users must check in and out at the check station.
2. Public access is prohibited 9 p.m.–5 a.m.
3. Fires are prohibited.

3. Walker SWA

To reach this property from Grand Junction, go 2 miles west on U.S. 6 & 50 to 24 Road, and south (left) on 24 Road and River Road to the parking area.

Entwined in thick riparian habitat growing on the banks of the Colorado River just southwest of Grand Junction, this wildlife area yields a wealth of wildlife viewing opportunities. Birds present during the seasons include bald eagles, herons, shorebirds, owls, and a wide variety of songbirds and waterfowl. Terrestrial species include gray fox, bobcats, beaver, deer, and raccoons. The area has an interpretive trail, parking, and toilets. It is closed October 1–March 31 to protect nesting waterfowl. Hunting is prohibited.

4. West Lake SWA
(Mesa County)

This wildlife area is a small lake located at the DOW regional offices in Grand Junction. The lake has fishing for stocked trout, bass, and crappie. Access to the lake is from the DOW parking area at 711 Independent Avenue.

5. Corn Lake SWA

This small lake sits beside the Colorado River at Corn Lake State Park southeast of Grand Junction. There is warm-water fishing in the lake and wildlife viewing opportunities. The property is located on Highway 141, 2 miles south of Business 70 at Clifton.

6. Jerry Creek Reservoirs SWA

Primary Use:	Warm-water fishing
Location:	Mesa County, about 30 miles northeast of Grand Junction, near Molina
Size:	Two reservoirs of approximately 500 acres each
Elevation:	5,500 feet
Division of Wildlife:	Area office in Grand Junction, 970-255-6100
Directions:	From Grand Junction, go 20 miles east on Interstate 70 to Highway 65 (Exit 49), and then 8 miles east (right) to Highway 330, and then about 2 miles east (left) to the parking area on the left. The entrance is well-marked.

These two reservoirs are out of sight but not out of the minds of anglers who have seen them. The secretive reservoirs lie hidden behind a pair of tall dams plugging up a deep gulch above Plateau Creek. The trail from the parking area to the lakes is a formidable climb over the dam, and the restrictions on fishing are prohibitive. But the vistas from the top are surprising, and the fishing might hold a surprise or two of its own.

Public use of this area is a sensitive issue. Users are advised to obey all rules and leave no trash behind—even if someone else dropped it. These deep reservoirs supply drinking water to Grand Junction.

Fishing

The reservoirs are managed as quality warm-water fisheries for largemouth bass and better-than-average bluegills.

1. Fishing is restricted to flies and lures only.
2. All fish must be returned to the water immediately.
3. Boating, floating, swimming, and wading are prohibited.
4. Ice fishing and public access to the frozen surface of the reservoirs are prohibited.

Hunting

Hunting is prohibited.

Watchable Wildlife

Waterfowl

Camping and Facilities

Camping is prohibited. Facilities include toilets at the parking area and at the reservoirs.

General Restrictions

1. All water contact activities are prohibited.
2. Pets and domestic animals including horses are prohibited.
3. Motorized and nonmotorized vehicles are prohibited.
4. Fires are prohibited.

Largemouth bass

7. Plateau Creek SWA

Primary Use:	Big-game hunting
Location:	Mesa County, 30 miles northeast of Grand Junction
Size:	1,350 acres
Elevation:	6,200 feet
Division of Wildlife:	Area office in Grand Junction, 970-255-6100
Directions:	From Grand Junction, go 20 miles east on Interstate 70 to Highway 65 (Exit 49), and then 8 miles east (right) to Highway 330, and then about 7½ miles east (left) to Sunnyside Road, and then north (left) ⅛ mile to the entrance. There is a sign for the property on Highway 330.

A monument at the entrance to this property honors District Wildlife Manager Harold D. Lanning (1939–1966) for his dedication to the DOW and commitment to improving wildlife habitat throughout Colorado. The wildlife area stretches across the hills north of Plateau Creek near the town of Collbran. The topography is rugged mesas, and foothills studded with piñon-juniper and sage. Access is difficult in wet weather, as evidenced by deep ruts in the dirt road.

Fishing

None

Hunting

Deer, elk, and turkey hunting opportunities exist on the property, and on thousands of adjoining acres in Grand Mesa National Forest to the north. This is in Game Management Unit 421.

Watchable Wildlife

Same as hunting

Camping and Facilities

Camping is permitted only during big-game seasons and is restricted to designated areas. There are no facilities.

General Restrictions

1. Vehicles are prohibited December 1–May 31.
2. Vehicles are restricted to designated roads.
3. Fires are prohibited.

The successful reintroduction of wild turkeys throughout Colorado is the comeback story of the century. Wild turkeys were hunted to near extinction in the early 1900s. Today, thanks to the combined efforts of the DOW and the National Wild Turkey Federation, wild turkeys can be found just about everywhere there is suitable habitat.

8. Garfield Creek SWA

Primary Use:	Big-game hunting
Location:	Garfield County, 3 miles south of Interstate 70 at New Castle
Size:	13,000 acres
Elevation:	6,000–9,000 feet
Division of Wildlife:	Area office in Glenwood Springs, 970-947-2920
Directions:	From Interstate 70 at New Castle (Exit 105), go 2 miles west and south on County Road 335 to County Road 312, and then 1 mile south (left) to the north end of the property. Parking areas are located on both sides of the road and well-marked with signs.

The bulk of this wildlife area lies cradled in the wide valley of lower Garfield Creek. Another tract sits higher in the Garfield Creek drainage at the western base of Sunlight Peak. Garfield Creek flows north from Sunlight Peak to the Colorado River. The terrain is mountainous and the vegetation is a mixture of riparian, sage, piñon-juniper, oak brush, open meadows, cultivated fields, and coniferous forest.

Fishing

None

Hunting

Elk, deer, Merriam's turkeys, and blue grouse are found in reasonable numbers on the property. This important wildlife area constitutes a complete ecosystem for elk, providing winter, transitional, and summer ranges. This is in Game Management Unit 42.

Watchable Wildlife

Same as hunting, plus golden eagles, bobcats, marmots, badgers, foxes, and weasels

Camping and Facilities

Camping is prohibited except for seven days before the beginning of regular big-game seasons through seven days after the end of regular big-game seasons. There are no facilities.

General Restrictions

1. Bicycles are prohibited off county roads.
2. Dogs are prohibited except when used as an aid to hunting.
3. Public access is prohibited December 1–July 15 except for spring turkey hunting below the junction, or small-game hunting above the junction, of County Roads 312 and 328.

9. Carbondale SWA

This SWA is a drift boat launching site and parking area located on the Roaring Fork River below the bridge at Carbondale. There is a short stretch of the river on the property for wading or fishing from the bank. Access is on the first gravel road north on Highway 82.

10. Basalt SWA

Primary Use:	Big-game hunting, shooting range
Location:	Eagle and Pitkin Counties, immediately north and east of Basalt
Size:	There is some question as to the actual size of this property but there are at least several hundred acres. It doesn't matter much anyway since the Christine and Basalt Units sit next to the White River National Forest.
Elevation:	7,500–9,000 feet
Division of Wildlife:	Area office in Glenwood Springs, 970-947-2920
Directions:	**Christine Unit:** From Basalt, go ½ mile west on Highway 82 (Business) to Homestead Road; turn right on the dirt road and go up the hill to the parking area and the shooting range.
	Basalt Unit: From Basalt, go 3 miles east on Forest Road 105 (Fryingpan River Road) to the property entrance on the left. The area is well-marked with signs.
	Watson Divide Unit: From Basalt, go 6 miles south on Highway 82. The property is located west of the highway and north of County Road 8. There are no signs.

This wildlife area consists of three tracts of land located near Basalt. Two large tracts stretch north from Basalt and from the Fryingpan River to the southern base of Basalt Mountain. They provide access to a variety of big-game and small-game hunting opportunities, and also provide fishing access to a short stretch of the Roaring Fork River. A third tract sits on a hill overlooking the river 6 miles south of town.

Fishing

The Fryingpan and Roaring Fork Rivers are classified as Gold Medal Water, and are managed for quality trout fishing. Both rivers are restricted to fishing with flies and lures only and all trout, except small brown trout, must be returned to the water immediately. Anglers may keep four brown trout less than 14 inches long; all others must be released.

Fishing access to the Roaring Fork River is located on Highway 82 about ½ mile north of Emma.

Christine Lake is stocked periodically with hatchery trout. Boating and water activities are prohibited on the lake.

Hunting

Big-game hunters use these properties for hunting and for access points to the southern slopes of Red Table Mountain and to the National Forest lands above Seven Castles. Deer, elk, and black bear hunting are rated good to excellent throughout the area. Other species in the area include bighorn sheep, rabbits, hares, blue grouse, bobcats, and mountain lions. This is in Game Management Unit 444.

Watchable Wildlife

Same as hunting

Camping and Facilities

Camping is allowed only during the big-game seasons. Camping is prohibited within ¼ mile of the Fryingpan River. Toilets are located only at the shooting range.

General Restrictions

1. Public access is prohibited December 1–April 15 except at Christine Lake and the shooting range.
2. Mountain bikes are prohibited.
3. Dogs are prohibited except for field trials February 1–March 31 on the Christine unit and August 1–September 30 on all units.
4. Alcohol is prohibited on the shooting range.
5. Fires are prohibited.

11. Coke Oven SWA

Primary Use:	Camping
Location:	Pitkin County, 40 miles east of Basalt
Size:	330 acres
Elevation:	8,500 feet
Division of Wildlife:	Area office in Glenwood Springs, 970-947-2920
Directions:	From Basalt, go 37½ miles east on Forest Service Road 105 (Fryingpan River Road) to the property. It is the first meadow that you come to after the road turns north and heads up the mountain. Look for the ovens on the south side of the meadow. There are no signs at the property.

This wildlife area covers a lush meadow near the base of Stellar Peak. The views are spectacular. Primitive but good campsites are available. A row of antique coke ovens stands at the edge of the meadow as a reminder of coal mining operations in the early 1900s.

Fishing

None

Hunting

The property is relatively small but it is surrounded by the White River National Forest. There is fair to good hunting for elk and deer, and excellent hunting for black bear. This is in Game Management Units 444 and 45.

Watchable Wildlife

Same as hunting

Camping and Facilities

Primitive camping, no facilities

Black bears are widely distributed throughout Colorado, found in both the foothills and mountains. Hunters may no longer hunt bears in spring, hunt over a baited area, or hunt with dogs.

12. Beaver Lake SWA (Marble)

Primary Use:	Trout fishing
Location:	Gunnison County, in Marble
Size:	40 acres
Elevation:	8,000 feet
Division of Wildlife:	Area office in Gunnison, 970-641-7060
Directions:	From Marble, go ¼ mile east on County Road 3 to the lake.

This small, shallow lake sits by the Crystal River just outside the town of Marble. With the Ragged Wilderness and Whitehouse Mountain looming in the distance, Beaver Lake is a scenic setting for canoeing, fishing, and observing waterfowl.

Fishing

Put-and-take fishing for stocked rainbows in the lake, and fishing for whitefish on the Crystal River

Hunting

Hunting is prohibited.

Watchable Wildlife

Waterfowl

Camping and Facilities

Camping is prohibited. There is a toilet at the parking area.

General Restrictions

1. Boating is prohibited, except by hand-propelled craft.
2. Fires are prohibited.

13. Escalante SWA

Primary Use:	Big-game, small-game, and waterfowl hunting
Location:	Delta County, north and west of Delta
Size:	7,500 total acres in all the tracts
Elevation:	5,000–7,500 feet
Division of Wildlife:	Area office in Montrose, 970-252-6000
Directions:	**Lower Roubideau Tract:** From Delta, go 4½ miles west on 5th Street (G Road) to the parking area on the left.
	Hamilton Tract: From Delta, go 2 miles west on 5th Street, then 2 miles northwest on G 50 Road to the parking area for south side of the property. To access the north parking area, go 5½ miles north of Delta on U.S. 50, and look for the signs on the left.
	Upper Roubideau and Peach Orchard Point Tracts: From Delta, go 6½ miles west on 5th Street (G Road), then take the right fork at the junction on Sawmill Mesa Road and go 11½ miles west to the properties. There are no signs for the property.
	Waterwheel and Gunnison River Tracts: From Delta, go 12 miles northwest on U.S. 50 to Escalante Canyon Road, then 3 miles southwest (left) to the south side of the Gunnison River Bridge. Park off the road on the left and walk 1 mile upstream to the areas. There are no signs for the properties.
	East Walker Tract: From Delta, go 12 miles northwest on U.S. 50 to Escalante Canyon Road, then 4 miles into the canyon. The property is marked with signs.
	Cap Smith Tract: From Delta, go 12 miles northwest on U.S. 50 to Escalante Canyon Road, then about 6 miles southwest into the canyon. There are several parking areas and signs.
	West Walker Tract: From Delta, go 12 miles northwest on U.S. 50 to Escalante Canyon Road, then 17 miles southwest into the canyon to Palmer Gulch Road, then 5 miles west (right), then 1¼ miles north, toward Tatum Ridge, and then about 6 miles northeast (right) on Tatum and Sowbelly Ridge Roads to the property.
	Picket Corral Tract: From Delta, go 12 miles northwest on U.S. 50 to Escalante Canyon Road, then 21 miles southwest into the canyon to the property.

Ten individual tracts of land are located in this intriguing and far-reaching wildlife area west of Delta. The varied tracts comprise a conglomerate of habitats, ranging in contrast from wet riparian bottomlands on the Gunnison River, to red-rock canyons in Escalante Creek, to broad mesas atop the Uncompahgre Plateau.

Lower Roubideau Tract is located at the confluence of Roubideau Creek and the Gunnison River 4 miles west of Delta. It has 2,500 acres consisting mostly of mature cottonwood riparian and wetland habitats. On the arid hills above the creek, vegetation changes quickly to rabbitbrush, cactus, grasses, and sunflowers.

Hamilton Tract is 400 acres of bottomland on the Gunnison River that adjoins Lower Roubideau. The habitat is a combination of riparian, willows, ponds, and cultivated wet meadows.

Upper Roubideau and Peach Orchard Point Tracts sit 20 miles southwest of Delta on Sawmill Mesa. Together, they total about 2,500 acres of arid, rocky terrain, sparsely vegetated in sage and piñon-juniper. The north end of the area plummets sharply into the canyon of the Dry Fork of Escalante Creek. The areas are important winter ranges for deer and elk.

Waterwheel and Gunnison River Tracts are small parcels of land located on the south side of the Gunnison River directly upstream (south) of the bridge at Escalante Canyon. Willows and tamarisk trees grow beside the river, and sage and cactus grow on the hillsides.

East Walker Tract straddles 4 miles of Escalante Creek, just inside the mouth of the canyon. Habitat here is a mix of cultivated fields, sagebrush, and a few tall cottonwoods beside the creek. The ruins of the Walker cabin are still standing and available for viewing. Henry Walker, a skilled bricklayer, built the cabin in 1911.

Cap Smith Tract is just up the creek from East Walker. It, too, has ruins of a cabin built in 1911. Captain Harry Smith was a tombstone carver and veteran of the Civil War. The cabin walls and nearby rock cliffs are beautifully engraved with names and insignias. This tract sits deep in the heart of the scenic canyon and has long views to the southwest.

West Walker Tract sits on Sowbelly Ridge on the north rim of Escalante Canyon. This 600-acre parcel is relatively flat and sparsely covered in sage, piñon, and juniper. It is used primarily as winter range for deer and elk. Access is difficult on rough roads.

Picket Corral Tract is located at the confluence of the middle and east forks of Escalante Creek, far back in Escalante Canyon. Fantastic views surround the 160-acre parcel of land vegetated with cottonwoods, willows, grass, sage, piñon, and juniper.

Fishing

Escalante Creek has marginal fishing for trout.

Hunting

The lower tracts located along the river and the creeks have hunting for deer, turkey, pheasant, quail, waterfowl and small game. The higher, drier tracts offer hunting for deer, elk, antelope, and small game. This area is in Game Management Unit 62.

Hunting is prohibited on Lower Roubideau Tract except for youths 15 and younger and their mentors. Mentors must be 18 or older and comply with hunter education requirements. Youths must be accompanied by mentors while hunting. Only one mentor per youth is permitted.

Watchable Wildlife

Same as hunting

Camping and Facilities

Primitive camping is available at all tracts. There are no facilities.

General Restrictions

1. Public access is prohibited on Hamilton and Lower Roubideau Tracts March 15–July 15 to protect nesting waterfowl.
2. Motor vehicles are restricted to established roads.

Opposite: Cap Smith Tract of the Escalante SWA in foreground, Picket Corral Tract in the distance

14. McCluskey SWA

Primary Use:	Big-game hunting and access to BLM and Gunnison National Forest
Location:	Delta County, 5 miles south of Paonia
Size:	1,600 acres
Elevation:	6,100–6,800 feet
Division of Wildlife:	Area office in Gunnison, 970-641-7060
Directions:	From Paonia, go 1½ miles west on J75 Drive (Matthews Lane) to County Road 3950, then ¾ mile south (left) to M75 Road, then 1 mile east (left) to County Road 4050, and then south (right) about 1 mile, crossing a cattle guard. The parking area is under the power lines.

Stretched across the foothills south of Paonia, this wildlife area provides important winter range and habitat for mule deer. Vegetation ranges from piñon-juniper in the flats, to a mixture of aspen, oak brush, and cottonwoods at higher elevations. This property, and the adjacent **Roeber SWA** (see p. 55), are wildlife easements that provide hunting opportunities and access to vast tracts of BLM and Forest Service lands.

Fishing

None

Hunting

Deer, elk, bear, and small game may be found on the property but the area is more important as winter range for deer. This is in Game Management Unit 53.

Watchable Wildlife

Same as hunting

Camping and Facilities

Overnight camping is prohibited. There are no facilities.

General Restrictions

1. Public access is prohibited from the day after the regular big-game season to April 30.
2. Public access is prohibited, except for hunting, fishing, and trapping.
3. Motor vehicles are prohibited, except on designated roads.
4. Dogs are prohibited.
5. Fires are prohibited.

15. Roeber SWA

To access this property from Paonia, go 1 mile south on 4100 Road (Onarga Avenue) to Lane N80, then 2 miles south and east (left) to 4200 Drive, and then 1 mile south (right) to the parking area.

This 1,000-acre property is adjacent to **McCluskey SWA** (see p. 54). Both properties are wildlife easements that provide hunting opportunities as well as access to vast tracts of BLM and Forest Service lands. Camping is prohibited, and there are no facilities. The restrictions are the same as McCluskey SWA.

16. Beaver Reservoir SWA
(Minnesota Creek)

Primary Use:	Hunting access
Location:	Gunnison County, Gunnison National Forest, 10 miles southeast of Paonia
Size:	40 acres
Elevation:	8,500 feet
Division of Wildlife:	Area office in Gunnison, 970-641-7060
Directions:	From Paonia, go about 5 miles southeast on 0.50 Drive to Forest Road 710, and then follow the road up the left side of the canyon to the reservoir.

This wonderfully remote and beautiful wildlife area sits high in the headwaters of Minnesota Creek on the western slopes of Mount Gunnison. Hunters and backpackers use it as a jumping-off point into the rugged Gunnison National Forest and the West Elk Wilderness. The road to the site is steep, narrow, and nearly impassable when it snows. A small clearing by the lake is a quiet, remote spot to camp in summer. The scenery is awesome!

Fishing

None, the reservoir is drawn down regularly for irrigation.

Hunting

Elk, deer, and bear are abundant throughout the area. A herd of 400–500 elk migrate through this area when weather pushes them out of summer pastures in the high country. The deer population is estimated at about 7,000 head. Hunting this steep, unforgiving country is not easy. Trails from the reservoir lead to Minnesota Pass, Elk Basin Pass, Browning Mountain, the Chain Mountains, and Cold Mountain. This is in Game Management Unit 53.

Watchable Wildlife

Same as hunting

Camping and Facilities

A limited number of camping and parking spaces are available at the lake. There are no facilities.

"Velvet brothers," mule deer bucks in velvet

17. Lake Irwin SWA

Primary Use:	Trout fishing
Location:	Gunnison County, 12 miles west of Crested Butte
Size:	Approximately 50 acres
Elevation:	10,512
Division of Wildlife:	Area office in Gunnison, 970-641-7060
Directions:	From Gunnison, go 30 miles north on Highway 135 to Crested Butte, then 6 miles west (left) on County Road 12 (Kebler Pass Road) to Forest Service Road 826, and then 1½ miles north (right) to the property. Or, from Gunnison go north on County Road 730 (Ohio Creek Road) to County Road 12 and then east (right) to Forest Service Road 826. The Forest service Road is limited to summer travel July–October, depending on snowfall.

An abundance of wildflowers and wild brook trout liven the atmosphere in this wildlife area located high in Gunnison National Forest west of Crested Butte. Old-growth forests of giant spruce and fir, with a dense understory of serviceberry and other shrubs, surround the lake. Wildflowers carpet the open meadows in July with red clover, cone flowers, bluebells, scarlet gilia, asters, flax, and many other species including the poisonous monkshood.

Fishing

The reservoir supports a thriving population of wild brook trout. Catchable rainbows are stocked periodically in summer.

Hunting

Hunting is prohibited.

Watchable Wildlife

Blue grouse

Camping and Facilities

Camping, toilets, and drinking water are available at the Forest Service campground at the lake. Also, there is a lodge and restaurant at the lake.

18. Spring Creek Reservoir SWA

Primary Use:	Trout fishing
Location:	Gunnison County, 30 miles northeast of Gunnison
Size:	Approximately 100 acres
Elevation:	10,000 feet
Division of Wildlife:	Area office in Gunnison, 970-641-7060
Directions:	From Gunnison, go 10 miles north on Highway 135 to Almont, then 6 miles northeast (right) on Forest Road 742 to Forest Road 744 (Spring Creek Road), and then 14 miles north (left) to the reservoir. The last 5 miles are rough, washboarded, and generally closed in winter.

Tucked away in the heavily timbered southern reaches of the Elk Mountains, Spring Creek Reservoir rests in a long valley cradled by 12,000-foot peaks.

Fishing

Catchable rainbow trout are stocked when they are available. Otherwise, fishing is limited to brown trout and a few brook trout.

Hunting

Hunting is prohibited on the property, but good opportunities exist for elk and deer hunting in the surrounding National Forest. Deer are more abundant here than in the rest of the Gunnison Basin.

Watchable Wildlife

Waterfowl

Camping and Facilities

Camping is plentiful at a Forest Service campground. Facilities include campsites, a boat ramp, toilets, and drinking water.

General Restrictions

No motor boats

19. Taylor River SWA

Primary Use:	Trout fishing
Location:	Gunnison County, Taylor River, 30 miles northeast of Gunnison
Size:	½ mile of fishing access
Elevation:	9,500 feet
Division of Wildlife:	Area office in Gunnison, 970-641-7060
Directions:	From Gunnison, go 10 miles north on Highway 135 to Almont, then 18 miles northeast (right) on Forest Road 742 to the property. You can't miss it; the battle lines are well-drawn.

Enormous trout lie in ambush below the dam at Taylor Park Reservoir. They wait for mysis shrimp washed through the outlet from the reservoir, and suck in thousands of the high-protein tidbits until their bodies grow close to the point of exploding. Commonly referred to as the Hog Trough, the ½-mile stretch of river on the property receives intense pressure from anglers. Fishing here resembles combat. It is a skirmish finding an unoccupied spot to cast a fly, and a battle landing the monster trout once hooked. The trout are fly-wise and finicky; they have seen a lot of imitations and only the best will fool them.

Fishing

Rainbows, browns, and brook trout to 10 pounds—and beyond.

1. Fishing is restricted to artificial flies and lures only.
2. All fish must be returned to the water immediately.
3. Public access is prohibited in the first 325 yards downstream from the dam.

Hunting

Hunting is prohibited.

Watchable Wildlife

None

Camping and Facilities

Camping is prohibited. Portable toilets are located in the parking areas.

General Restrictions

Parking is prohibited, except in designated areas.

20. Almont Triangle SWA

Primary Use:	Big-game hunting, winter range for elk
Location:	Gunnison County, 1 mile north of Almont
Size:	640 acres
Elevation:	8,000 feet
Division of Wildlife:	Area office in Gunnison, 970-641-7060
Directions:	From Gunnison, go 10 miles north on Highway 135 to Almont. Continue on Highway 135, 1 mile northwest to the sign and access road on the right.

This popular big-game hunting area is situated in the hills between the East and Taylor Rivers just north of Almont. It is good for deer but better for elk, especially in the late season. Elk winter here on the sage-covered hills and open, grassy meadows.

Fishing

None

Hunting

Elk, deer, bighorn sheep, and small game can be found here. Both blue and sage grouse nest in the area. Bighorn sheep from the Taylor River herd use this area in winter. This is in Game Management Unit 54, and Bighorn Sheep Unit S26.

Watchable Wildlife

Same as hunting

Camping and Facilities

None

General Restrictions

Public access is prohibited November 15–March 31.

21. Cabin Creek SWA

Primary Use:	Big-game hunting
Location:	Gunnison County, 20 miles northeast of Gunnison
Size:	The actual size of the SWA is vague, but it adjoins BLM lands to the south and Gunnison National Forest to the east.
Elevation:	9,000–10,500 feet
Division of Wildlife:	Area office in Gunnison, 970-641-7060
Directions:	From Gunnison, go 2 miles north on Highway 135 to County Road 10 (Lost Canyon Road), then 8 miles east (right) to Forest Service Road 604, and then south (right) into the property.

This property sits in the foothills on the eastern rim of the Gunnison Basin. The terrain consists of low ridges and hills separating creeks and gulches. Vegetation is a mixture of grassy meadows, sage, aspen, and coniferous forests. The wildlife area is an important winter range for elk and deer.

Fishing

None

Hunting

The deer population is stronger here in Game Management Unit 55 than other units in the Gunnison Basin, but the overall size of the herd has decreased in recent years. Elk hunting is better here in the late season. The area receives heavy use during all of the big-game seasons. Both blue and sage grouse are found here. Check current regulations for closures on sage grouse hunting.

Watchable Wildlife

Same as hunting

Camping and Facilities

There is primitive camping in several established campgrounds. A classic outhouse stands duty among the aspen at one of the big-game camps.

General Restrictions

Public access is prohibited December 1–March 31 to protect wintering herds of big game.

22. Leaps Gulch SWA

From the northern edge of Gunnison, go northeast on County Road 10 (paved) to Forest Road 743, then approximately 5 miles to the first closed road on the left past Forest Road 604 (the road to Cabin Creek SWA). The property is approximately 3 miles north of Forest Road 604, and access is by foot or horseback via the closed road. This is in Game Management Unit 55.

The terrain and habitat here are similar to **Cabin Creek SWA** (see p. 63). The area is critical winter range for elk and deer and closed to public access December 1–March 31.

23. Gunnison River SWA
(Van Tuyl and Redden)

Primary Use:	Trout fishing
Location:	Gunnison County, 1 mile northwest of downtown Gunnison
Size:	About 1 mile of river
Elevation:	7,700 feet
Division of Wildlife:	Area office in Gunnison, 970-641-7060
Directions:	From Gunnison, go north on Highway 135 to County Road 13 on the north edge of town, then ¼ mile west (left) and bear left onto Tincup Drive. Follow Tincup west about 3 blocks to Palisade City Park. Parking for the trail to the river is located on the north side of the park.

Straddling the Gunnison River below the cliffs on the northwest outskirts of Gunnison, this wildlife area sees more fishermen in drift boats than on the banks. A short hike from the parking area puts anglers on this stretch of quality water.

Fishing

This stretch of the river is a quality brown trout fishery. The brown trout population occasionally is augmented with stockings of fingerling rainbow trout. The ½-mile-long trail from the parking area to the river crosses a marshy field that may be standing in water during wet months.

Hunting

None

Watchable Wildlife

Waterfowl

Camping and Facilities

Camping is prohibited. Restrooms are located at Palisade City Park.

General Restrictions

Access is by foot only (no bicycles).

24. Gunnison SWA

Primary Use:	Hunting, fishing, archery range
Location:	Gunnison County, 6 miles west of Gunnison
Size:	2,800 acres
Elevation:	8,500 feet
Division of Wildlife:	Area office in Gunnison, 970-641-7060
Directions:	From Gunnison, go 6 miles west on U.S. 50 to the entrance and sign on the right.

Tucked away in the rolling hills west of Gunnison, this significant wildlife area embraces a large portion of lower Beaver Creek Valley above the confluence at the Gunnison River. In addition to hunting and fishing, the property plays important roles for wildlife. Elk and deer migrate down from the high country to winter in the broad valley, and waterfowl nest along the creek. Wetlands on the property were greatly enhanced through a cooperative effort by the DOW, Great Outdoors Colorado, and Ducks Unlimited.

Fishing

There are two separate fisheries on West Beaver Creek, one above the barrier waterfall, and one below. Above the waterfall, the stream is managed as a reclamation stream for native Colorado River cutthroat trout. Below the barrier, are self-sustaining populations of wild brown and brook trout.

Hunting

The Beaver Creek drainage is a major big-game hunting area and very popular with elk hunters. The SWA provides hunting opportunities and important access to BLM, Forest Service, and wilderness lands to the north. There is a limited amount of duck hunting on the creek and the wetlands located on the south end of the site. This area is in Game Management Unit 54.

Watchable Wildlife

Same as hunting

Camping and Facilities

Camping is restricted to designated areas. Overnight parking is allowed at the Beaver Creek trailhead, located at the north end of the property. There is an archery range and several parking areas.

General Restrictions

1. Public access is prohibited December 1–March 31.
2. Beaver Creek Trail is restricted to foot or horseback travel only.

25. Centennial SWA

Primary Use:	Winter range for big game
Location:	Gunnison County, 12 miles west of Gunnison
Size:	1,800 acres
Elevation:	8,000 feet
Division of Wildlife:	Area office in Gunnison, 970-641-7060
Directions:	From Gunnison, go 12 miles west on U.S. 50 to the DOW sign at the dirt access road just past Stevens Campground, and then north (right) into the property.

This SWA lies in the sage-covered hills north of Blue Mesa Reservoir. The property was acquired by the DOW to conserve critical winter range for deer and elk, and to protect important breeding grounds and habitat for Gunnison sage grouse.

Fishing

None

Hunting

This wildlife area is critical winter range for a large herd of deer. Elk and deer hunting is only fair on the actual property, but this SWA provides hunting access to BLM and Forest Service lands to the north. A pack trail from the SWA leads to the southern end of the West Elk Wilderness. This is in Game Management Unit 54.

Watchable Wildlife

Gunnison sage grouse leks are located here, and the property is closed during mating season. The sage grouse also nest and raise their broods here. Sage grouse and other wildlife can be viewed when the property opens June 30.

Camping and Facilities

Camping is prohibited, and there are no facilities. A sign at the property entrance says camping is permitted in designated areas only, but searching for a designated area is futile because there aren't any.

General Restrictions

1. Public access is prohibited December 1–June 30 to protect wintering big game and nesting sage grouse.
2. Vehicle travel is limited in accordance with posted regulations.

26. Sapinero SWA

Primary Use:	Big-game hunting
Location:	Gunnison County, 15 miles west of Gunnison
Size:	7,000 acres
Elevation:	7,500–9,000 feet
Division of Wildlife:	Area office in Gunnison, 970-641-7060
Directions:	From Gunnison, go 15 miles west on U.S. 50 to the property signs. Access roads enter the property at East Elk Creek and Red Creek.

This expansive sweep of land north of Blue Mesa Reservoir was the first property acquired by the DOW using funds provided by the Pitman-Robertson Act of 1937. The funds are collected through a federal tax on firearms. The wildlife area is critical winter range for deer and elk, but is open for hunting, camping, and hiking at other times of the year. The topography of the area is marked by deep draws and riparian creek drainages, separated by grassy, flat-topped ridges and rock outcroppings.

Fishing

The creeks have self-sustaining populations of small brown and brook trout.

Hunting

Although the deer herd has declined in recent years, elk are numerous and well-distributed throughout Game Management Unit 54. In addition to big-game hunting, there also is hunting for rabbits, snowshoe hares, blue grouse, and sage grouse.

Watchable Wildlife

Nesting waterfowl

Camping and Facilities

Primitive camping is permitted on the property. There are no facilities.

General Restrictions

1. Vehicles must remain on roads.
2. Snowmobiles are prohibited.

Southwest Colorado

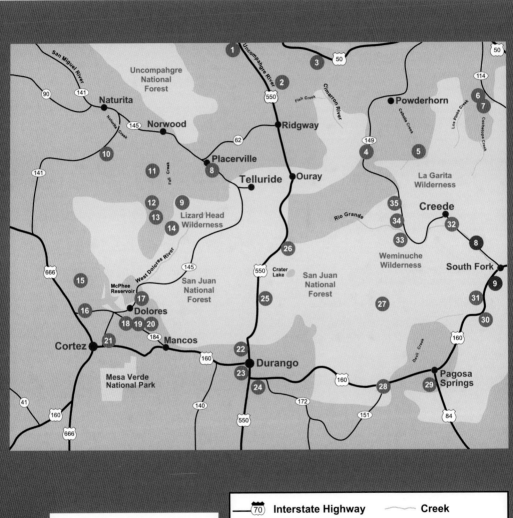

See map on page 216 for South Central Region in which 8 and 9 belong.

🛡70	Interstate Highway	〰 Creek
⬭50	U.S. Highway	〰 River
⬭318	State Highway	🟦 Lake
●	City or Town	🟦 Wilderness Area
❶	State Wildlife Areas	🟦 National Park

State Wildlife Areas located south and west of Gunnison are numerous and diverse. Some offer excellent trout fishing in scenic mountain lakes and streams, while others, at lower elevations, are managed for warm-water species such as bass and northern pike. The southwest region is the historical range of two native trout species, the Rio Grande cutthroat and the Colorado River cutthroat. Anglers are required to recognize these native trout and release them back into the water immediately.

Big- and small-game hunting in the southwest region is some of the best that Colorado has to offer. Many of the wildlife areas, such as **Billy Creek** and **Cimarron**, are huge tracts of land that are managed primarily as winter range for elk and deer, and are closed during winter, but open to big-game hunting in the fall. The Uncompahgre Plateau west of Montrose is a stronghold for Merriam's turkeys. Although waterfowl hunters often overlook the southwest region, there are huntable populations of ducks in the wildlife areas located on the upper Rio Grande.

Wildlife Areas in Southwest Colorado

1. Chipeta Lakes SWA

To reach this property from Montrose, go 3 miles south on U.S. 550 to Chipeta Drive, and then ½ mile north (right) to the lake.

This wildlife area is a small warm-water lake in a parklike setting just south of Montrose. It is a nice place for picnics and family outings. The lake has fishing for bass and panfish. Camping is prohibited. Facilities include portable toilets, trash receptacles, and a picnic shelter.

2. Billy Creek SWA

Primary Use: Big-game hunting

Location: Montrose and Ouray Counties, 7–20 miles south of Montrose

Size: 5,000 acres in all tracts

Elevation: 6,300–9,000 feet

Division of Wildlife: Area office in Montrose, 970-252-6000

Directions: **Colona Tract:** From Montrose, go approximately 7 miles south on U.S. 550 to Government Springs Road, and then 2 miles west (right) to the marked access road.

Billy Creek Tract: From Montrose, go 16 miles south on U.S. 550 to the gravel road beside the DOW house, then go east (left) over the bridge and follow the dirt road to the property.

Beckett Tract: From Montrose, go 18 miles south on U.S. 550 to the access road at County Road 4, and then east (left) ½ mile to the property.

Carmichael Tract: From Montrose, go 21 miles south on U.S. 550 to where the highway widens and then turn east (left), drive through the ranch yard, and continue 1¼ miles east on the dirt road to the property.

The four tracts of land on this sizable piece of property provide hunting access to land in the Uncompahgre River valley between Ridgway and Montrose. The topography and habitat zones are similar in all tracts, and consist of rolling hills with sage, piñon-juniper, and oak brush, wide drainages with cottonwood bottoms and grassy meadows, and flat-topped ridges sparsely forested in pine. A few dirt roads cut through the properties, permitting access to back areas. These roads become extremely slick when wet. Four-wheel-drive vehicles with chains are a must.

Fishing

None

Hunting

Although deer numbers remain low in this area, the elk herd is in good condition. All of the tracts in the SWA can have good hunting for elk, depending on weather. Early snows in the high country often push elk down to winter. Other huntable species include black bears, small game, and band-tailed pigeons. This is in Game Management Unit 65.

Watchable Wildlife

At Billy Creek Tract, a parking area is located on a hill where a wintering elk herd can be observed in the meadows.

Camping and Facilities

Primitive camping is available on all of the tracts. There are no facilities.

General Restrictions

1. Public access is prohibited on all tracts January 1–March 31 to protect wintering big game.
2. Snowmobiles are prohibited on the Colona Tract.
3. Motor vehicles are prohibited, except on designated roads in and parking areas.

3. Cimarron SWA

Primary Use:	Big-game hunting
Location:	Montrose County, 25 miles southeast of Montrose
Size:	6,000 acres
Elevation:	7,500–9,500 feet
Division of Wildlife:	Area office in Montrose, 970-252-6000
Directions:	From Montrose, go 23 miles east on U.S. 50 to Little Cimarron Road, then 2 miles south (right) to the sign and the access road, and then 2 miles southwest on the access road to the parking area.

Spreading wide across the northern lap of the mesa dividing the Little Cimarron and Big Cimarron drainages, this significant wildlife area provides important winter range for big game and habitat for small game and nesting waterfowl. The lower portions of the site consist of moderate to steep grades, blanketed by sage and interspersed with oak brush. The higher reaches have a mixture of sage, aspen, spruce, and fir. In addition to the Cimarron River, which borders the SWA on the west, there are small creeks and beaver ponds scattered about.

Fishing

Trout fishing is marginal in the Cimarron River.

Hunting

Big-game hunting success on this expansive tract of land is directly related to the amount of snowfall in the high country to the south. The elk stay high until winter forces them down to their winter range on the SWA, where hunting can be very good later in the season. A limited number of roads and restrictions on motor vehicle travel reduce hunting pressure and add to the quality hunting experience. Other hunting opportunities exist for waterfowl on the numerous beaver ponds, and for blue grouse in the aspen forests.

Watchable Wildlife

Same as hunting

Camping and Facilities

Camping is prohibited. There are no facilities.

General Restrictions

1. Motor vehicles are prohibited, except on designated roads.
2. Parking is prohibited more than 30 feet off designated roads.
3. Snowmobiles are prohibited.
4. Fires are prohibited.
5. Discharge of firearms is prohibited in the designated safety zones.

4. Lake Fork of the Gunnison River SWA

Located 5½ miles north of Lake City on Highway 149, this fishing easement provides public access to outstanding brown trout fishing on the Lake Fork. The access road drops sharply away from the highway and soon narrows to a one-lane road that ends at the parking area. The easement runs north for approximately 3 miles. Access is limited to 20 feet on either side of the river. In this stretch, there is a solid population of self-sustaining brown trout up to 20 inches long and a few rainbow trout in the hog class. Fishing is restricted to flies and lures only. Camping is prohibited.

The DOW has other fishing easements on the Lake Fork with fishing for cutthroat trout, rainbow trout, and kokanee salmon. These easements are marked with signs on Highway 149. See the current fishing brochure for regulations.

5. Cebolla Creek SWA

Primary Use:	Trout fishing and big-game hunting
Location:	Hinsdale County, Upper Cebolla Creek, 15 miles south of Powderhorn
Size:	1,400 acres
Elevation:	8,800–10,000 feet
Division of Wildlife:	Area office in Gunnison, 970-641-7060
Directions:	From Highway 149 at Powderhorn, go 15 miles south on County Road 27 to the property.

This venerable wildlife area has been a favorite spot with campers, anglers, and big-game hunters for many years. Cebolla Creek runs down the middle of the property, with cliffs and steep hills rising sharply to the east and the west. A footbridge across the creek gives access to the area west of the property. The creek is flanked by mature cottonwoods and spruce, and willows and alder line the banks. The hills are forested in spruce and fir, with sagebrush and grass dominating the gentler slopes and the benches above the creek.

Fishing

Cebolla Creek has a healthy population of self-sustaining brown trout up to 18 inches, and a few rainbows. The stretch of water on the SWA gets a lot of fishing pressure because there is very little public water elsewhere in the valley. Additional fishing access is found about 5 miles upstream from the SWA where the valley widens and Cebolla Creek traces the northern boundary of La Garita Wilderness.

Hunting

Big-game hunting for elk and deer is by limited license only. You may not hunt here with an over-the-counter license. Other species to hunt include bighorn sheep and blue grouse. This is in Game Management Units 66 and 67.

Watchable Wildlife

Bighorn sheep can be seen on the cliffs east of the SWA.

Camping and Facilities

Primitive campsites are scattered around the SWA under the canopy of large blue spruce and cottonwood trees near the river. There are no facilities or trash barrels. Camping is restricted to 14 consecutive days.

General Restrictions

See Hunting.

6. Cochetopa SWA

Primary Use: Trout fishing and duck hunting

Location: Saguache County, Cochetopa Creek, 30 miles southeast of Gunnison

Size: Approximately 5 miles of fishing access

Elevation: 9,000 feet

Division of Wildlife: Area office in Gunnison, 970-641-7060

Directions: From Gunnison, go 8 miles east on U.S. 50 to Highway 114, then 18 miles south (right) to County Road NN14, then south (right) to the DOW boundary signs on the right. Access to the creek is via stiles and fence crossings at marked areas beside the road.

The name Cochetopa rolls reluctantly off the tongues of the anglers and hunters who know this place. If two streams ever deserved the status of Wild Trout Water, they are Cochetopa Creek and its tributary Los Pinos Creek. And if there were designations for Wild Duck Water, they would qualify for that, too. The creek wander through the valley, cutting their way through grassy meadows and thick stands of willows.

The wildlife area runs north, straddling Cochetopa Creek from Dome Lakes to the confluence of Los Pinos Creek. Portions of the SWA are a wildlife easement on the Coleman Ranch. This is a working ranch with cattle grazing in the fields and by the creek. Free-running pets are not permitted.

Fishing

Cochetopa Creek and Los Pinos Creek run parallel through most of the upper portion of the SWA, converging at the north end. Both have healthy, self-sustaining populations of wild brown and brook trout, and a few rainbows. The average size trout is about 12 inches, but a few of the brown trout grow much larger.

1. Fishing is restricted to artificial flies and lures only.
2. All trout must be returned to the water immediately.

Hunting

Both creeks are good for duck hunting. A handful of decoys placed in a wide bend is usually all that is needed to attract ducks flying out from nearby Dome Lakes. Thick patches of willows near the banks are ideal natural blinds. The creeks are also good for jump shooting. Stealth and patience are needed to get close to the ducks before they jump. Elk and deer hunting are by limited license. This is in Game Management Unit 66.

Watchable Wildlife

Waterfowl

Camping and Facilities

Camping is prohibited. There are no facilities.

General Restrictions

1. Access is by foot only from designated parking areas.
2. Dogs are prohibited.

7. Dome Lakes SWA

Primary Use:	Trout fishing and waterfowl hunting
Location:	Saguache County, Cochetopa Creek, 30 miles southeast of Gunnison
Size:	200 acres
Elevation:	8,700 feet
Division of Wildlife:	Area office in Gunnison, 970-641-7060
Directions:	From Gunnison, go 8 miles east on U.S. 50 to Highway 114, then 18 miles south (right) to County Road NN14, then 5 miles south (right) to the lakes.

The Dome Lakes are two small reservoirs located on Cochetopa Creek in Gunnison National Forest. The lakes are easily accessed from county roads and offer fishing for stocked rainbows, wild brown trout, and wild brook trout.

Fishing

Fishing in the upper lake is fair for stocked rainbows and wild brown trout. The lower lake has a good population of wild brook trout. Although motor boats are permitted, the best fishing is from small boats, canoes, or belly boats.

Hunting

There are plenty of ducks on the lakes until duck season opens. Hunting can be excellent during the first season, but the lakes are small and it doesn't take much hunting pressure to push the ducks out of the area. Additional waterfowl hunting is available downstream from the lakes on Cochetopa Creek. A fair number of ducks nest throughout the valley.

Watchable Wildlife

Waterfowl

Camping and Facilities

Camping is permitted at the upper lake, except from October 1 through the last day of waterfowl season. Facilities include toilets at both lakes and drinking water.

8. San Miguel SWA

From Placerville, go approximately 2 miles east on Highway 145 to reach the property.

Located on the San Miguel River south of Placerville, this fishing easement gives anglers access to a short stretch of the river. The trout population is mostly brown trout that are stocked as fingerlings. Catchable-sized rainbows are stocked when they are available.

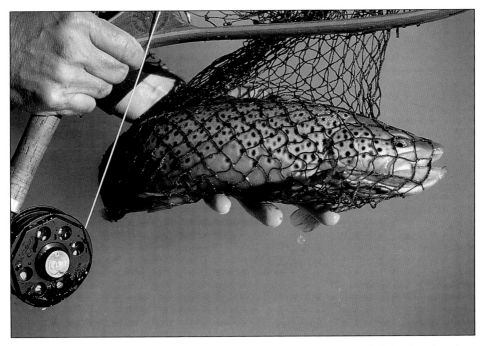

Most brown trout populations in Colorado are self-sustaining. During fall spawning season, male brown trout may be identified by their vibrant colors and hooked jaws.

9. Woods Lake SWA

Primary Use:	Trout fishing
Location:	San Miguel County, 15 miles southwest of Telluride
Size:	160 acres with about 30 acres of water
Elevation:	9,500 feet
Division of Wildlife:	Area office in Durango, 970-247-0855
Directions:	From Highway 145 at the Telluride cutoff, go 9 miles west on Highway 145 to Forest Service Road 618 (Fall Creek Road), then 9 miles south (left) to the property. The parking area is past the National Forest campground. Or, from Ridgway go 23 miles southwest on Highway 62 (over Dallas Divide) to Highway 145 at Placerville, then 3½ miles east (left) on Highway 145 to Fall Creek Road (turn right).

The Lizard Head Wilderness looms large over this beautiful small lake perched in a high valley south of the San Miguel River. The ragged crowns and jagged peaks of a string of Fourteeners radiate across the head of the valley. A thick forest of dark timber grows right to the lake's shores. There is not a prettier place in the state to paddle a canoe in search of trout.

Fishing

At this time, the lake is home to a population of wild, self-sustaining brook trout. In the future, the brook trout will be removed, and the lake will be managed as a brood lake for native Colorado River cutthroat trout. A barrier dam below the lake will prevent brook trout from reentering from Fall Creek. Fishing is by artificial flies and lures only.

Hunting

None

Watchable Wildlife

Waterfowl

Camping and Facilities

Camping is prohibited at the SWA, but a recently renovated National Forest campground is located just below the lake. There is a level parking area, a toilet, and a boat launching area at the SWA. Boating is prohibited except by craft propelled by hand, wind, or electric motor.

General Restrictions

See Fishing.

10. Dry Creek Basin SWA

Primary Use:	Big-game hunting
Location:	San Miguel County, 50 miles southwest of Montrose
Size:	8,000 acres total, including 1,200 acres in the southeastern tract
Elevation:	6,000–8,000 feet
Division of Wildlife:	Area office in Montrose, 970-252-6000
Directions:	From Naturita, go 3 miles east on Highway 145 to Highway 141, then approximately 13 miles south (right) to the main body of the property. To reach the more remote southeastern tract, go 11 miles south on Highway 141 to County Road U29, then 2 miles east (left) to County Road 31U, and then 6 miles south (right) to the access road and parking area on the right.

At first sight, this far-off and expansive basin near the Utah border appears like the land that time forgot. Signs of civilization are few and far between. Closer inspection reveals a history of mining and ranching in the area. The wildlife area consists of two large tracts of land located within a few miles of each other. Terrain and habitats on both tracts range from the sage-filled floor of the basin, to mesas and ridges covered in piñon-juniper, oak brush, and other shrubs.

Fishing

None

Hunting

Elk and deer hunting in the basin ranges from slow in the early seasons to good in the late season. The basin is important winter range for big game, but it takes a considerable amount of snowfall to push them down from summer and transitional ranges. Small-game hunting includes doves, rabbits, and sage grouse. This is in Game Management Unit 70.

Watchable Wildlife

Bald and golden eagles in winter

Camping and Facilities

Camping is restricted to designated areas. There are no facilities.

General Restrictions

1. The southeast tract is restricted to foot or horseback travel only.
2. Snowmobiles are prohibited.
3. Vehicles must remain on roads.

11. Miramonte Reservoir SWA

Primary Use:	Trout fishing
Location:	San Miguel County, 15 miles south of Norwood
Size:	800 acres including 400 surface acres of water
Elevation:	7,500 feet
Division of Wildlife:	Area office in Montrose, 970-252-6000
Directions:	From Norwood, go 1½ miles east on Highway 145 to Forest Service Road 610 (Dolores-Norwood Road), then 13 miles south to County Road L 40, then 2½ miles west (right) to the reservoir.

Miramonte Reservoir is a choice destination for fishing, waterfowl hunting, and a host of recreational activities. The reservoir is located in the middle of a flat, sage-filled basin immediately north of Lone Cone Mountain.

Fishing

Miramonte Reservoir is a put-and-grow trout fishery. Each year the DOW stocks 70,000–90,000 fingerling (5-inch) rainbow trout. Growth rate for the fingerlings is moderate and the average-size fish caught is 16–18 inches.

Hunting

Duck hunting is good at the reservoir, especially near the Naturita Creek inlet.

Watchable Wildlife

Ospreys, and a variety of ducks and shorebirds

Camping and Facilities

Camping is restricted to designated areas located at the two fee campgrounds. Facilities include level campsites for trailers and tents, picnic shelters, toilets, drinking water, fire rings, dump stations, trash barrels, and boat ramps.

General Restrictions

1. Discharging firearms or bows is prohibited, except while waterfowl hunting.
2. Waterskiing is prohibited 5 p.m.–10 a.m.
3. Waterskiing and jetskiing are prohibited except in designated areas.
4. Vehicles are restricted to roads and parking areas.

12. Lone Cone SWA

Primary Use:	Big-game hunting
Location:	Dolores County, 25 miles south of Norwood
Size:	5,000 acres
Elevation:	8,000–9,000 feet
Division of Wildlife:	Area office in Durango, 970-247-0855
Directions:	From Norwood, go 1½ miles east to Forest Road 610 (Dolores-Norwood Road), then travel 22 miles south and west (right) following the primary road at all turns. Just past a high meadow with a radio tower, the road drops quickly and switches back to the west. The access road to the property is on the south (left) side of the switchback. There is a red metal gate at the entrance. Turn south (left) and follow the road down the hill to the parking area.

This wildlife area sits in the heart of prime elk and deer country, surrounded on three sides by private land. The eastern edge of the property borders and provides access to the San Juan National Forest. Consequently, the property receives moderate to heavy hunting pressure. The terrain is broken and hilly, with numerous small creeks. The habitat is dense oak brush and other deciduous shrubs mixed with aspen, spruce, and fir. Open grassy meadows sit atop some of the hills and ridges. Beaver ponds and willow marshes are numerous.

Fishing

Marginal fishing opportunities exist for brook trout in the streams and beaver ponds.

Hunting

Elk, deer, black bear, and blue grouse are found on the property. This is in Game Management Units 70 and 71.

Watchable Wildlife

Same as hunting

Camping and Facilities

Several good campsites are located by the creek at the end of the access road. The best spots are taken early but there is ample space in the parking area and meadow. Facilities include drinking water from a domestic well, and horse corrals. This secluded wildlife area is a great place to camp and hike in the summer.

General Restrictions

Snowmobiles are prohibited.

13. Groundhog Reservoir SWA

Primary Use:	Trout fishing
Location:	Dolores County, 25 miles northeast of Dolores
Size:	Approximately 500 acres of water
Elevation:	9,000 feet
Division of Wildlife:	Area office in Durango, 970-247-0855
Directions:	From Dolores, go 25 miles north on Forest Service Road 526 to Forest Service Road 533 and then 5 miles east (right) to the reservoir.

Groundhog Reservoir is a funky little out-of-the-way place to camp, launch the boat, and kick back to the 1950s, when scenes like this were common at remote mountain reservoirs. Some folks like it so much they come here every summer to troll away the days fishing for trout, and idle away the evenings visiting with campground neighbors. The pace here would be slow, if there were one. Some supplies are available at the Groundhog America store on the property.

Fishing

Groundhog Reservoir is managed as a put-and-grow fishery. It is stocked with 2-inch fingerling rainbows and Colorado River cutthroat trout. There is a thriving population of crawfish in the reservoir, and a few trout big enough to eat them. Ice fishing is rated as excellent, but the road to the reservoir is not maintained in winter and access is by cross-country skis or snowmobiles.

Hunting

None

Watchable Wildlife

Waterfowl

Camping and Facilities

Campsites, restrooms, toilets, and a store are available at Groundhog America, the concessionaire at the reservoir.

General Restrictions

1. Boating is prohibited if it creates a white-water wake.
2. Fishing is prohibited in the Nash and Groundhog Creek inlets upstream for ½ mile, April 15–July 15.

14. Fish Creek SWA

Primary Use:	Access to big-game hunting
Location:	Dolores County, 25 miles northeast of Dolores
Size:	300 acres
Elevation:	9,000 feet
Division of Wildlife:	Area office in Durango, 970-247-0855
Directions:	From Dolores, go 12 miles north on Highway 145 to Forest Service Road 535, then 12 miles north (left) to the access road on the left. Cross the cattle guard and drive past the private residences 1½ miles to the parking area.

Located in the rugged county north of the West Dolores River, this out-of-the-way wildlife area plays a big role in providing hunting access to the south side of Black Mesa and to the San Juan National Forest. The large graveled parking area can accommodate several horse trailers and campers during hunting seasons. The topography of the area is mountainous, with creek drainages heavily timbered in spruce and fir. There are areas of dense oak brush and open grassy meadows.

Fishing

There is marginal fishing for small brook trout in Fish Creek.

Hunting

The wildlife area straddles 2 miles of Fish Creek. Big-game hunting is permitted in the wildlife area, but the area is small and better suited for small game like blue grouse, rabbits, and snowshoe hares. A Forest Service trail heads east into the National Forest from the parking area, following Fish Creek around the south side of Black Mesa. Deer and elk hunting are better here during the early season. This is in Game Management Unit 71.

Watchable Wildlife

Same as hunting

Camping and Facilities

Camping is prohibited, except during big-game hunting seasons.

15. Lone Dome SWA

Primary Use:	Trout fishing
Location:	Dolores County, Dolores River below McPhee Reservoir, 20 miles north of Cortez
Size:	1,700 acres, including 10 miles of fishing access on the Dolores River
Elevation:	7,000 feet
Division of Wildlife:	Area office in Durango 970-247-0855
Directions:	From Cortez, go 21 miles north on U.S. 666 to County road DD (stay right), then 1 mile east (right) to County Road 16, then 3 miles north (left) to the USFS sign at the access road, and then 1½ miles east (right) to Bradfield Bridge.

There may be trouble in paradise but it's paradise all the same. The beautiful Dolores River below McPhee Reservoir is the perfect setting for a trophy trout fishery. The river bends and glides through the narrow valley in a series of long riffles, fast runs, and deep pools. Mature cottonwoods and ponderosas stand tall over the banks, and hay meadows stretch out on the valley floor. Lofty outcroppings and sheer rock walls adorn the valley walls. The trouble lies in the cold fact that the river has great potential as a quality trout fishery, but lacks the flow of water necessary to make it happen. Low flows during the hot summer months are devastating to trout and aquatic insect populations. Water flows are determined by irrigation needs, and are beyond the DOW's control.

Fishing

Undaunted by the low flows, the DOW continues successfully to manage the river for quality trout fishing, stocking it periodically with fingerling rainbow and cutthroat trout. Fishing for rainbows and cutthroats is hard to predict, ranging from fair to excellent. The most reliable fishing is for the river's venerable brown trout. Browns to 20 inches are not uncommon.

1. Fishing is by flies and lures only.
2. All trout must be returned to water immediately.

Hunting

Dolores Canyon and the San Juan National Forest land to the northeast are highly-rated locations for turkey hunting, with an over-the-counter license. Other hunting opportunities exist for deer, elk, black bears, dove, and blue grouse. This is in Game Management Unit 711.

Watchable Wildlife

Same as hunting

Camping and Facilities

Camping is prohibited on the SWA but there is a comfortable USFS campground with toilets and potable water located at Bradfield Bridge, on the north end of the property.

General Restrictions

1. Overnight parking is prohibited, except in designated areas.
2. Fires are prohibited.

16. Narraguinnep Reservoir SWA

From Cortez, go 10 miles north on U.S. 666 to Highway 184, and then 2 miles east (right) to the reservoir.

Narraguinnep is a 600-acre irrigation reservoir located 11 miles north of Cortez and 7 miles west of Dolores. It is managed as a warm-water fishery with walleye as the primary species. Walleye to 18 inches are common. Other species include channel catfish, yellow perch, and an unwanted population of stunted northern pike. There is no size or bag limit on pike. Camping is prohibited. Facilities include toilets and a concrete boat ramp. Waterfowl hunting is permitted. The reservoir has moderate fluctuations in water level.

17. Dolores River SWA

To reach this property from Dolores, go 5 miles east on Highway 145 to the access road on the right. The entrance is well-hidden by trees.

This little stretch of water on the Dolores River is difficult to locate and hardly worth the effort. Fishing is marginal for rainbow and brown trout. Kokanee snagging is permitted November 15–December 31. Camping is prohibited, and so is fishing in the rearing ponds.

18. Puett Reservoir SWA

From Mancos, go 11 miles north and west on Highway 184 to County Road 33, then 1 mile south (left) to road P.4, and then 1½ miles east (left) to access the reservoir.

Located about halfway between Dolores and Mancos, this small (about 300-acre) irrigation reservoir sits at the end of a dead-end road surrounded by farms. It is a warm-water fishery managed primarily for walleye and smallmouth bass, but there is a population of northern pike, too. There is a concrete boat ramp, but low water levels make it difficult to use. The lake is subject to extreme water fluctuations. Watchable wildlife include osprey, great blue herons, Canada geese, and a variety of ducks. Waterfowl hunting is permitted. Camping is prohibited.

Mallard drakes

19. Summit Reservoir SWA

Primary Use:	Fishing and waterfowl hunting
Location:	Montezuma County, 10 miles northeast of Cortez
Size:	About 500 acres
Elevation:	7,500 feet
Division of Wildlife:	Area office in Durango, 970-247-0855
Directions:	From U.S. 160 in Mancos, go 9 miles north and west on Highway 184 to the sign at the access road on the left, and then ¼ mile south (left) to the parking area.

Summit is the largest of three reservoirs located along the Dominguez/Escalante Memorial Highway between Mancos and Dolores. The landscape is relatively flat with a few low hills forested in a mixture of pine and oak brush.

Fishing

The lake is managed primarily as a warm-water fishery for largemouth and smallmouth bass, and has fair-to-good fishing for both. All bass less than 15 inches long must be returned to the water immediately. The lake is stocked periodically with rainbow trout. Although there is a good concrete boat ramp, it often doesn't reach the water during summer when the lake is low. The lake is ideal for belly boats and other small craft that can be launched by hand. There are plenty of places to fish from shore and there is a rock rubble dam.

Hunting

The reservoir has shallow bays that can be very good for duck hunting.

Watchable Wildlife

Waterfowl

Camping and Facilities

Camping is prohibited. Facilities include a toilet and a boat ramp.

General Restrictions

Boating is prohibited if it creates a white-water wake.

20. Joe Moore Reservoir SWA

Primary Use:	Fishing
Location:	Montezuma County, 15 miles northeast of Cortez
Size:	100 acres
Elevation:	7,500 feet
Division of Wildlife:	Area office in Durango, 970-247-0855
Directions:	From Cortez, go 16 miles east on U.S. 160 to Highway 184 at Mancos, then 2½ miles northwest (left) to County Road 40, and 4 miles north (right) to the reservoir.

Joe Moore is one of those spots that you probably wouldn't visit unless you lived nearby. It is a small, quiet, warm-water reservoir surrounded by pine trees. The reservoir is used for irrigation, and the water level can be very low in summer.

Fishing

The reservoir is stocked with hatchery trout when they are available, and it has a decent population of largemouth bass.

Hunting

Waterfowl

Watchable Wildlife

Same as hunting

Camping and Facilities

There are several nice primitive campsites, a toilet, and a boat ramp.

General Restrictions

Boating is prohibited if it creates a white-water wake.

21. Totten Reservoir SWA

Primary Use:	Warm-water fishing
Location:	Montezuma County, 3 miles northeast of Cortez
Size:	Approximately 500 acres of water
Elevation:	6,000 feet
Division of Wildlife:	Area office in Durango, 970-247-0855
Directions:	From Cortez, go 3 miles east on U.S. 160 to County Road 29, and then 1 mile north (left) to the reservoir.

Totten is a medium-sized irrigation reservoir located in the open farmland just outside of Cortez. It is a nice facility for picnicking, fishing, and waterfowl hunting.

Fishing

The reservoir is managed as a warm-water fishery for largemouth bass, catfish, and bluegill. There is also a small population of northern pike. There is no bag or possession limit for pike. All bass less than 15 inches long must be returned to the water immediately.

Hunting

Waterfowl hunting is permitted except in the inlet area, as posted.

Watchable Wildlife

Same as hunting

Camping and Facilities

Camping is prohibited. Facilities include toilets, a picnic shelter, and a concrete boat ramp.

General Restrictions

1. Boating is prohibited if it creates a white-water wake.
2. Public access is prohibited along the north shore March 1–May 31.
3. Public access is prohibited from one hour after sunset to one hour before sunrise, except for fishing.
4. Fires are prohibited.

22. Perins Peak SWA

Primary Use:	Big-game and small-game hunting
Location:	La Plata County, 3 miles west of Durango
Size:	13,000 acres total
Elevation:	7,000–8,500 feet
Division of Wildlife:	Area office in Durango, 970-247-0855
Directions:	**Tract A:** From Durango, go 4 miles west on U.S. 160 to County Road 207 (Lightner Creek Road), then 2 miles north (right) to County Road 208. County Road 208 is the access road.
	Tract B: From Durango, go 5 miles west on U.S. 160 to Victory Coal Mine. The access trail passes through ½ mile of private property to the SWA boundary.

Due to the close proximity to Durango, and because the main tract straddles a public road, this property gets a lot of recreational use by hikers and mountain-bikers. A parking area at the north end of Tract A provides an access point into the San Juan National Forest.

Fishing

None

Hunting

Big-game hunting for elk, deer, and black bears, and small-game hunting for Merriam's turkeys and blue grouse. This is in Game Management Unit 74.

Watchable Wildlife

Same as hunting

Camping and Facilities

Camping is prohibited, except during elk and deer seasons. There are no facilities.

General Restrictions

1. Public access is prohibited from the last day of deer and elk seasons to March 31.
2. Public access is prohibited east of County Road 208 and north of U.S. 160 April 1–July 15.
3. Snowmobiles are prohibited.
4. Discharging firearms or bows is prohibited, except while hunting.

23. Bodo SWA

Primary Use:	Hunting and hiking
Location:	La Plata County, 1 mile south of Durango
Size:	7,500 acres
Elevation:	7,000–7,500 feet
Division of Wildlife:	Area office in Durango, 970-247-0855
Directions:	From Durango, go 1 mile south on U.S. 160 to County Road 211, then ¼ mile west (right) to the sign marking the eastern boundary of the SWA. County Road 211 runs west through the middle of the property.

This wildlife area covers a wide swath of land in a basin just south of Durango. Bodo is important for conserving habitat and providing a variety of hunting and recreational opportunities. The basin is cradled between Smelter Mountain to the north and a high ridge to the south. Vegetation is a mixture of sage, oak brush, and grasses on the basin floor, and coniferous forests on the north-facing slopes of the ridge. Basin Creek flows east through the property to the Animas River.

Fishing

None

Hunting

Deer, elk, and small game including blue grouse, doves, rabbits, and band-tailed pigeons

Watchable Wildlife

Same as hunting

Camping and Facilities

None

General Restrictions

1. Discharging firearms or bows is prohibited except while hunting.
2. Fires are prohibited.
3. Snowmobiles are prohibited.

24. Pastorius Reservoir SWA

From Durango, go 7 miles southeast on U.S. 160 to Highway 172, then 2 miles south (right) to County Road 302, and then ½ mile west (right) to the lake.

Pastorius is an 80-acre parklike irrigation reservoir located in the farmland 8 miles southeast of Durango. The lake is managed as both a warm- and a cold-water fishery, with largemouth and smallmouth bass, bluegill, and trout. The minimum size for bass is 15 inches. The reservoir is stocked periodically with fingerling and catchable-sized rainbow trout. Waterfowl hunting is allowed. Camping is prohibited. Boating is prohibited, except for craft propelled by hand or electric motor.

25. Haviland Lake SWA

Primary Use:	Trout fishing
Location:	La Plata County, 20 miles north of Durango
Size:	200 acres
Elevation:	8,500 feet
Division of Wildlife:	Area office in Durango, 970-247-0855
Directions:	From Durango, go 18 miles north on U.S. 550 to Forest Service Road 671, and then ½ mile east (right) to the lake.

This is a nice little fishing hole with easy access, good facilities, and great mountain scenery. And you can barely hear U.S. 550 traffic buzzing over the hill.

Fishing

The lake receives heavy fishing pressure, especially after hatchery trucks deliver their loads of catchable-sized rainbow trout. Fishing for the lake's thriving population of brook trout is better right after ice-out. There is easy wading along the shoreline and plenty of weed beds to cast a fly over.

Hunting

Waterfowl hunting is permitted, but the area is close to homes.

Watchable Wildlife

Same as hunting

Camping and Facilities

Camping is prohibited at the SWA, but a Forest Service campground at the lake has camping, toilets, and drinking water. There are fishing platforms and a gravel boat ramp.

General Restrictions

Boating is prohibited, except for craft propelled by hand or electric motor.

26. Andrews Lake SWA

From Durango, go 39 miles north on U.S. 550 to the access road, and then east (right) ½ mile to the lake. The lake is open to day use only.

Andrews Lake is a small, alpine lake located 1 mile south of Molas Pass. Mountain vistas are tremendous in every direction. The lake is stocked periodically with catchable-sized hatchery trout, when they are available. A trail leads to small fishing piers located around the lake. The SWA also serves as the trailhead and parking for the Colorado Trail and the trail to Crater Lake. The access road and parking areas are paved, and there are modern toilets.

27. Williams Creek Reservoir SWA

Primary Use:	Trout fishing
Location:	Hinsdale County, San Juan Mountains, 30 miles northwest of Pagosa Springs
Size:	500 acres
Elevation:	8,500 feet
Division of Wildlife:	Area office in Durango, 970-247-0855
Directions:	From Pagosa Springs, go 2½ miles west on U.S. 160 to Forest Service Road 600 (which becomes Forest Road 631), then 30 miles northwest (right) to the signs at Forest Service Road 640, and then 1 mile east (right) to the reservoir.

Williams Creek has all the right stuff. Imagine a mountain reservoir surrounded by stunning scenery and inhabited by an illusive community of wild, trophy-class brook trout. Add a stock of Snake River cutthroats and then season the mix with a self-sustaining population of wild (yes, wild!) kokanee salmon. The reservoir is easily accessed and immensely popular in summer.

Fishing

The lake is managed as a put-and-grow fishery, stocked periodically with fingerling Snake River cutthroat trout. The lake receives a considerable amount of fishing pressure. There are no size restrictions, but the trout grow fast and the ones that avoid being caught for a few years will grow to 14–16 inches. The most challenging fishing at the lake is for a little-known and evasive population of big brook trout. The big brook trout are easier to catch right after ice-out in spring and right before the lake freezes in fall. A unique opportunity exists here to fish for a population of self-sustaining kokanee salmon that are holdovers from the days when they were stocked by the DOW.

Hunting

Waterfowl

Watchable Wildlife

Same as hunting

Camping and Facilities

Camping is available for a fee at two nearby National Forest campgrounds. Facilities include toilets and a boat ramp.

General Restrictions

1. Waterskiing is prohibited.
2. Sailboards are prohibited.

28. Devil Creek SWA

Primary Use:	Hunting
Location:	Archuleta County, 17 miles west of Pagosa Springs
Size:	560 acres
Elevation:	6,800–7,500 feet
Division of Wildlife:	Area office in Durango, 970-247-0855
Directions:	From Pagosa Springs, go 17 miles west on U.S. 160 to Forest Road 627, then about 1½ miles north (right) to the property. There are no boundary signs or parking areas. Park at the earthen barricade and follow the creek upstream.

The ridges and knobs overlooking Devil Creek are prime habitat for Merriam's turkeys and mule deer. Old-growth ponderosas tower over a dense understory of Gambel oak, serviceberry, and other deciduous shrubs. The property straddles 2 miles of the creek and adjoins the San Juan National Forest. Access is by foot or horseback only.

Fishing

None

Hunting

Hunting is reported as good to excellent for deer, turkey, blue grouse, and other small game. This is in Game Management Unit 77.

Watchable Wildlife

Same as hunting

Camping and Facilities

Overnight camping is prohibited in the wildlife area, and there are no facilities. Primitive camping is available in the National Forest. There are several campgrounds nearby on U.S. 160.

General Restrictions

1. Snowmobiles are prohibited.
2. Fires are prohibited.

29. Echo Canyon Reservoir SWA

Primary Use:	Fishing
Location:	Archuleta County, 4 miles south of Pagosa Springs
Size:	200 acres
Elevation:	7,000 feet
Division of Wildlife:	Area office in Durango, 970-247-0855
Directions:	From Pagosa Springs, go 1 mile east on U.S. 160 to U.S. 84, then 4 miles south (right) to the sign and access road on the right.

The state-record largemouth bass was caught here in 1997. It measured 22½ inches long and weighed 11 pounds, 6 ounces. The reservoir lies in the low hills south of Pagosa Springs. A service road travels around the north side of the lake, providing easy access to fishing and waterfowl hunting.

Fishing

Fishing is good for largemouth bass, sunfish, and yellow perch, and the reservoir is stocked annually with catchable-sized (10-inch) rainbow trout. There is good access to shoreline fishing and a fishing jetty is located on the north shore.

1. All largemouth and smallmouth bass between 12 and 15 inches long must be returned to the water immediately.
2. There is no bag or possession limit for yellow perch.

Hunting

Waterfowl

Watchable Wildlife

Same as hunting

Camping and Facilities

Camping is prohibited. Facilities include several parking areas, toilets, a boat ramp, and a jetty.

General Restrictions

1. Waterskiing is prohibited.
2. Fires are prohibited.

Largemouth bass

30. Alberta Park Reservoir SWA

Primary Use:	Trout fishing
Location:	Mineral County, Wolf Creek Pass
Size:	60 acres of water; the high water mark is the boundary.
Elevation:	10,000 feet
Division of Wildlife:	Area office in Durango, 970-247-0855
Directions:	From South Fork, go 18 miles southwest on U.S. 160 to the Wolf Creek Ski Area, then south (left) through the ski parking area and continue 1¾ miles on Forest Service Road 391 to the reservoir.

Alberta Park Reservoir is Colorado's premier fishery for trophy-sized Rio Grande cutthroat trout. This is a special place for anglers interested in catching native trout. The reservoir lies in a narrow creek drainage directly below Wolf Creek Ski Area and the Continental Divide.

Fishing

In 2000, the average-size Rio Grande cutthroat in the reservoir was approximately 13 inches long. DOW biologists expect some of the cutthroats to reach 20 inches in a few years. Although anglers must release all the cutthroats they catch, they are encouraged to keep the brook trout.

1. Fishing is restricted to artificial flies and lures only.
2. All cutthroat trout must be returned to the water immediately.
3. The daily bag limit for brook trout is four fish plus an additional 10 fish less than 8 inches long.

Hunting

Hunting is prohibited.

Watchable Wildlife

Waterfowl

Camping and Facilities

Camping is prohibited. There are no facilities except a small gravel boat ramp. Campsites with full facilities are available at Forest Service campgrounds in the vicinity.

General Restrictions

Fires are prohibited.

31. Big Meadows Reservoir SWA

Primary Use:	Trout fishing
Location:	Mineral County, 10 miles southwest of South Fork
Size:	100 acres
Elevation:	9,200 feet
Division of Wildlife:	Area office in Montrose, 970-252-6000
Directions:	From South Fork, go 10 miles southwest on U.S. 160 to Forest Road 410 (Big Meadows turnoff), and then 2 miles west (right) to the reservoir.

Although it receives heavy use during the summer tourist season, this reservoir manages to keep one thing a secret—almost.

Fishing

Big Meadows is managed as a put-and-take fishery, stocked periodically with 10-inch-long hatchery rainbows. This keeps the tourists happy, but the real news here is the outstanding fishing for a wild, self-sustaining population of brook trout—and some of them grow large. Fishing is better near the inlet, especially in late summer and early fall, when the brook trout are spawning. Brook trout spawn on gravel beds in flowing water. The trail west from the reservoir follows the inlet creek into the Weminuche Wilderness. And by the way, there is also a small population of Rio Grande cutthroat trout in the reservoir. All cutthroats must be returned to the water immediately!

Hunting

Hunting is prohibited.

Watchable Wildlife

Waterfowl

Camping and Facilities

Camping is prohibited at the SWA, but there is a Forest Service campground on the south side of the reservoir. The SWA has a boat ramp and toilets.

General Restrictions

See Hunting and Fishing.

32. Creede SWA

This area is situated on the Rio Grande near the old fish hatchery south of Creede. There is a limited amount of fishing here on a short stretch of the river. From Creede, go 1½ miles southeast on Highway 149 to an unmarked road on the right, and then ½ mile south (right) to the river. There is a parking area with a picnic bench.

33. Road Canyon Reservoir SWA

Primary Use:	Trout fishing
Location:	Hinsdale County, upper Rio Grande, 25 miles west of Creede
Size:	100 acres
Elevation:	9,000 feet
Division of Wildlife:	Area office in Monte Vista, 719-587-6900
Directions:	From Creede, go 25 miles west and north on Highway 149 to Forest Service Road 520, and then 4 miles west (left) to the reservoir.

Road Canyon is the first and southernmost in a trio of SWAs located in the headwaters of the Rio Grande west of Creede. Cradled in a long valley at the northern edge of the Weminuche Wilderness, the reservoir has great views to go along with the fishing. There are two reservoirs here, but the upper lake is quite small. Access is kept open year-round.

Fishing

Road Canyon is managed as a put-and-grow fishery and stocked periodically with fingerling rainbows. It gets an occasional booster shot of catchable-sized (10-inch) hatchery rainbows when they are available. The lake is loaded with weeds and teeming with aquatic insects. Trout grow rapidly in the rich waters.

Hunting

Waterfowl

Watchable Wildlife

The reservoirs are loaded with ducks in late summer.

Camping and Facilities

Camping is prohibited, but a Forest Service campground is located just west of the reservoir. Facilities at the SWA include toilets and a boat ramp.

General Restrictions

Boating is prohibited if it creates a white-water wake.

Rainbow trout

34. Brown Lakes SWA

Primary Use:	Trout fishing
Location:	Hinsdale County, upper Rio Grande, 25 miles west of Creede
Size:	500 acres
Elevation:	9,800 feet
Division of Wildlife:	Area office in Montrose, 970-252-6000
Directions:	From Creede, go 25 miles west on Highway 149 to Forest Service Road 515 (Hermit Lakes Road), then 1½ miles west (left) to the property.

Brown Lakes is a shallow reservoir located in the scenic valley of Hermit Lakes Creek in the headwaters of the Rio Grande. The lake is managed as a cold-water fishery and has easy access on county roads.

Fishing

Trout do well in the shallow, weedy lakes. The lakes are stocked with hatchery rainbows when they are available, and it has a healthy population of wild brook trout.

Hunting

If the large number of ducks on these lakes in September is an indication, the opening day of duck season in October should be outstanding.

Watchable Wildlife

Waterfowl

Camping and Facilities

Camping is prohibited. Facilities include toilets and a boat ramp on the upper lake. Camping is available at the Forest Service campground east of the lower lake.

35. Rito Hondo Reservoir SWA

From Creede, go 35 miles west and north on Highway 149 to Forest Service Road 513, and then 2 miles north (left) to the fork, and then right to the reservoir.

Rito Hondo is a 40-acre reservoir resting in a high meadow just below the Continental Divide in the headwaters of the Rio Grande. The reservoir is managed as a put-and-grow trout fishery stocked periodically with fingerling rainbows and cutthroats, and there is a healthy population of self-sustaining brook trout. There is a Forest Service campground with toilets and a gravel boat ramp. Boating is prohibited, except for craft propelled by hand, wind, or electric motor. The lake is rated good for ice fishing.

North Central Colorado

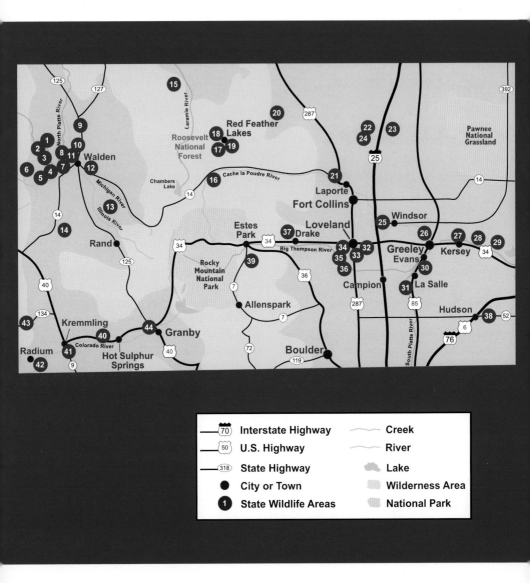

	Legend	
🛣 70 Interstate Highway	～ Creek	
🛡 50 U.S. Highway	～ River	
🛡 318 State Highway	🌊 Lake	
● City or Town	▦ Wilderness Area	
① State Wildlife Areas	▦ National Park	

The north central region has more State Wildlife Areas than any other. Covering both sides of the Continental Divide, it encompasses the headwaters of the North Platte River, the Colorado River, the Laramie River, and the entire Cache la Poudre River and Big Thompson River drainages.

Trout fishing opportunities seem endless here. They range from lunker brown trout fishing at North Delaney Butte Reservoir, to premium trout fishing on the Colorado River at **Hot Sulphur Springs SWA**, to small streams like Raspberry Creek at **Irvine SWA**, in the headwaters of the North Platte River. Anglers can fish for native greenback cutthroat trout in the headwaters of the North Fork of the Poudre River at **Cimarron SWA**.

Of the many wildlife areas in the north central region with big-game hunting, none are more important or impressive than **Cherokee SWA**, which stretches along the North Fork of the Poudre from the Laramie Mountains to the foothills. (Not to mention the thousands of acres along the Colorado River at **Radium SWA!**)

Wildlife Areas in North Central Colorado

1. Lake John SWA

Primary Use:	Trout fishing
Location:	Jackson County, North Park, 10 miles northwest of Walden
Size:	565 acres of water, 282 acres of land
Elevation:	8,100 feet
Division of Wildlife:	Area office in Steamboat Springs, 970-870-2197
Directions:	From Walden, go 8 miles west on County Road 12W to County Road 7 and then 7 miles north (right) to the access road, and 2 miles west (left) to the property.

Lake John is the largest and most popular reservoir in North Park. It has a well-earned reputation for producing trophy-sized trout. The reservoir's weedy substrate is awash in scuds and aquatic insects, resulting in a remarkable growth rate of stocked fingerling trout. With shoreline camping and a four-fish bag limit on trout, Lake John is popular with anglers of the lawn chair, propped rod, and bait-fishing persuasion.

Fishing

Every year, 200,000 rainbow trout and Snake River cutthroat trout fingerlings are pumped into Lake John. By the end of their second summer, the 5-inch fish have grown to 16 inches, and by their third summer, the ones that have survived the onslaught of anglers will have grown to 20 inches. However, Lake John is subject to winter kill and many trout never live through a hard winter. Lake John is managed as a put-and-grow-and-take fishery, and receives an incredible 150,000 hours of fishing pressure annually.

Hunting

Waterfowl

Watchable Wildlife

Sage grouse, osprey, and waterfowl

Camping and Facilities

Primitive camping is permitted around the shores of the lake. Facilities include toilets, boat ramps, and picnic tables with shade shelters. A private campground with electric hookups and a dump station is located on the premises.

General Restrictions

Waterskiing and sailboards are prohibited.

Rainbow trout grow quickly to trophy size in Lake John.

2. Richard SWA

Primary Use:	Trout fishing
Location:	Jackson County, North Fork of the North Platte River, adjacent to Lake John SWA
Size:	Approximately 2,000 acres and 6 miles of river access
Elevation:	8,100 feet
Division of Wildlife:	Area office in Steamboat Springs, 970-870-2197
Directions:	**Richard East (North Platte River):** From Walden, go 8 miles west on County Road 12W to County Road 7, then 7 miles north (right) to the access road, and 2 miles west (left) to Lake John SWA. The parking area for Richard SWA is located at the southwest corner of Lake John.
	Richard West (hunting access only): From Walden, go 13 miles west on 12W to the area, which is situated on the west side of Sheep Mountain and marked by DOW signs. There is no access to the North Platte from this area.

Richard SWA is situated south of **Lake John** (see p. 116). This wildlife area is typical of the North Platte River, with a meandering stream sparsely vegetated with willows.

Fishing

This stretch of the North Fork of the North Platte River is a brown trout fishery with fish ranging in size from fingerlings to 20 inches.

1. Fishing is by artificial flies and lures only.
2. Bag and possession for trout is two fish.

Hunting

Deer, elk, antelope, sage grouse, and waterfowl hunting opportunities are available. Richard West provides hunting access on Sheep Mountain. Hunting is prohibited within 200 yards of a building.

Watchable Wildlife

Same as hunting

Camping and Facilities

Campsites and toilets are available at Lake John.

General Restrictions

See Hunting and Fishing.

3. Delaney Butte Lakes SWA

Primary Use:	Trout fishing
Location:	Jackson County, North Park, 10 miles west of Walden
Size:	435 acres of water and 2,132 acres of land
Elevation:	8,100 feet
Division of Wildlife:	Area office in Steamboat Springs, 970-870-2197
Directions:	From Walden, go ½ mile west on Highway 14 to County Road 12W, then 5 miles west (right) to County Road 18, then west (straight) 4½ miles to County Road 5, then ½ mile north (right) to the property.

Bundled together at the base of Delaney Butte, three extremely fertile reservoirs serve up a smorgasbord of superb trout fishing. Rock outcroppings and small groves of aspen adorn the top of the landmark butte, but the general landscape is treeless and dominated by sagebrush. Each lake is individually managed for different species of trout and fishing methods, but all share in the common goal of providing quality trout fishing.

Fishing

In general, all three lakes offer excellent opportunities for fly fishing in summer, and ice fishing in winter. The damselfly and *callibaetis* mayfly hatches that occur in early summer are peak times for dry-fly fishing.

North Delaney is classified as Gold Medal Water and considered the finest brown trout fishery in the state. There is a sizable, healthy, self-sustaining population of large brown trout, many exceeding 20 inches. The DOW supplies its fish hatcheries with brown trout eggs and milt from here.

East Delaney is a rainbow trout factory operating at peak efficiency. After reclamation in 1998 to remove unwanted suckers, the lake was stocked with rainbows and a few browns. Their rate of growth has been remarkable. The average size in 1999 was 18 inches and climbing. East Delaney boasts the highest catch rate of the three lakes.

South Delaney is managed as a Snake River cutthroat and rainbow trout fishery, with heavy focus on the cutthroats. Big trout swim these waters. Trout weighing more than five pounds are not rare. Some are much larger.

Hunting

Waterfowl, deer, and small game

Watchable Wildlife

Sage grouse, nighthawks, pronghorn antelope, and a variety of waterfowl are common in this region of North Park.

Camping and Facilities

Primitive campsites are located on the shorelines around all three lakes. Facilities include boat ramps, restrooms, and picnic shelters.

General Restrictions

1. Artificial flies and lures only (this includes ice fishing).
2. Bag and possession for trout is two fish.
3. At North Delaney Lake, brown trout 14–20 inches must be returned to the water immediately.
4. Boating is prohibited if it creates a white-water wake.
5. Sailboards are prohibited.

4. Manville SWA

Primary Use:	Trout fishing
Location:	Jackson County, North Park, 10 miles southwest of Walden
Size:	1 mile of stream fishing on the Roaring Fork of the North Platte River
Elevation:	8,000 feet
Division of Wildlife:	Area office in Steamboat Springs, 970-870-2197
Directions:	From Walden, go 5 miles west on County Road 12W to County Road 18, then 4½ miles west (straight) to County Road 5, and then ¼ mile south (left) to the parking area at the bridge.

Located just a long cast south of **Delaney Butte Lakes** (see p. 119), Manville SWA gives access to 1 mile of trout fishing on the Roaring Fork.

Fishing

Primarily a brown trout fishery, the Roaring Fork is a tributary to the North Platte. The trout are small but willing, averaging only 6–10 inches, and this is a great place for beginning fly fishers. The North Platte River is not on public land. Do not trespass.

1. Fishing is by artificial flies and lures only.
2. The bag and possession for trout is two fish of any size.
3. Fishing is prohibited on the North Platte River.

Hunting

Hunting is prohibited.

Watchable Wildlife

Moose are common in the area, and they can be aggressive toward humans. Do not approach them, especially cows with calves.

Camping and Facilities

None

General Restrictions

See Hunting and Fishing.

5. Irvine SWA

Primary Use:	Trout fishing
Location:	Jackson County, North Park, 15 miles west of Walden
Size:	About 4 miles of fishing access
Elevation:	8,200 feet
Division of Wildlife:	Area office in Steamboat Springs, 970-870-2197
Directions:	From Walden, go 5 miles west on County Road 12W to County Road 18, then west (straight) 4½ miles to County Road 5, then ½ mile south (left) to County Road 22, and then 2½ miles southwest (right) to the DOW sign. The access road is the driveway to the ranch, and the parking area is in the rancher's yard. The lower parking area (which can be seen from County Road 22) offers access to the confluence of Raspberry and Beaver Creeks.

Raspberry Creek is a soggy little wiggle of water flowing out of the Mount Zirkel Wilderness to join other little streams in the headwaters of the North Platte River. This gem of a small stream receives very little fishing pressure because it is nearly impossible to find, and you feel like you're trespassing when you do.

Fishing

There are wild populations of both brown and brook trout in Raspberry Creek. The browns average 13 inches long and the brook trout average 12 inches. Small and heavily willowed, the stream is challenging, yet rewarding. For the best fishing, follow the creek upstream to the west of Pitchpine Mountain.

1. Fishing is by artificial flies and lures only.
2. Access is limited to the stream corridor.

Hunting

Hunting is prohibited.

Watchable Wildlife

Moose are common in the area, and they can be aggressive toward humans. Do not approach them, especially cows with calves.

Camping and Facilities

None

General Restrictions

See Hunting and Fishing.

6. Odd Fellows SWA

Primary Use: Trout fishing

Location: Jackson County, North Park, 15 miles west of Walden

Size: 2 miles of stream access

Elevation: 8,200 feet

Division of Wildlife: Area office in Steamboat Springs, 970-870-2197

Directions: From Walden, go 5 miles west on County Road 12W to County Road 18, then 4½ miles west (straight) to County Road 5, then ½ mile south (left) to County Road 22, and then 2½ miles southwest (right) to the signed access road on the right. The access road goes to the right of the ranch house and through the barnyard to a narrow bridge over an irrigation ditch. Over the bridge, the two-track road takes off to the north, heading up and around the east slope of Pitchpine Mountain. After passing three barbed-wire gates, cattle guards, and another narrow bridge over yet another irrigation ditch, the road ends at a fenced parking area beside the creek. Please respect private property by staying on the established road and closing all the gates.

Down in a valley, around a mountain, and behind a working ranch flows a small stream with a string of beaver ponds and a thriving population of wild brown trout. To say that Odd Fellows is off the beaten path is an understatement. Finding the parking area is not easy, but is worth the effort, because the fishing is good. So are the views of Red Canyon and the Mount Zirkel Wilderness. Odd Fellows is the place to test your fly-fishing skills against a master brown trout. And watch out for the moose!

Fishing

A hearty population of brown trout continues to survive and grow here, in spite of extremely low flows in the stream from irrigation demands in late summer and fall. Brown trout over 16 inches long are common, but catching these wild and wary fish is never easy, and fishing is made even more difficult when the flow is low. Fishing is by artificial flies and lures only.

Hunting

Hunting is prohibited.

Watchable Wildlife

Moose are common in the area, and they can be aggressive toward humans.
Do not approach them, especially cows with calves.

Camping and Facilities

None

General Restrictions

See Hunting and Fishing.

7. Verner SWA

Primary Use:	Trout fishing
Location:	Jackson County, North Platte River, 5 miles west of Walden
Size:	About 1 mile of fishing access on the North Platte, downstream from the bridge on County Road 12W
Elevation:	8,000 feet
Division of Wildlife:	Area office in Steamboat Springs, 970-870-2197
Directions:	From Walden, go 5 miles west on County Road 12W to County Road 18, then ½ mile west (straight) to the access road on the right.

This wildlife area is easily accessed from a parking area that is visible from County Road 12W. The scenery is good, but the fishing in this stretch of the North Platte is marginal.

Fishing

Fishing for the resident brown trout in this stretch of the North Platte is challenging. The trout are smallish, 8–10 inches. Fishing is by artificial flies and lures only.

Hunting

Hunting is prohibited.

Watchable Wildlife

Moose are common in the area, and they can be aggressive toward humans. Do not approach them, especially cows with calves.

Camping and Facilities

None

General Restrictions

1. Public access is limited to the fenced area along the river.
2. Stay by the river. Do not cut across fields.

Brook trout

8. Brownlee SWA

Primary Use:	Trout fishing
Location:	Jackson County, North Platte River, 5 miles west of Walden
Size:	1¼ miles of fishing access
Elevation:	8,000 feet
Division of Wildlife:	Area office in Steamboat Springs, 970-870-2197
Directions:	From Highway 14 west of Walden, go 5½ miles west on County Road 12W, then ½ mile west (straight) on County Road 18 to the signed access road on the right. The parking area sits over the hill, hidden from view of County Road 18.

Brownlee SWA is located on the North Platte River ½ mile downstream from **Verner SWA** (see p. 124). The Brownlee property doesn't receive a great deal of fishing pressure, even though the fishing is much better on this stretch of the river. The river is a ½-mile hike from the parking area on a hill overlooking the river. The views from the parking area are some of the best in North Park. Sweeping panoramas of the Continental Divide, the Mount Zirkel Wilderness, and the Medicine Bow Mountains provide the backdrop for fly fishing in this "postcard" stretch of the North Platte River.

Fishing

From the parking lot on the hill it's about a ½-mile hike to the river. The river winds across the valley floor in a series of horseshoe bends. Brownlee and the adjacent **Verner SWA** offer 2½ miles of combined fishing access on the North Platte River. Although there aren't great numbers of trout on this stretch of the river, there are some browns that measure 21–22 inches. Catchable rainbows are stocked periodically.

1. Fishing is by flies and lures only.
2. Bag and possession limit for trout is two fish.

Hunting

None

Watchable Wildlife

Waterfowl

Camping and Facilities

None

General Restrictions

See Fishing.

Large numbers of Canada geese nest in North Park.

9. Cowdrey Lake SWA

Primary Use: Trout fishing

Location: Jackson County, 7 miles north of Walden

Size: 80 acres of water

Elevation: 8,000 feet

Division of Wildlife: Area office in Steamboat Springs, 970-870-2197

Directions: From Walden, go 7½ miles north on Highway 125 to the signed access road on the left.

This little reservoir is a good place to catch lots of stocked rainbow trout, and to avoid the crowds at the more popular SWAs such as nearby **Lake John** (see p. 116) and **Delaney Butte Lakes** (see p. 119).

Fishing

The catch rate is higher here than at other North Park reservoirs, due to heavy stockings with both catchable (10-inch) and sub-catchable rainbow trout. Cowdrey also is rated good to excellent for ice fishing. The lake is shallow and may winter-kill from thick ice. The DOW posts signs at the lake when this happens.

Hunting

Waterfowl hunting is allowed on the reservoir, but the north shore of the lake is private property, and you can guess where the ducks go. The land on the west shore is part of the SWA and a fair spot to set out decoys. The only access to the west shore is by boat.

Watchable Wildlife

Waterfowl

Camping and Facilities

Camping is allowed in the parking area. There is a good boat ramp and a toilet.

General Restrictions

1. Boating is prohibited if it creates a white-water wake.
2. Sailboards are prohibited.

10. Diamond J SWA

Primary Use:	Trout fishing and duck hunting
Location:	Jackson County, North Park, just north of Walden
Size:	3,129 acres, including 6 miles of the Michigan River and about 1 mile of the Illinois River
Elevation:	8,100 feet
Division of Wildlife:	Area office in Steamboat Springs, 970-870-2197
Directions:	From Walden, there are signed parking areas located 1½ and 4 miles north of town on Highway 125. Also, there is access on the west side of the property from County Road 15 north of Walden Reservoir. The property is bounded on the east by Highway 125, on the west by County Road 15, on the south by the town of Walden, and on the north by private property.

The Michigan and Illinois Rivers run through this gem of a wildlife area just north of Walden. The smaller Illinois River parallels for about a mile before its confluence with the Michigan River on the southern portion of the property. The Michigan continues another 5 miles before exiting the north end of the wildlife area. The only thing to rival the trout fishing on the Michigan River might be the duck hunting on the Illinois.

Fishing

The Michigan River is a first-rate brown trout fishery, and the meandering river supports a robust, self-sustaining population. Although the browns aren't native, they are nonetheless wild in every sense. Electro-fishing surveys conducted by the DOW in 2000 showed 700 brown trout per mile, and nearly half of them were over 14 inches long. The survey also revealed the presence of large fish, many over 18 inches long. The Illinois River is not a fishery.

1. Fishing is by artificial flies and lures only.
2. Bag and possession limit is two fish.

Hunting

The Illinois River runs close enough to Walden Reservoir that it gets splattered with ducks spilling over from the lake. Both jump shooting and pass shooting can be very productive on days when the ducks spend the day flying to and from the lake. Decoy hunting is good, too, particularly farther downstream on the Michigan River.

Watchable Wildlife

Waterfowl

Camping and Facilities

Camping is permitted in the city-owned camping areas, as indicated by signs at the parking areas. There are no facilities. Camping and toilets are located nearby at Cowdrey Reservoir.

General Restrictions

Hunting is prohibited east of Highway 125.

11. Walden Reservoir SWA

Primary Use:	Waterfowl hunting
Location:	Jackson County, ½ mile west of Walden
Size:	739 acres
Elevation:	8,000 feet
Division of Wildlife:	Area office in Steamboat Springs, 970-870-2197
Directions:	From Walden, go ¼ mile west on County Road 12W to County Road 15, then north (right) to the reservoir.

This wide, shallow pool of water is a reliable spot to observe and hunt waterfowl. Walden Reservoir is the largest body of water in an extensive network of wetlands located in the vicinity of Walden. The shallow, weedy reservoir is the perfect environment for waterfowl.

Fishing

None

Hunting

Waterfowl and mourning doves

Watchable Wildlife

During warmer months, the reservoir teems with hundreds of Canada geese, shorebirds, and a large variety of ducks.

Camping and Facilities

None

Mourning dove

12. Murphy SWA

Primary Use:	Trout fishing
Location:	Jackson County, North Park, Michigan River at Walden
Size:	5 miles of river
Elevation:	8,100 feet
Division of Wildlife:	Area office in Steamboat Springs, 970-870-2197
Directions:	From Walden, go 1 mile east on County Road 12 to the property.

The Murphy fishing lease opens 5 miles of tough fishing on the Michigan River in the boggy meadows east of Walden. Brown trout rest easy in the deep channels that braid through the property.

The Michigan River splits into five channels in this soggy maze of braided and difficult water. Willows and alders crowd the riverbanks, making backcasts nearly impossible. The low-lying fields adjacent to the river ooze with water in spring, giving rise to a nation of mosquitoes. As fortune would have it, though, these hostile waters are home to large brown trout.

Hunting

Hunting is prohibited.

Watchable Wildlife

Waterfowl

Camping and Facilities

None

General Restrictions

See Hunting.

13. Owl Mountain SWA

From Walden, go 13 miles southeast on Highway 14 to County Road 25, then 6 miles south (right) to County Road 27, and then right 2 miles to the property.

Owl Mountain rises from the rolling floor of North Park in the southeast corner of the valley. This 920-acre wildlife area ranges in elevation from 8,500 to 9,300 feet, and has hunting for elk, deer, and blue grouse. Vegetation is dominated by sage on the lower portions and by aspen and pine on top of the mountain.

14. Seymour Lake SWA

Primary Use:	Trout fishing
Location:	Jackson County, North Park, 10 miles west of Rand
Size:	81 acres
Elevation:	8,200 feet
Division of Wildlife:	Area office in Steamboat Springs, 970-870-2197
Directions:	From the town of Rand at the south end of the valley, go 4 miles north on Highway 125 to County Road 28, then 10 miles west (left) to County Road 11, and then south (left) 3½ miles to the reservoir.

Although shallow and prone to winter kill from thick ice, Seymour has a lot to offer anglers and campers. Trout grow at an almost unbelievable rate, gorging on the staggering numbers of aquatic insects living in the lake's weedy substrate. Rainbow trout fingerlings that survive just two years will grow to 17 inches and weigh several pounds.

Fishing

Seymour is managed as a put-and-take fishery, stocked annually with rainbow trout. Fishing is good in winter, too, and this is a great place to take kids ice fishing. However, don't wait until late winter, because thick ice often depletes the water of oxygen and kills the trout.

Hunting

Hunting is prohibited.

Watchable Wildlife

American white pelicans, cormorants, egrets, herons, and a host of ducks can be viewed in spring and summer.

Camping and Facilities

Camping is permitted in the parking areas.
Facilities include a boat ramp and toilets.

General Restrictions

1. Public access is limited to the immediate shoreline around the reservoir.
2. Boating is prohibited if it creates a white-water wake.
3. Sailboards are prohibited.

15. Hohnholz Lakes SWA

Primary Use:	Trout fishing, wildlife watching
Location:	Larimer County, Laramie River, 50 miles northwest of Fort Collins
Size:	80 acres
Elevation:	8,000 feet
Division of Wildlife:	Area office in Fort Collins, 970-472-4300
Directions:	From Colorado Highway 14 at Chambers Lake, at the upper end of Poudre Canyon, go 30 miles north on the Laramie River Road (County Road 103) to the property.

Set off by itself in the northern reaches of the Laramie River valley near the Wyoming state line, this wildlife area has two nice lakes and about 1 mile of fishing on the Laramie River. Despite its remote setting, it receives moderate to heavy use in summer.

Fishing

Hohnholz Lake #2 (Little Hohnholz) is stocked with catchable rainbow trout and sub-catchable Snake River cutthroats. Ice fishing is good.

Hohnholz Lake #3 (Big Hohnholz) is managed as a quality fishery for brown trout and Snake River cutthroats. The cutthroats average 16–18 inches.

Laramie River has a decent population of brown trout and there is a good hatch of giant stoneflies *(Pteronarcys californica)* in May.

1. Fishing in the Laramie River is by artificial flies and lures only, and the bag and possession for trout is two.
2. Fishing in Hohnholz #3 is by artificial flies and lures only.

Hunting

Waterfowl

Watchable Wildlife

Sandhill cranes often visit the Laramie River Valley in June. Other watchables include golden eagles, American white pelicans, pronghorn antelope, and a variety of ducks, including cinnamon teal and common goldeneyes.

Camping and Facilities

Camping is permitted only at the designated area. Restrooms are located at the camping and parking areas.

General Restrictions

1. Camping is not permitted at the parking areas at the lakes.
2. Boating is prohibited except for craft propelled by hand, wind, or electric motor.
3. Sailboards are prohibited.

The Sofa Pillow dry fly closely imitates this large stonefly. Fly-fishers sometimes refer to these big bugs as willow flies or salmon flies.

16. Bliss SWA

Primary Use:	Trout fishing
Location:	Larimer County, Cache la Poudre River, 40 miles west of Fort Collins
Size:	352 acres
Elevation:	7,700–9,000 feet
Division of Wildlife:	Area office in Ft. Collins, 970-472-4300
Directions:	From the intersection of Highway 287 and Highway 14 (Ted's Place), go 40 miles west on Highway 14 to the property. The camping area is on the south (left) side of the highway. The property is divided into two parcels of land along the river. Look for the green and white DOW signs marking the boundaries.

Straddling 1 mile of the Poudre River in the scenic upper reaches of Poudre Canyon, this wildlife area is one of the few places on the river that has no-fee camping and public access to fishing.

Fishing

The upper Poudre River (above the fish hatchery) is managed as a wild-trout fishery for brown trout. Additional fishing access is located downstream at the fish hatchery. The brown trout in this stretch range in size from 6 to 17 inches.

Hunting

Bighorn sheep inhabit the canyon walls. The terrain is steep on both sides of the river, making access to the top difficult. This is in Game Management Unit 8 and Bighorn Sheep Units S1 and S19.

Watchable Wildlife

Same as hunting

Camping and Facilities

There is a level, open parking area with a toilet and several primitive campsites near the river.

General Restrictions

Boat launching and takeout are prohibited.

17. West Lake SWA (Larimer County)

Primary Use:	Trout fishing
Location:	Larimer County, Red Feather Lakes, 30 miles northwest of Fort Collins
Size:	38 acres
Elevation:	8,200 feet
Division of Wildlife:	Area office in Fort Collins, 970-472-4300
Directions:	From the town of Red Feather Lakes, go 1 mile east on Red Feather Lakes Road to the property.

West Lake is one of several small lakes situated in the area around Red Feather Lakes. Although managed as a put-and-take fishery, it is capable of producing an occasional big trout.

Fishing

West Lake is managed as a put-and-take trout fishery, stocked with 10-inch long hatchery rainbows. However, this little body of water has surprised a few anglers in the past with brown trout weighing 7–8 pounds.

Hunting

Hunting is prohibited.

Watchable Wildlife

Waterfowl

Camping and Facilities

Camping is available at a Forest Service campground.

General Restrictions

Boating is prohibited, except for craft propelled by hand, wind, or electric motor.

18. Dowdy Lake SWA

Primary Use:	Trout fishing
Location:	Larimer County, Red Feather Lakes, 30 miles northwest of Fort Collins
Size:	120 acres of water
Elevation:	8,250 feet
Division of Wildlife:	Area office in Fort Collins, 970-472-4300
Directions:	From the town of Red Feather Lakes, go 1 mile northeast on the USFS access road to the boat ramp and camping area.

Dowdy is one of several lakes situated around Red Feather Lakes that are stocked with catchable trout.

Fishing

Dowdy Lake is stocked with catchable and sub-catchable rainbow trout.

Hunting

Waterfowl

Watchable Wildlife

Same as hunting

Camping and Facilities

USFS campground (fee). Facilities include a boat ramp and toilets.

General Restrictions

Boating is prohibited if it creates a white-water wake.

19. Parvin Lake SWA

Primary Use:	Trout fishing
Location:	Larimer County, Red Feather Lakes, 30 miles northwest of Fort Collins
Size:	62 acres of water, 180 acres of land
Elevation:	8,100 feet
Division of Wildlife:	Area office in Fort Collins, 970-472-4300
Directions:	From the town of Red Feather Lakes, go 2 miles east on Red Feather Lakes Road to the entrance.

Parvin Lake has the best trout fishing and the best scenery in the Red Feather Lakes area. It is a popular destination for belly boaters who don't mind the short hike to the lake. Anglers are required to check in and out of the check station at the entrance.

Fishing

Parvin Lake has excellent trout fishing from belly boats. In 2000, the lake was opened to ice fishing, but bait (including Power Bait) is not allowed.

1. Fishing is by artificial flies and lures only.
2. Bag and possession limits are posted at the check station.

Hunting

Waterfowl

Watchable Wildlife

Ospreys nest on the island in the center of the lake.

Camping and Facilities

Overnight camping is prohibited. There is a toilet at the parking area.

General Restrictions

1. Boating is prohibited, except belly boats for fishing.
2. Oars are not allowed.
3. Walk-in access only from the parking area at the check station.

20. Cherokee SWA

Primary Use: Fishing and hunting

Location: Larimer County, 30 miles northwest of Fort Collins

Size:
Lower Unit: 2,701 acres
Middle Unit: 4,481 acres
Upper Unit: 4,960 acres
Lone Pine Unit: 6,880 acres

Elevation: 6,200–8,600 feet

Division of Wildlife: Area office in Fort Collins, 970-472-4300

Directions: **Lower Unit:** From Fort Collins, go 22 miles north on U.S. 287 to Cherokee Park Road (County Road 80C), then 6 miles west (left) to the parking area on the south (left) side of the road.

Middle Unit: From U.S. 287, go 10 miles west (left) on Cherokee Park Road to the parking area and access roads on the north (right) side of the county road.

Upper Unit: From U.S. 287, go 22 miles west (left) on Cherokee Park Road to the unit. Stay left on County Road 80C at the junction with County Road 59.

Lone Pine Unit: From Fort Collins, go 20 miles north on U.S. 287 to Red Feather Lakes Road (County Road 74E) then 8 miles west (left) to the parking area on the right.

Trout fishing, hunting, and wildlife viewing opportunities abound on this very important and expansive block of public lands. The wildlife area encompasses four large tracts, totaling more than 19,000 acres and stretching all the way from the foothills to the Laramie Mountains.

The adjoining tracts provide a continuous, uninterrupted migration route for deer and elk in their seasonal movements between the foothill and montane habitat zones. Semidesert shrubs such as juniper, sage, rabbitbrush, and mahogany dominate vegetation in the grassy foothills. As the terrain rises, the dry shrubs give way to scrub oak interspersed with ponderosas and grasses. The montane zone is a mixture of aspen and coniferous forests, with parklike mountain meadows.

The diversity of habitat in the different zones supports a variety of wildlife. Some areas provide winter range for deer and elk, and others have habitat for smaller species, including the endangered Preble's meadow jumping mouse.

Fishing

Lower Unit: No fishing.

Middle Unit: Excellent fishing on the North Fork of the Poudre River for brown trout. The stretch from Bull Creek upstream to Divide Creek is catch-and-release and fishing by flies and lures only. Brown trout range in size from 12 to 17 inches. This stretch is reached by taking the west (left) access road from the parking area. East of the property, the river flows into Halligan Reservoir, a private lake stocked with rainbows. Some of the big rainbows migrate upriver into the SWA in spring, and big browns do the same in fall. Taking the east (right) access road from the parking area puts you within walking distance of this stretch.

Upper Unit: There is good fishing for greenback cutthroat trout in George and Cornelius Creeks. Fishing for the cutthroats is strictly catch and release, but you may keep a regular limit of brown trout and brook trout; harvesting the browns and brookies helps the cutthroat population. Also you can fish for browns in the North Fork of the Poudre. The upper portion is steep and tight, and the river tumbles over large boulders, creating deep pools of pocket water. The lower stretch flows into a hay meadow where its banks grow thick with alders and willows.

Lone Pine Unit: Lone Pine Creek has marginal fishing for brown trout.

Hunting

Big-game species on the property include deer, elk, and mountain lion. Small-game species include blue grouse, rabbits, and doves. This is in Game Management Unit 191.

Watchable Wildlife

Same as hunting

Camping and Facilities

Camping is allowed. Toilets are located at the parking areas.
The upper unit has excellent primitive camping in aspen groves.

General Restrictions

In all units, vehicles, bicycles, and horses are limited to existing roads and trails, however horses may be used off-road as an aid to big-game hunting.

Lone Pine and Lower units:

1. Closed to public access after the last day of deer and elk season through June 14, except for lawful mountain lion hunting.
2. Open to public access from June 15 to the Saturday before archery season.

Middle and Upper units: Closed to public access March–Memorial Day.

21. Watson Lake SWA

Primary Use:	Warm-water fishing
Location:	Larimer County, 2 miles west of Laporte and 6 miles northwest of Fort Collins
Size:	139 acres
Elevation:	5,100 feet
Division of Wildlife:	Area office in Fort Collins, 970-472-4300
Directions:	From Laporte, go 1 mile west on County Road 54G (the main road through town) to County Road 28 (Rist Canyon Road), then 1 mile west (left) to the property entrance on the west side of the river.

A parklike atmosphere pervades this well-developed wildlife area beside the Cache la Poudre River near Laporte.

Fishing

Watson Lake is undergoing a transition from a put-and-take trout fishery to a cool-water fishery for smallmouth bass, tiger muskies, and sauger. If all goes well, the saugers will provide milt to hatcheries to fertilize walleye eggs for saugeye production. Smallmouth bass and tiger muskie fishing is expected to be good after the populations are established. Fishing is good from the shoreline and from belly boats.

Hunting

Hunting is prohibited.

Watchable Wildlife

Waterfowl

Camping and Facilities

Overnight camping is prohibited. Facilities include a wheelchair-accessible fishing pier, picnic benches, shade shelters, a nature trail, and toilets.

General Restrictions

1. Boating is prohibited, except belly boats for fishing.
2. Ice fishing is prohibited.
3. Discharging firearms or bows is prohibited.
4. Ice skating is prohibited.
5. Swimming and sail-boarding are prohibited.
6. Use or possession of live minnows is prohibited.

22. Wellingon Reservoir #4 *and* Smith Lake SWA

Primary Use:	Warm-water fishing
Location:	Larimer County, 2 miles northwest of Wellington
Size:	Two small lakes with a total of 135 acres of water
Elevation:	5,200 feet
Division of Wildlife:	Area office in Fort Collins, 970-472-4300
Directions:	From Interstate 25 at the Wellington exit (Exit 278), go 2 miles west on County Road 62E, then 1 mile north to Wellington Reservoir, and then 1½ miles north to Smith.

Situated in the farmland north of Fort Collins, these small reservoirs are stocked with warm-water fish.

Fishing

The lakes have warm-water fishing for bass, sunfish, and catfish.

Hunting

Hunting is prohibited.

Watchable Wildlife

Waterfowl

Camping and Facilities

Overnight camping is prohibited at both reservoirs. Facilities include restrooms and boat ramps.

General Restrictions

1. Boating is prohibited if it creates a white-water wake.
2. Discharging firearms or bows is prohibited.

Anglers in spring often fly-fish for crappies.

23. Wellington SWA

Primary Use:	Waterfowl hunting
Location:	Larimer County, northeast of Fort Collins and east of Interstate 25
Size:	2,700 total acres
Elevation:	5,200 feet
Division of Wildlife:	Area office in Fort Collins, 970-472-4300
Directions:	**Wellington Unit:** From I-25 at Wellington exit (Exit 278), go ½ mile north on the service road to County Road 64, and then 1½ miles east to the parking areas on the north and south sides of the road.
	Cobb Unit: From I-25 at the Highway 14 exit (Exit 269), go 5 miles north on the east service road to County Road 56, and then 1½ miles east to the property.
	Schware Unit: From I-25 at Highway 14, go 7 miles north on the east service road to County Road 60, and then 1 mile east to the property.

This wildlife area comprises three separate units that feature several ponds and small lakes for waterfowl hunting. The areas are near Fort Collins and receive heavy use from September through the end of waterfowl season, or until the ponds freeze over.

Fishing

None

Hunting

Waterfowl, dove, rabbit, and pheasant

Watchable Wildlife

Same as hunting

Camping and Facilities

None

General Restrictions

1. Boating is prohibited, except for hand-propelled boats used as an aid in waterfowl hunting (putting out and picking up decoys, and retrieving downed waterfowl).
2. Access is prohibited on Wellington and Schware Units March 15–July 15.
3. Access is prohibited on Wellington Unit from the first day of the regular waterfowl season to the first day of pheasant season except Saturdays, Sundays, Mondays, and legal holidays.
4. Horseback riding is prohibited, except at Cobb Unit during field trials.

24. Douglas Lake SWA

Primary Use:	Fishing
Location:	Larimer County, 7 miles north of Fort Collins
Size:	565 acres
Elevation:	5,000 feet
Division of Wildlife:	Area office in Fort Collins, 970-472-4300
Directions:	From the Wellington exit at Interstate 25 (Exit 278), follow Highway 1 a total of 5½ miles west, then south, then west again to County Road 15, then go 1 mile north (right) to County Road 60, ¼ mile west (left) to La Vina Drive, and then north (right) to the property.

Douglas is the largest of the State Wildlife Areas located in the farmlands north of Fort Collins. It is stocked with hatchery trout.

Fishing

Although stocked with catchable-sized (10-inch) rainbow trout, the lake also has fair fishing for smallmouth bass and yellow perch. Ice fishing for yellow perch varies from spotty to excellent for perch up to 13 inches long.

Hunting

Hunting is prohibited.

Watchable Wildlife

Waterfowl

Camping and Facilities

Overnight camping is prohibited. Facilities include boat ramps, large parking areas, and toilets.

General Restrictions

1. Boating is prohibited if it creates a white-water wake.
2. Discharging firearms or bows is prohibited.
3. Sailboards, sailboats, and ice skating are prohibited.
4. Other restrictions are posted at the property.

25. Frank SWA

Primary Use:	Fishing and waterfowl hunting
Location:	Larimer County, Cache la Poudre River, 2 miles west of Windsor
Size:	640 acres
Elevation:	4,800 feet
Division of Wildlife:	Area office in Fort Collins, 970-472-4300
Directions:	From Interstate 25 at the Windsor exit (Exit 262), go 2½ miles east on Highway 392 to County Road 13, then ½ mile south (right) to the parking area.

Hunting is allowed at this time, but the future is uncertain because of housing subdivisions that have all but surrounded this onetime unique wildlife area. The property receives a lot of use from nearby residents walking dogs.

Fishing

The wildlife area consists of several gravel pits and ponds located on both sides of the Poudre River. The ponds have fishing for warm-water species, including catfish and largemouth bass. The back ponds receive less fishing pressure.

Hunting

Waterfowl hunting is by reservation only and is determined by a lottery drawing held in mid-October. For more information on the drawing and reservations, call 970-472-4432 weekday afternoons.

Watchable Wildlife

Waterfowl

Camping and Facilities

None

General Restrictions

1. Hunting is prohibited, except with shotguns and bows.
2. Fires are prohibited.
3. Discharging firearms or bows is prohibited, except while hunting.
4. Smallmouth and largemouth bass must be 15 inches or longer.

26. Seeley Reservoir SWA

Primary Use:	Fishing, picnicking
Location:	Weld County, 3 miles north of Greeley
Size:	118 acres
Elevation:	4,700 feet
Division of Wildlife:	Area office in Fort Collins, 970-472-4300
Directions:	From Greeley, go 3 miles north on 35th Avenue.

Seeley Reservoir is being surrounded by housing development from Greeley.

Fishing

The lake is stocked with catchable-sized rainbow trout.

Hunting

None

Watchable Wildlife

American white pelicans, cormorants, Canada geese, and ducks are common at the lake.

Camping and Facilities

Camping is prohibited. A toilet is located at the west parking area.

General Restrictions

1. Public access is prohibited from one hour after sunset to one hour before sunrise, except for fishing.
2. Fishing is prohibited, except on the west shoreline or from boats one-half hour after sunset to one-half hour before sunrise.
3. Discharging firearms or bows is prohibited.
4. Fires are prohibited.

27. Mitani–Tokuyasu SWA

Primary Use:	Waterfowl and dove hunting
Location:	Weld County, South Platte River, 5 miles east of Greeley
Size:	54 acres
Elevation:	5,000 feet
Division of Wildlife:	Area office in Fort Collins, 970-472-4300
Directions:	From U.S. 85 in Greeley, go 5 miles east on Highway 263 to the property access road on the south (right) side of the highway.

Vandalism, littering, and unauthorized use plague this unique little property located at the confluence of the South Platte and Cache la Poudre Rivers, east of Greeley.

Fishing

None

Hunting

Waterfowl and doves

Watchable Wildlife

Same as hunting

Camping and Facilities

None

General Restrictions

1. Day use only.
2. Discharging firearms or bows is prohibited, except while hunting.
3. Fires are prohibited.

28. Nakagawa SWA

Primary Use:	Small-game hunting
Location:	Weld County, 10 miles east of Greeley
Size:	158 acres
Elevation:	4,600 feet
Division of Wildlife:	Area office in Fort Collins, 970-472-4300
Directions:	From Kersey, go 5 miles east on U.S. 34 to County Road 61, then 2 miles north (left) to the property.

This little wildlife area is located near, but not on, the South Platte River.

Fishing

None

Hunting

Dove, deer, and small game can be hunted on this small patch of bottomland lying just north of the South Platte River.

Watchable Wildlife

Same as hunting

Camping and Facilities

None

General Restrictions

1. Discharging firearms or bows is prohibited, except while hunting.
2. Fires are prohibited.

29. Centennial Valley SWA

Primary Use:	Waterfowl hunting
Location:	Weld County, South Platte River, 15 miles east of Greeley
Size:	853 acres
Elevation:	4,500 feet
Division of Wildlife:	Area office in Fort Collins, 970-472-4300
Directions:	From Greeley, go 14 miles east on U.S. 34 to Weld County Road 50, then 1½ miles east (left) to County Road 380 and the parking area.

This new wildlife area features public access to premium waterfowl hunting on the South Platte River near Greeley. Public use is managed for quality hunting and regulated by a lottery system.

Fishing

None

Hunting

Waterfowl

Watchable Wildlife

Same as hunting

Camping and Facilities

None

General Restrictions

1. Waterfowl, turkey, and deer hunting are by reservation only through a lottery drawing. Call 1-800-846-9453 for more information.
2. Public access is prohibited during all waterfowl seasons except Saturdays, Sundays, Mondays, and holidays.
3. All hunters must use their designated hunting zone and check in and out of the check station on the property.
4. Hunting is by shotgun, archery, and muzzle-loader only.
5. Small game and waterfowl hunting is prohibited the opening weekend of the regular plains rifle season.
6. Outside of spring turkey season, the property is closed to public access March 1–August 31, except the trail designated for wildlife observation.

7. Dogs are not allowed, except as an aid to hunting. Field trials and dog training are prohibited.
8. Target practice is prohibited.
9. Fires are prohibited.
10. Closed to recreational horse use.

30. Brower SWA

To access the property from U.S. 85 in Evans, go 1 mile east on 37th Street to the parking area east of the river.

Located on the South Platte River at the town of Evans, this 69-acre parcel of land has access to waterfowl and small-game hunting. Public access prohibited March 1–August 31. Camping is prohibited. There are no facilities.

31. Webster SWA

From U.S. 85 at La Salle, go 2¼ miles southwest on County Road 394 to the property. Look for the DOW sign on the north (right) side of the road.

Webster is a 158-acre parcel of farmland situated near the South Platte River southwest of Evans. The property is open to waterfowl and small-game hunting. Camping is prohibited. There are no facilities. Discharging firearms or bows is prohibited, except shotguns, muzzle-loaders and bows while hunting.

32. Big Thompson Ponds SWA

Primary Use:	Warm-water fishing
Location:	Larimer County, Interstate 25 service road, 4 miles east of Loveland
Size:	50 acres
Elevation:	5,000 feet
Division of Wildlife:	Area office in Fort Collins, 970-472-4300
Directions:	From Interstate 25 at the Highway 402 exit (Exit 255), take the east service road north ¾ mile to the underpass, cross west (left) under I-25 and go north (right) on the west service road to the property.

The Big Thompson Ponds are a collection of old gravel pits adjacent to the Big Thompson River.

Fishing

The ponds have fishing for largemouth bass, smallmouth bass, and sunfish. All bass under 15 inches must be released immediately.

Hunting

Waterfowl

Watchable Wildlife

Cormorants, great blue herons, shorebirds, and waterfowl

Camping and Facilities

Camping is prohibited. A toilet is located at the parking area.

General Restrictions

1. Boating is prohibited, except for belly boats used for fishing.
2. Discharging firearms or bows is prohibited except when hunting.
3. Dog training is prohibited.
4. Fires are prohibited.

Largemouth bass

33. Simpson Ponds SWA

Primary Use: Warm-water fishing, waterfowl hunting

Location: Larimer County, Big Thompson River, 1 mile southeast of Loveland

Size: 44 acres

Elevation: 4,900 feet

Division of Wildlife: Area office in Fort Collins, 970-472-4300

Directions: From Interstate 25 at the Highway 402 exit (Exit 255) go 2 miles west to County Road 9E, and then ½ mile north (right) to the parking areas on the left side of the road.

The Simpson Ponds are flooded gravel pits adjacent to the Big Thompson River.

Fishing

Largemouth bass, bluegill, and channel catfish

Hunting

The wildlife area is small, and competition for hunting spots is intense. However, the waterfowl hunting can be worth the effort. The river and the ponds, which are flooded gravel pits beside the river, attract good numbers of geese and ducks. Dove hunting can be good here, too.

Watchable Wildlife

Same as hunting

Camping and Facilities

None

General Restrictions

1. Discharging firearms or bows is prohibited, except while hunting.
2. Boating is prohibited, except belly boats for fishing.
3. Fires are prohibited.

34. Boedecker SWA

Primary Use:	Warm-water fishing
Location:	Larimer County, 3 miles southwest of Loveland
Size:	308 acres of water
Elevation:	5,000 feet
Division of Wildlife:	Area office in Fort Collins, 970-472-4300
Directions:	From Loveland, go 2 miles west on First Street to County Road 21 and ½ mile south (left) to the reservoir.

Boedecker Reservoir has a large parking area.

Fishing

Largemouth bass, crappie, and bluegill

Hunting

Waterfowl

Watchable Wildlife

Same as hunting

Camping and Facilities

Overnight camping is prohibited. There is a boat ramp and a toilet.

General Restrictions

1. Fishing is prohibited from boats from November 1 to the end of the waterfowl season.
2. Boating is prohibited if it creates a white-water wake.
3. Discharging firearms or bows is prohibited, except while hunting.
4. Sailboards are prohibited.

35. Lon Hagler SWA

Primary Use:	Fishing
Location:	Larimer County, 3 miles southwest of Loveland
Size:	201 acres of water
Elevation:	5,000 feet
Division of Wildlife:	Area office in Fort Collins, 970-472-4300
Directions:	From the town of Campion, go 3¼ miles west on County Road 14W, then 1½ miles north (right) on County Road 21S, and then 1½ miles west (left) to the entrance.

Lon Hagler Reservoir is heavily stocked with hatchery rainbows, and is considered to have the best tiger muskie fishing north of Denver. A well-maintained archery range is located on the property.

Fishing

Although the reservoir is managed as a put-and-take fishery with catchable rainbows, it has a solid population of yellow perch and a number of large tiger muskies.

Hunting

None

Watchable Wildlife

Waterfowl

Camping and Facilities

Camping is permitted in designated areas. Facilities include toilets, a boat ramp, a nature trail, and an archery range.

General Restrictions

1. Use permit is required.
2. Boating is prohibited if it creates a white-water wake.
3. Sailboats and sailboards are prohibited.

Practice at the Lon Hagler SWA archery range

36. Lonetree Reservoir SWA

Primary Use: Fishing

Location: Larimer County, 5 miles southwest of Loveland

Size: 502 acres of water

Elevation: 5,000 feet

Division of Wildlife: Area office in Fort Collins, 970-472-4300

Directions: From the town of Campion, go 3½ miles west on County Road 14W to Lonetree Drive and then 1 mile south (left) to the entrance.

Lonetree Reservoir is noted as one of the best warm-water fisheries on the Front Range. It has good boat ramps and the picnic area is shaded by large cottonwood trees.

Fishing

Fishing is rated as good to excellent for wipers, walleye, and catfish.

Hunting

Waterfowl (mostly pass-shooting ducks)

Watchable Wildlife

Great blue herons

Camping and Facilities

Overnight camping is prohibited. Facilities include toilets, boat ramps, and picnic shelters.

General Restrictions

1. Fishing is prohibited from boats from November 1 through the last day of waterfowl season.
2. Fishing is prohibited in the outlet canal.
3. Boating is prohibited if it creates a white-water wake.
4. Public access is prohibited in the heron nesting closure area.
5. Sailboards and surfboards are prohibited.
6. Special size and bag restrictions for bass, walleye, and wipers.
7. Fires are prohibited.

37. North Fork SWA

To access this property from U.S. 34 at Drake, go ¼ mile west on Devil's Gulch Road to the parking area, on the site of the old fish hatchery.

Located on the North Fork of the Big Thompson River near the old fish hatchery at Drake, this small property has about one mile of trout fishing on the North Fork. The North Fork is a narrow stream with a few brown trout and even fewer rainbows. Public access is prohibited, except for fishing.

38. Banner Lakes SWA

Primary Use:	Waterfowl hunting
Location:	Weld County, 30 miles northeast of Denver
Size:	934 acres
Elevation:	5,000 feet
Division of Wildlife:	Area office in Brush, 970-842-6300
Directions:	From Interstate 76 at Hudson (Exit 31), go 4 miles east on Highway 52 to the property. The property is situated on both sides of the highway. Parking areas are well-marked.

Banner Lakes is a chain of ponds and small lakes located in the rolling hills east of Hudson. This wildlife area receives heavy hunting pressure from Metro Area duck hunters.

Fishing

There are catfish, sunfish, and largemouth bass in the lakes.

Hunting

Despite heavy use, this strip of wetlands attracts a lot of ducks. The property is divided into 13 areas, each containing a pond or a small lake. Reservations are available at 800-846-WILD (9453). Sunken duck blinds are located at most of the areas; using them is optional.

Watchable Wildlife

Excellent for waterfowl when the property opens to public access on July 15 (after nesting season).

Camping and Facilities

No overnight camping. There is a toilet at the check station.

General Restrictions

1. Public access is prohibited north of Highway 52 April 1–July 15.
2. Public access is prohibited from the first day of the regular waterfowl season to the first day of the pheasant season except on Saturdays, Sundays, Mondays, and legal holidays.
3. Fishing is prohibited during the regular waterfowl season. Boating is prohibited except for craft propelled by hand.
4. Hunters must check in and out at the check station when it is open.
5. Field trials are prohibited, except for February 1–March 31 and August 1–September 30.
6. Discharging firearms or bows is prohibited, except while hunting or training dogs.

39. Twin Sisters SWA

From the town of Allenspark, go 4 miles north on Highway 7 to County Road 82 at Meeker Park, then east (right) 1 mile to County Road 82E. Go southeast (right) 2 miles to Forest Road 119, then north (left) 2½ miles to Forest Road 325, and then 1 mile west (left) to the property.

This wildlife area sits south of Estes Park in Roosevelt National Forest. It consists of one square mile of heavily-timbered forest on the western slope of the Twin Sisters Mountain Range. Altitudes on the property range from 9,000 to 10,500 feet. Access is difficult on four-wheel-drive roads, the boundaries are vague, and the area is surrounded by National Forest. The primary use is hunting for deer, elk, and blue grouse.

40. Hot Sulphur Springs SWA

Primary Use: Trout fishing

Location: Grand County, Colorado River, west of Hot Sulphur Springs

Size: 1,200 total acres and approximately 5 miles of fishing access to the Colorado River

Elevation: 7,500 feet

Division of Wildlife: Area office in Hot Sulphur Springs, 970-725-6200

Directions: **Beaver Creek Unit:** From Hot Sulphur Springs, go 3 miles west on U.S. 40 to the Colorado River and turn south (left) at the east end of the bridge.

Hot Sulphur Springs Ranch Unit: Same as above except turn south (left) at the west end of the bridge. The DOW office is located here.

Paul F. Gilbert Fishing Area: Same as above

Lone Buck Unit: From Hot Sulphur Springs, go 3½ miles west on U.S. 40 to the property and the sign on the south (left) side of the highway.

Byers Canyon Rifle Range: North side of U.S. 40 at the Lone Buck Unit.

Jenny Williams Unit: From Hot Sulphur Springs, go 3 miles west on U.S. 40 to County Road 50 and 2 miles south (left) to the property. There are no signs; look for a gate on the east (left) side of the road.

Breeze Unit: From Parshall, go ½ mile west and look for the two parking areas on the left side of U.S. 40.

Kemp Unit: From Parshall, go ½ mile east on U.S. 40 to County Road 3, turn south (right) over the Colorado River bridge, and look for the two parking areas on the west (right) side of the road. The second parking area has the best access to the Williams Fork River.

There are eight individual units in this wildlife area and all but two are fishing easements or leases on the Colorado River. The Beaver Creek, Hot Sulphur Springs Ranch, Paul F. Gilbert, and Lone Buck units are bunched together along the Colorado River west of the U.S. 40 bridge. The Kemp and Breeze Units are located west of Parshall, and include a stretch of the Williams Fork River that remains open in winter. The Colorado River Valley is wide through here, shouldered by low rolling hills. The river bottom is lush cottonwood riparian habitat, thick with willow and alder.

Fishing

This stretch of the Colorado River was once home to a prized population of rare self-sustaining rainbow trout. The rainbows spawned here every spring until whirling disease wiped them out. Now that the rainbows are gone, this stretch of river is fast becoming a first-rate brown trout fishery. Brown trout are resistant to the disease and are flourishing in the river. The browns are wild, wily, and superior in many ways to the rainbows they replaced.

The Colorado River is a typical freestone stream consisting of pools, runs, and riffles. It is ideal for fly fishing. Mayflies, caddisflies, stoneflies, and midges hatch throughout the summer months, with hatches often overlapping each other.

Hunting

Marginal hunting opportunities exist for both big game and small game. Hunting is the primary use of the Jenny Williams Unit, which is a winter range for deer and elk.

Watchable Wildlife

Same as hunting

Camping and Facilities

Camping is permitted only in the Lone Buck and Beaver Creek Units.
Facilities include toilets and a rifle range.

General Restrictions

1. In all units, fishing is by flies and lures only, and all trout must be returned to the water immediately.
2. Discharging firearms or bows is prohibited in Beaver Creek and Lone Buck campgrounds and in the Paul F. Gilbert Fishing Area.
3. Fires are prohibited.
4. Jenny Williams Unit is closed to public use from the last day of big-game season until May.

41. Junction Butte SWA

Primary Use: Hunting

Location: Grand County, 3 miles south of Kremmling

Size: 1,450 acres

Elevation: 7,700–8,500 feet

Division of Wildlife: Area office in Hot Sulphur Springs, 970-725-6200

Directions: From Kremmling, go 3 miles south on Highway 9 to County Road 387, and then ½ mile east (left) on the dirt road.

This wildlife area covers the majority of Junction Butte, a solitary mountain standing south of the Colorado River. The area is closed to the public except during big-game hunting seasons.

Fishing

None

Hunting

Deer, elk, and blue grouse

Watchable Wildlife

Same as hunting

Camping and Facilities

None

General Restrictions

1. Closed to public use from the end of big-game season until September.
2. Hang gliding is prohibited.
3. Motor vehicles are limited to established roads.

42. Radium SWA

Primary Use: Hunting and fishing

Location: Grand County, Colorado River, 15 miles southwest of Kremmling

Size: 1,200-plus acres

Elevation: 7,000–8,700 feet

Division of Wildlife: Area office in Hot Sulphur Springs, 970-725-6200

Directions: From Kremmling, go 2½ miles south on Highway 9 to County Road 1 (Trough Road) and then west (right) 12 miles to the first tract of land, which is marked by DOW signs on the south (left) side of the road.

To reach Blacktail Creek, and the tracts located on the north side of the Colorado River, continue west on County Road 11 and turn north (right) toward Radium. After crossing the bridge over the river, bear right on County Road 11 and look for the DOW signs.

This intriguing wildlife area includes several huge tracts of land located on both sides of the Colorado River. Hunting, fishing, and other outdoor opportunities abound within the wildlife area, and on thousands of acres in the surrounding BLM lands. The rugged terrain features steep canyons, gulches, cottonwood creek bottoms, dry hills dotted with piñon and juniper, and grassy mountain meadows. These tracts of land are critical winter ranges for elk and deer.

Fishing

The Colorado River has fishing for rainbow and brown trout. Blacktail Creek has fishing for brook trout.

Hunting

Hunting opportunities exist in the area for elk, deer, black bear, mountain lion, rabbit, grouse, and waterfowl. This is in Game Management Units 15, 27, 36, and 37.

Watchable Wildlife

Species common to the area include golden eagles, bobcats, pine martens, badgers, and golden-mantled ground squirrels (rock squirrels).

Camping and Facilities

Primitive camping is allowed throughout the area. There are no facilities, except at the Forest Service campground located on County Road 11 at Sheep Creek.

General Restrictions

1. Vehicles are restricted to established roads.
2. Discharge of firearms is prohibited in designated safety zones and around hay meadows and buildings.

43. Rock Creek SWA

Primary Use:	Trout fishing and big-game hunting
Location:	Routt County, Gore Pass, 20 miles west of Kremmling
Size:	About 200 acres
Elevation:	8,500 feet
Division of Wildlife:	Area office in Steamboat Springs, 970-870-2197
Directions:	From Kremmling, go 6 miles north on U.S. 40 to Highway 134, then west (left) over Gore Pass (elevation 9,527 feet) 14 miles to Forest Road 206, and then south (left) 2 miles to the property.

Rock Creek meanders on gentle grades through a broad meadow surrounded by low hills forested in pine and aspen. This wildlife area is a nice place for a family fishing or camping trip. Or just to stop for a picnic. The Rock Creek stagecoach line ran through here. Stop and explore the remains of the station.

Fishing

Rock Creek is the ideal stream for beginning fly fishers. There are no trees to snag a back cast and plenty of brookies to catch. The stream has beaver ponds on the upper end of the property.

Hunting

There is hunting in Routt National Forest for elk, deer, and black bear. This is in Game Management Unit 15.

Watchable Wildlife

Moose from North Park have expanded their range into this area. They can be aggressive toward humans. Do not approach them, especially cows with calves.

Camping and Facilities

Camping is permitted at the wildlife area and in the National Forest. There are no facilities.

44. Windy Gap
(Watchable Wildlife Area)

Primary Use:	Waterfowl observation
Location:	Grand County, Windy Gap Reservoir on the Colorado River, at the intersection of U.S. 40 and Highway 125
Size:	100 acres
Elevation:	8,000 feet
Division of Wildlife:	Area office in Hot Sulphur Springs, 970-725-6200
Directions:	From Granby, go 2 miles west on U.S. 40.

There is plenty to see and hear at this popular rest area located on U.S. 40 west of Granby.

Fishing

Fishing is prohibited.

Hunting

Hunting is prohibited.

Watchable Wildlife

A wide variety of waterfowl including shorebirds and pelicans

Camping and Facilities

Overnight camping is prohibited. Facilities include restrooms, drinking water, picnic tables with shade shelters, information kiosks, coin-operated viewing scopes, and an interpretive trail.

General Restrictions

1. Public access is prohibited outside of the viewing area.
2. Closed to public access from sunset to sunrise.

American white pelicans are common sights at many Colorado reservoirs.

Central Colorado

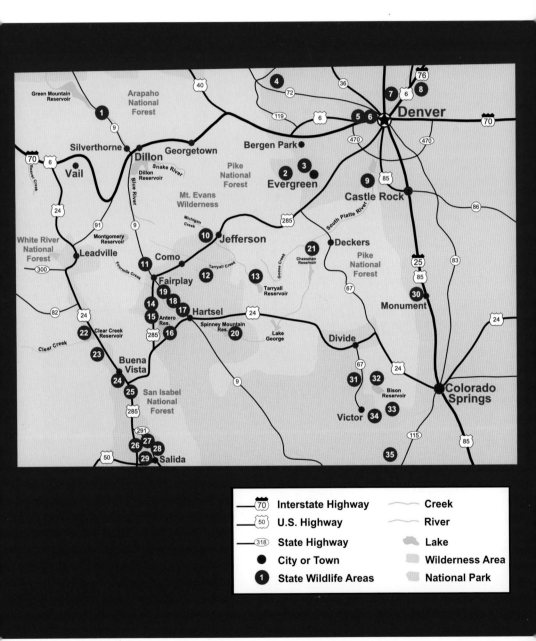

Green Mountain Reservoir
Arapaho National Forest
1
9
40
4
72
36
76
7
6
8
119
6
5 **6**
Denver
70
470
470
Silverthorne
Dillon
Georgetown
Bergen Park
Snake River
Pike National Forest
2 **3**
9
85
Vail
70 6
Beaver Creek
Dillon Reservoir
Blue River
Evergreen
Castle Rock
86
24
Mt. Evans Wilderness
285
South Platte River
91
9
Michigan Creek
10 **Jefferson**
21 **Deckers**
25
83
White River National Forest
Montgomery Reservoir
Leadville
11 Como
Tarryall Creek
12
Goose Creek
Cheesman Reservoir
Pike National Forest
85
300
Fourmile Creek
Fairplay
13
67
30
82
19
Tarryall Reservoir
Monument
24
14 **18**
15 Antero Res.
17 **Hartsel**
24
Spinney Mountain Res.
20
Lake George
Divide
24
22 Clear Creek Reservoir
16
67
Clear Creek
23
Buena Vista
9
31 **32**
24
Bison Reservoir
Colorado Springs
24
25 San Isabel National Forest
Victor **34** **33**
285
115
85
291
26 **27**
28
35
50
29 Salida

🛡 70	Interstate Highway	～	Creek
🛡 50	U.S. Highway	～	River
318	State Highway	▨	Lake
●	City or Town	▨	Wilderness Area
1	State Wildlife Areas	▨	National Park

T he central region covers the Front Range from Denver south to Pueblo, and west to the Continental Divide. Included in this region are South Park and the upper Arkansas River Valley. Some of the most heavily used of all SWAs are found in South Park at **Tarryall Reservoir**, **Antero Reservoir**, **Spinney Mountain**, and **Tomahawk**. Others, such as **Champion SWA**, located on the Arkansas River, and **Beaver Creek SWA**, offer good trout fishing without the crowds.

Wildlife Areas in Central Colorado

1. Blue River SWA

Primary Use:	Trout fishing
Location:	Summit County, Blue River, north of Silverthorne
Size:	Several miles of access to the Blue River
Elevation:	9,000 feet
Division of Wildlife:	Area office in Hot Sulphur Springs, 970-725-6200
Directions:	All three parking areas are located on Highway 9 and are well-marked with DOW signs.
	Sutton Unit: 7 miles north of Silverthorne
	Eagle's Nest Unit: 9 miles north of Silverthorne
	Blue River Unit: 17 miles north of Silverthorne

This wildlife area consists of three individual leases scattered along the Blue River between Silverthorne and Green Mountain Reservoir. These areas provide public fishing access to Gold Medal Water.

Fishing

The Blue River, from Dillon Reservoir downstream to the Colorado River, is classified as Gold Medal Water. "Cold Medal Water" is a more accurate description. Even in summer, the water runs icy cold in the Blue. Trout fishing is marginal most of the year, with an occasional mayfly hatch to liven things up. The Blue River unit, located at the first bridge upstream from Green Mountain Reservoir, has a run of kokanee salmon in fall. Snagging is permitted September 1–December 31.

Hunting

Hunting is prohibited.

Watchable Wildlife

There is a watchable wildlife interpretive trail at the Blue River Unit. Songbirds, waterfowl, raptors, and deer frequent the area.

Camping and Facilities

None

General Restrictions

Discharging firearms or bows is prohibited.

Rainbow trout

2. Mount Evans SWA

Primary Use:	Big-game and blue grouse hunting
Location:	Clear Creek County, 20 miles west of Evergreen
Size:	3,500 acres
Elevation:	8,300–10,500 feet
Division of Wildlife:	Area office in Denver, 303-291-7227
Directions:	From Interstate 70 at the Evergreen exit (Exit 252), go 8 miles south on Highway 74 to Upper Bear Creek Road (Evergreen Lake), then go 6 miles west (right) to the fork in the road. Take the right fork and follow the signs 3 miles to the entrance. The parking areas are well-marked.

A fantastic place in its own right, this property also provides access to the Mount Evans Wilderness Area. The terrain in the wildlife areas is rugged, but not extreme. The mountains are forested in Douglas fir, with a sparse understory of shrubs. The landscape is marked with creeks, wet meadows, and grassy parks.

Fishing

Bear Creek is loaded with small brookies and a few brown trout. The creek flows through a narrow valley in a series of pools, runs, riffles, and beaver ponds. Access to the valley is from a hiking trail at the first parking area. The trail goes south over the hill and down to the creek.

Hunting

Elk, deer, and bighorn sheep hunting is by limited licenses issued in a drawing. The area is open for turkey hunting in fall but there aren't many around. Small-game hunting opportunities exist for squirrels, rabbits, snowshoe hares, and blue grouse. This area is in Game Management Unit 39.

Watchable Wildlife

Same as hunting

Camping and Facilities

Camping is available at Camp Rock, but the road is open only from June 15 until the day after Labor Day. Camp Rock is located in a narrow valley at the end of Camp Rock Road on the western boundary of the property. The camping area has eight primitive sites situated beside a small stream and shaded by tall ponderosas. There is a toilet, but no drinking water. A high-clearance, four-wheel-drive vehicle is recommended on Camp Rock Road. From here, trails lead south and west to the Bear Track Lakes area of the Mount Evans Wilderness.

General Restrictions

1. Public access is prohibited January 1–June 14.
2. Dogs must be on a leash, except when hunting.
3. Motorized vehicles are prohibited during archery and muzzle-loader seasons, beginning the day after Labor Day.
4. Vehicles are allowed during big-game rifle seasons, beginning the Wednesday before the start of the first season, and ending on the last day of the third season.
5. Camping is limited to five days, except during big-game seasons, at designated campgrounds.
6. Mountain bikes are prohibited on trails and permitted only on established roads.

3. Bergen Peak SWA

Primary Use:	Hiking
Location:	Jefferson County, 2 miles southwest of Bergen Park
Size:	Approximately 500 acres
Elevation:	8,500–9,600 feet
Division of Wildlife:	Area office, Denver, 303-291-7227
Directions:	From Bergen Park, go west on County Road 103 (Squaw Pass Road) to Sinton Road, then almost 3 miles south (left) to the parking area. Access on the south side of the SWA is from the Elk Meadows Trailhead, which is located on Stagecoach Road 1¼ miles west of Highway 74 in Evergreen.

Big-game hunting is allowed at this wildlife area situated on the outskirts of Evergreen and Bergen Park. Access into the property is by foot or horseback only, from the parking area. Mountain bikes are prohibited!

Fishing

None

Hunting

Elk are numerous in these suburban foothills. The elk herd is often seen in Elk Meadows, the wide meadow on Highway 74 between Evergreen and Bergen Park. Deer and elk hunting are by limited licenses only. This is in Game Management Unit 391.

Watchable Wildlife

Same as hunting

Camping and Facilities

None

General Restrictions

1. Public access is prohibited, except by foot or horseback.
2. Dogs must be on a leash, except when hunting small game.

An elk hunter carrying trophy antlers pushes through deep snow in the black timber.

4. Gross Reservoir SWA

From Boulder, go west on Baseline Road to Flagstaff Mountain Road and then 7 miles southwest (left) to the reservoir.

Gross Reservoir is a water-supply reservoir located in the mountains southwest of Boulder. The reservoir is not considered a viable fishery due to drastic fluctuations in the water level, and the absence of aquatic vegetation. There is a small run of kokanee salmon at the inlet. Boats and floating devices are prohibited. The primary uses of the property are hiking, picnicking, and sunbathing.

5. Ward Pond SWA

To access the property from the Ward Road exit on Interstate 70 in Wheatridge (Exit 266), go north ½ mile on Ward Road to the parking area on the east (right) side of the road.

Fishing at this Metro Area pond is strictly for fun. Fishing is restricted to artificial flies and lures, and all fish must be returned to the water immediately. Bass fishing is reported as good. A trail leads around the 5-acre pond, but a belly boat is necessary to reach the best fishing areas. Public access is prohibited, except for fishing. Portable toilets are located at the parking area.

6. Lowell Ponds SWA

Lowell Ponds are a pair of old gravel pits situated north of Denver beside Clear Creek at Lowell Boulevard and 56th Way, and are visible from Interstate 76 (east of Exit 2). They are managed as warm-water fisheries for largemouth bass and sunfish. The minimum size for bass is 15 inches. There is a long list of restrictions that prohibit everything except fishing during daylight hours.

7. Grandview Ponds SWA

Located in Thornton north of Denver, at 104th Avenue and Colorado Boulevard, these ponds sit in a parklike setting surrounded by subdivisions and shopping centers. There is fishing for largemouth bass, smallmouth bass, catfish, and sunfish. There are no facilities. Use is restricted to daylight hours.

8. White Horse SWA

Lying at the southern boundary of Barr Lake State Park northeast of Denver, this 480-acre property is a conservation and recreation lease restricted to youth/mentor waterfowl hunting. To hunt here, youths and their mentors must attend an orientation class before getting a reservation number. Call the DOW at 303-291-7227 for information.

9. Sharptail Ridge SWA

This new wildlife area is closed to public access for now. It is a conservation easement, consisting of roughly 700 acres in Douglas County. The purpose of the easement is to protect an indigenous population of prairie sharp-tailed grouse. This property may open sometime in the future for elk and deer hunting on an extremely limited basis.

Elk

10. Teter SWA

Primary Use:	Elk hunting and trout fishing
Location:	Park County, South Park, 4 miles west of Jefferson
Size:	950 acres
Elevation:	9,500 feet
Division of Wildlife:	Area office in Denver, 303-291-7227
Directions:	From Jefferson, about 40 miles southwest of Denver, go 2 miles south on U.S. 285 to County Road 35, then 2 miles northwest (right) to the parking area on the left. Or, from Fairplay go 13 miles northeast on U.S. 285 to County Road 35, then left 2 miles.

This quiet wildlife area straddles a mile of Michigan Creek in the northwest corner of South Park. The creek winds its way through a corridor of thick willows in a grassy meadow. Elk often graze here in winter.

Fishing

Michigan Creek is one of those small streams that you can step across in many places but might surprise you by the size of trout it harbors. In the stream, undercut banks tangled with willow roots provide effective hiding places for the stream's resident brown trout. And above the stream, dense willows create a formidable obstacle for fly casters. Accomplished fly fishers will appreciate this challenging water.

Fishing tip: Larger brown trout prey on longnose suckers, which are native to the drainage. A good fly for imitating the suckers is a size-6, olive-colored Wooly Bugger.

Hunting

Elk, deer, and waterfowl

Watchable Wildlife

Same as hunting

Camping and Facilities

None

General Restrictions

1. Parking is prohibited, except in the designated areas.
2. Fires are prohibited.

11. Alma SWA

From Fairplay, go 7 miles north on Highway 9 to County Road 4, then ¼ mile northwest (left) to the property.

This wildlife area straddles 2 miles of the Middle Fork of the South Platte River below Montgomery Reservoir, 8 miles northwest of Fairplay. Fishing in the creek and the beaver ponds is marginal for brown and brook trout. A few ducks nest in the area. The area is open for deer, elk, and waterfowl hunting, but hunting is not prudent given such a small amount of land and considering the houses neighboring the property. Overnight camping is allowed. Toilets are located at the parking areas. This is in Game Management Units 49 and 500.

12. Reinecker Ridge SWA

Primary Use:	Elk hunting
Location:	Park County, South Park, 5 miles east of Fairplay
Size:	12,000 acres
Elevation:	9,000 feet
Division of Wildlife:	Area office in Denver, 303-291-7227
Directions:	From U.S. 285 at Como, go 8 miles southeast on County Road 15 (Elkhorn Road) to the DOW sign, and then 2 miles west (right) on the dirt road to the property. Or from Hartsel, go 5 miles east on U.S. 24 to County Road 15, and then 15 miles north (left) to the sign. The dirt road is not maintained and turns into gumbo when wet. A four-wheel-drive vehicle is necessary to reach the wildlife area.

Reinecker Ridge rises from the relatively flat, treeless floor of South Park, providing woodland habitat and shelter for wildlife. The long, rolling, round-topped ridge is sculpted with groves of aspen interspersed with stands of pines, and open grassy meadows. This wildlife area contains important wintering range and calving grounds for elk. The ridge runs north and south, stretching from U.S. 285 at Como to U.S. 24 at Hartsel.

Fishing

None

Hunting

Elk are the primary interest, but the ridge also has hunting for deer, antelope, and small game. Big-game hunting is by limited license only. Additional public hunting is available nearby at Mud Springs State Trust Lands. This is in Game Management Unit 50.

Watchable Wildlife

Same as hunting

Camping and Facilities

No overnight camping, no facilities

General Restrictions

1. Public access is prohibited January 1–May 1.
2. Fires are prohibited.

13. Tarryall Reservoir SWA

Primary Use:	Trout fishing
Location:	Park County, South Park, 18 miles southeast of Jefferson
Size:	886 acres (175 acres of water)
Elevation:	9,000 feet
Division of Wildlife:	Area office in Denver, 303-291-7227
Directions:	From the town of Jefferson on U.S. 285, go 18 miles southeast on County Road 77 to the reservoir. Or, from U.S. 24 a mile west of Lake George, go 22 miles northwest on County Road 77 (Tarryall Road) to the reservoir.

This venerable fishing hole tucked away in a picturesque valley between the Tarryall Mountains and Puma Hills has remained a reliable trout fishery for many years. Good fishing is available from shore, jetty, motor boat, canoe, or belly boat. Tarryall Reservoir is a popular weekend camping and fishing destination, and receives heavy use in summer.

Fishing

The trout population is boosted annually with shots of a mixture of sub-catchable (fingerling) rainbow and Snake River cutthroat trout, and about 20,000 catchables (10-inch trout). Weeds fill the shallow water near shore in summer, and bank fishing is difficult. Belly boats and other small craft are needed for fishing the outer edge of the weeds.

Trout fishing usually is better beyond the weeds, in open water 10–15 feet deep. Trout often cruise along the weed beds foraging on the nymphs of aquatic insects such as caddisflies, Hexagenia mayflies, damselflies, and midges, and small crustaceans like scuds (freshwater shrimp). Fly fishing is good with nymph flies such as the Halfback Nymph, Prince Nymph, or Gold-Ribbed Hare's Ear.

Tarryall Creek itself has a fair population of trout; there is about ½ mile of public fishing on the creek directly above the reservoir.

Northern pike also thrive here, and some grow large; 10-pounders are not uncommon. The best fishing is usually in May, when the pike move into the shallows. Pike anglers who practice "catch and eat" contribute greatly to the overall well-being of both the pike and the trout populations.

Hunting

Waterfowl hunting can be good until the lake ices up, usually sometime in the middle of November. Opening days and weekends usually are swarming with duck hunters. Get there early to secure a spot on the popular bay on the northwest end of the reservoir.

Watchable Wildlife

Same as hunting

Camping and Facilities

Good campsites are available near the water at five different campgrounds located around the lake. Facilities include boat ramps and toilets. There is no drinking water.

General Restrictions

Public access is prohibited from the dam, spillway, and outlet structures.

A duck hunter and Chesapeake Bay retriever huddle in the willows at Tarryall Reservoir.

14. Knight–Imler SWA

Primary Use:	Trout fishing
Location:	Park County, South Fork of the South Platte River, 5 miles above Antero Reservoir
Size:	Approximately 2 miles of fishing access
Elevation:	9,000 feet
Division of Wildlife:	Area office in Denver, 303-291-7227
Directions:	From Fairplay, go 10 miles south on U.S. 285 to the parking areas east (left) of the highway.

Despite heavy use, this 2-mile-long stretch of the South Platte River continues to provide good brown trout fishing.

Fishing

A stable population of wild brown trout resides in this stretch of the river. The river bends and twists through wet meadows, making deep undercuts in the banks. Add to this a few riffles, runs, and pools, and you have a model environment for brown trout. In fall, a few cutthroat trout, splake, and larger brown trout migrate into the river from Antero Reservoir. Anglers should take care not to wade through spawning redds or otherwise harass the spawning trout.

Fishing tip: The alert brown trout bolt for cover under the cutbanks when danger approaches. Anglers should stalk the browns from downstream, walking quietly, keeping a low profile, and making long casts with dry flies and nymphs. There are several good caddis and mayfly hatches throughout the warm months. By late summer, the fields flanking the river are jumping with grasshoppers. The Madam X fly is a fair imitation of a hopper.

Hunting

Hunting is prohibited.

Watchable Wildlife

Waterfowl

Camping and Facilities

None

General Restrictions

1. Fishing is by artificial flies and lures only.
2. All trout between 12 and 20 inches must be released immediately.
3. The bag limit for trout is two, and no more than one can be longer than 20 inches.
4. Public access is prohibited beyond 25 feet of the center of the river.

Snake River cutthroat at Antero Reservoir

15. 63 Ranch SWA

Primary Use:	Trout fishing
Location:	Park County, South Park, 15 miles south of Fairplay
Size:	1,200 acres
Elevation:	9,500 feet
Division of Wildlife:	Area office in Denver, 303-291-7227
Directions:	From Fairplay, go 15 miles south on U.S. 285 to the DOW property sign and entrance on the left. Or, from Antero Junction go 5½ miles north on U.S. 285.

The South Fork of the South Platte River wiggles through stretch of Gold Medal Water in a series of sharp bends and tight curves. The wildlife area is located directly upstream from Antero Reservoir, and supports a stable population of resident brown trout.

Fishing

Angling pressure is heavy on this stretch of the river during the summer. As with the **Knight-Imler SWA** (see p. 190) upstream, the best fishing at 63 Ranch SWA occurs in fall when spawning trout migrate into the river from Antero Reservoir. Anglers should take precautions against wading through spawning areas. Fishing is restricted to flies and lures only.

Hunting

Waterfowl

Watchable Wildlife

Same as hunting

Camping and Facilities

Camping is prohibited. There are no facilities.

General Restrictions

See Fishing.

16. Antero Reservoir SWA

Primary Use:	Trout fishing, waterfowl hunting
Location:	Park County, South Park, 5 miles southwest of Hartsel
Size:	5,000 acres
Elevation:	9,000 feet
Division of Wildlife:	Area office in Denver, 303-291-7227
Directions:	From Hartsel, go 5 miles southwest on U.S. 24 to the access roads marked by DOW signs. The first access road leads to the north side of the reservoir and the inlet area. The second road goes to a boat ramp and camping area on the south side of the reservoir.

Big, beautiful, and famous for its trout fishing, this wildlife area is a favorite year-round destination for anglers. Trout grow quickly here, feasting on the abundance of aquatic insects and crustaceans that inhabit the weedy substrate. They can go from 5-inch fingerlings to 5-pound bruisers in as few as four years.

Below the dam, a habitat improvement project in the South Fork of the South Platte River promises to enhance fishing and waterfowl hunting in that area. The project also will rechannel portions of the river to provide spawning habitat for trout.

Fishing

Antero Reservoir was treated with rotenone in 1997, ridding the lake of suckers. After the reclamation, the reservoir was stocked with rainbow, brown, and cutthroat trout, and splake. Splake, which are lake trout/brook trout hybrids, were stocked into Antero as 2-inch fingerlings in 1999. High numbers of adult splake and brown trout can hold the sucker population in check.

Ice fishing is a favorite winter activity here. Trout cruise the substrate all winter, looking for scuds and other invertebrates. The trouts' preference for tiny ice jigs necessitates the use of thin line and light tackle. Hooking a big trout on light tackle and coaxing it through a small hole is not an easy feat. Use caution when on the ice, always making safety your top priority.

Hunting

Opening day of the first split waterfowl season draws a fair number of waterfowl hunters, but there is plenty of shoreline for all to spread out. A few Canada geese will remain in the area through the first season, but the best waterfowl hunting is for ducks. A diverse and sizable number of ducks nest in South Park. Waterfowl hunting is also permitted on the river below Antero Dam.

Watchable Wildlife

Same as hunting

Camping and Facilities

Camping is allowed in the parking areas. Facilities include restrooms, and a boat ramp on the south side of the reservoir.

General Restrictions

1. Boating is prohibited 9 p.m.–4 a.m.
2. Public access is prohibited on the west face of the dam, along south and west shorelines, and on the island, except for waterfowl hunting.
3. Ice fishing shelters must be portable.

17. Badger Basin SWA

Primary Use:	Trout fishing
Location:	Park County, Hartsel
Size:	22 miles of fishing access limited to 25 feet on either side of the center of the rivers
Elevation:	8,000 feet
Division of Wildlife:	Area office in Denver, 303-291-7227
Directions:	**Fourmile Creek:** Parking for Fourmile Creek is located at the junction of Highway 9 and U.S. 24, 1 mile west of Hartsel.
	Middle Fork of the South Platte: There are three parking areas located on the Middle Fork. Go north on the main street from Hartsel and follow the gravel road to the signs.
	South Fork of the South Platte: The parking areas for South Fork are located on Highway 9 east and west of town.

In the vicinity around Hartsel, there are more than 22 miles of public trout fishing on streams located in Badger Basin SWA. The streams are the Middle and South Forks of the South Platte River, and Fourmile Creek. Unfortunately, fishing in the streams is marginal and the fish run small. The future, however, is promising, now that grazing has stopped and stream improvement projects are in the plans.

Fishing

South Fork of the South Platte from Hartsel to Antero Reservoir lacks the habitat to support trout year-round. This section is stocked periodically with catchable-sized rainbow trout to improve angling opportunities. The river below Hartsel is also stocked periodically with catchable rainbows, but habitat is better in this stretch and it supports a population of brown trout.

Fourmile Creek doesn't receive a lot of fishing pressure, and fishing can be pretty good when the flow is high. Right after spring runoff is usually a good time. The small creek flows into the South Fork from the north through the open meadow west of Highway 9. It is nearly invisible from the highway.

Middle Fork of the South Platte has better habitat and a good population of resident brown trout. Although the average trout is small, there are enough brown trout over 16 inches to sanction the Middle Fork as Gold Medal Water.

Hunting

None, fishing access only

Watchable Wildlife

Birds seen in the area include mountain bluebirds, ravens, ducks, geese, and raptors.

Camping and Facilities

None

General Restrictions

1. Parking in designated areas only.
2. Public access is allowed only from designated parking areas, and is prohibited beyond the fenced and posted easements.

Brown trout

18. Buffalo Peaks SWA

Primary Use:	Trout fishing
Location:	Park County, South Park, 7 miles north of Hartsel
Size:	3 miles of fishing access along the river
Elevation:	9,000 feet
Division of Wildlife:	Area office in Denver, 303-291-7227
Directions:	From Hartsel, go 7 miles north on Highway 9 to the river at Garo and turn east (right) on the private road to the parking areas. The first parking area is located just past the first cattle guard, and the last one is located at the bridge on the south end of the property.

The Middle Fork of the South Platte River meanders across the open floor of South Park on the upper half of this wildlife area, then winds through a boggy patch of willows at Red Hill before emerging again onto open ground. The south end of the property borders **Tomahawk SWA** (see p. 198). This stretch of Gold Medal Water is home to a robust population of wild brown trout. The views of the Mosquito Range aren't bad, either.

Fishing

A thriving population of brown trout and a few rainbow trout inhabit all parts of the river. Due to easy access and a central location, the river sees lots of fishermen in the summer. Angling pressure makes the browns skittish, but it doesn't stop them from eating. It does, however, make the larger fish picky about what they eat, and that makes them difficult to catch.

1. Fishing is restricted to flies and lures only.
2. All trout 12–20 inches must be returned to the water immediately.
3. Bag and possession limit for trout is two fish, and no more than one may be longer than 20 inches.

Hunting

No hunting, fishing access only

Watchable Wildlife

Deer and ducks

Camping and Facilities

No overnight camping, no facilities

General Restrictions

See Hunting and Fishing.

19. Tomahawk SWA

Primary Use:	Trout fishing
Location:	Park County, 5 miles north of Hartsel
Size:	3,400 acres
Elevation:	9,000 feet
Division of Wildlife:	Area office in Denver, 303-291-7227
Directions:	From Hartsel, go 5 miles north on Highway 9 to the DOW sign marking the access road on the right. Follow the access road over the hill to the parking area. Or, from Fairplay go 10 miles south on Highway 9 to the access road.

Brown trout rule on this premium stretch of Wild Trout Water. The wildlife area straddles 2 miles of the Middle Fork of the South Platte River downstream of **Buffalo Peaks SWA** (see p. 197). The river winds in and out of a maze of marshes and willows, eroding deep cutbanks on the outside bends, and spreading thin over gravel riffles. A small run of brown trout from Spinney Mountain Reservoir spawns here in fall.

Special Note: The river is scheduled to be closed to fishing from September 1, 2002 to January 1, 2003, while DOW biologists study the spawning success of brown trout that migrate into this stretch of the river from Spinney Mountain Reservoir.

Fishing

There is a self-sustaining population of resident brown trout and a few stocked rainbows. In the past, brown trout have migrated up from Spinney Mountain Reservoir to spawn on the gravel riffles in this stretch. Anglers should avoid wading in the redds.

Dry fly fishing can be good for anglers who stalk quietly upstream and make long delicate presentations to the shy browns hiding under the cutbanks. Dawn and dusk are the best times to see trout feeding at the surface.

1. Fishing is prohibited September 1, 2002–January 31, 2003, for a brown trout spawning study.
2. Fishing is by artificial flies and lures only.
3. All trout 12–20 inches must be returned to the water immediately upon catch.
4. Bag and possession limit for trout is two fish, and not more than one may be longer than 20 inches.

Hunting

Aside from the river, this property includes a large tract of land on the west slope of Reinecker Ridge for hunting elk, deer, and small game. Duck hunting on the river is spotty because of heavy use by anglers.

Watchable Wildlife

Same as hunting

Camping and Facilities

None

General Restrictions

Fires are prohibited.

20. Spinney Mountain SWA

Primary Use:	Trout and pike fishing
Location:	Park County, South Platte River, 8 miles east of Hartsel
Size:	3,000 acres
Elevation:	9,000 feet
Division of Wildlife:	Area office in Denver, 303-291-7227
Directions:	From Hartsel, go 8 miles east on County Road 59 to the access road.

The saga of Spinney Mountain Reservoir is the story of the rise and fall of the heavy-weight champion of Colorado trout lakes. This remarkable trout factory was once one of the best trophy-trout fisheries in the West. Five-pound brown, rainbow and Snake River cutthroat trout were commonplace, and trout weighing more than 10 pounds were caught every year. The reservoir suffers now from the results of loose regulations, and greedy overharvesting during the glory years, and from the subsequent explosion of the northern pike population.

Will Spinney rise again? The habitat is still there, unharmed and rich as ever, only now it's ruled by the sharp teeth of the pike. Time will tell, but biologists hope to reduce the number of big pike by removing the bag limit, and by asking anglers to keep all the pike they catch. The end result, they hope, will be a population of stunted pike. And then they can stock 10-inch trout in late fall when the pike's metabolism slows. The trout will grow 3 inches over the winter and be too large for the stunted pike to eat when they wake up in spring.

In the meantime, Spinney Mountain Reservoir is a super pike fishery with a few large trout hanging on for dear life.

Fishing

Both the reservoir and the South Platte River below are within the SWA and are both designated as Gold Medal Water.

1. Fishing is by artificial flies and lures only.
2. Bag and possession limit in the reservoir is one trout more than 20 inches.
3. In the river, all trout must be returned to the water immediately.
4. Ice fishing is prohibited.

Hunting

Waterfowl

Watchable Wildlife

Mountain bluebirds, ravens, waterfowl, and antelope are common in the area.

Camping and Facilities

Camping is prohibited. Facilities include boat ramps and toilets.

General Restrictions

1. The reservoir is closed from one-half hour after sunset to one-half hour before sunrise.
2. A State Parks Pass is required at the reservoir.
3. The reservoir is closed until complete ice-out in spring.
4. Fires are prohibited.

21. Cheesman Reservoir SWA

Primary Use:	Trout fishing and kokanee snagging
Location:	Douglas County, 5 miles southwest of Deckers and about 35 miles southwest of Denver
Size:	Approximately 3 miles of shoreline fishing access to Cheesman Reservoir
Elevation:	7,000 feet
Division of Wildlife:	Area office in Denver, 303-291-7227
Directions:	From Deckers, go 5 miles southwest on County Road 126, then 3 miles south (left) on Forest Service Road 211 to the reservoir.

If you take time to read all the rules, restrictions, and closures imposed by the Denver Water Board, you may run out of time for fishing. The bottom line is that you may do nothing here except fish from the bank in designated areas during daylight hours. The irony is that the fishing is terrible, unless you consider kokanee snagging as fishing. The water level in the reservoir fluctuates drastically from spring to fall.

Fishing

Fishing is prohibited on the north shore of the reservoir west of the dam. It is a long hike around the lake to the inlet, but "they" say that is where the best trout fishing is found. Access to the Goose Creek inlet is via the trail heading south from the parking area. Goose Creek is the place to snag kokanee salmon in September.

A trail heading east from the parking area leads to the South Platte River below Cheesman Dam. It is 1 mile to the river, and the trail is very steep below the dam. Fishing on the river is catch and release, by flies and lures only.

Hunting

Hunting is prohibited.

Watchable Wildlife

Bald eagles are often seen in Cheesman Canyon in winter.

Camping and Facilities

Camping is prohibited. Toilets are located at the parking area.

General Restrictions

There are too many to list here. Check the DOW's fishing brochure for current regulations.

22. Clear Creek Reservoir SWA

Primary Use:	Trout fishing
Location:	Chaffee County, 13 miles north of Buena Vista
Size:	500 acres
Elevation:	9,000 feet
Division of Wildlife:	Area office in Salida, 719-530-5520
Directions:	From Buena Vista, go 13 miles north on U.S. 24, then 1 mile west (left) on County Road 390.

Clear Creek is a medium-sized reservoir situated in the Arkansas River Valley just off Highway 24 between Buena Vista and Leadville. It has good fishing year-round for trout and kokanee salmon.

Fishing

Clear Creek Reservoir is relatively shallow and has good aquatic plant growth. This results in the fast growth of the trout and kokanee salmon that are stocked as 5-inch fingerlings. Species include Snake River cutthroats, rainbow, and brown trout, and kokanee salmon. Clear Creek Reservoir is rated as one of the best in the area for ice fishing.

Hunting

Waterfowl

Watchable Wildlife

Same as hunting

Camping and Facilities

Overnight camping is prohibited. Facilities include boat ramps and toilets.

General Restrictions

Fishing is prohibited from the dam, spillway, and outlet downstream to U.S. 24.

23. Heckendorf SWA

From Buena Vista, go 5 miles north on U.S. 24 to County Road 361 and then 1 mile west (left) to the property.

Heckendorf is a 640-acre tract of land sitting on a shelf above the Arkansas River. The terrain is virtually flat, with only a shallow draw to break the landscape. The area is used for big-game and small-game hunting and as winter range for elk. Camping is prohibited and there are no facilities.

24. Buena Vista River Park SWA

Two blocks east of downtown Buena Vista on Main Street, there is a parking area with access to the Arkansas River. A trail leads to ½ mile of fishing access. There is no boating access.

Arkansas River at Champion SWA

25. Champion SWA

To reach this property from the junction of U.S. 285 and 24, go ¾ mile south to the fenced parking area on the east side of U.S. 285. A trail from the parking area leads down to the river.

Champion is a small fishing lease that provides access to about 1 mile of the Arkansas River, 3 miles south of Buena Vista. Judging from the overgrown condition of the trail, this access doesn't receive much use. This is a nice stretch of river for dry-fly fishing, especially during the annual Mother's Day caddisfly hatch.

26. Big Bend SWA *and*
27. Arkansas River/Salida SWA

Upstream from Salida there is a complicated assembly of individual fishing leases that provides public access to short stretches of the Arkansas River. All of these properties have parking areas that are well-marked with signs and restrictions. The properties are located off County Roads 154, 160, 163, and 166.

Arkansas River at Big Bend SWA

28. Sands Lake SWA

From Salida, go ½ mile north on Highway 291 to the sign for the property on the east (right) side of the road. Hunting is prohibited. Facilities include a fishing pier and toilets.

Trout fishing is good at this small lake located on the outskirts of Salida, if you can get your bait past the regiment of begging ducks. Sands Lake is managed as a put-and-take trout fishery and stocked with catchable-sized rainbows. The lake is highly productive and never freezes. Many of the stockers carry over from year to year and grow quickly. This is a great place to teach kids how to fish.

29. Franz Lake SWA

From Salida, go ¾ mile north on Highway 291, then ¾ mile west (left) on County Road 154 to the lake.

Franz Lake is located 1 mile north of the Mount Shavano Fish Hatchery. It is a pretty lake in a parklike setting, with a view of the Collegiate Range. It is primarily a fishing property, managed as a put-and-take fishery with 10-inch rainbow trout.

30. Monument Lake SWA

Monument Lake is a 10-acre lake located in downtown Monument. It is stocked periodically with hatchery trout. Go west on 3rd Street, west on 2nd Street at the Post Office, and then cross the railroad tracks to the entrance. There are no facilities.

31. Dome Rock SWA

Primary Use:	Big-game hunting
Location:	Teller County, Pike National Forest, 5 miles south of Divide
Size:	6,980 acres
Elevation:	8,000–9,800 feet
Division of Wildlife:	Area office in Colorado Springs, 719-227-5200
Directions:	From Divide, go 5 miles south on Highway 67 to County Road 61 (Rainbow Valley Road), then ¾ mile on the right fork, to the parking area.

Thousands of acres of rolling mountains timbered with ponderosa pine, Douglas fir, aspen, mountain mahogany, and scrub oak interspersed with broad mountain meadows make this wildlife area an ideal habitat for elk and mule deer.

Fishing

Fourmile Creek has marginal fishing for brown trout.

Hunting

This is elk country. It is also in Game Management Unit 581.

Watchable Wildlife

Same as hunting

Camping and Facilities

None

General Restrictions

1. Public access is restricted to foot or horseback only from the parking lot and connecting trails for Mueller State Park.
2. Public access is prohibited December 1–July 15 on Spring Creek and Dome View trails, and on Dome Rock Trail from Jackrabbit Lodge. This is critical winter range and calving grounds for elk.
3. Dogs are prohibited.
4. Fires are prohibited.
5. Rock climbing is prohibited.
6. Mountain bikes are prohibited.

Opposite: Traditional archery hunters prefer the classic styling and feel of the long bow.

32. Pikes Peak SWA

Primary Use:	Bighorn sheep hunting
Location:	Teller County, 5 miles south of Pikes Peak, on the eastern slopes of Sheep Mountain
Size:	640 acres
Elevation:	10,200–11,000 feet
Division of Wildlife:	Area office in Colorado Springs, 719-227-5200
Directions:	The property is located just northeast of Bison Reservoir, but there is no access from Bison Reservoir Road. The only access is by foot or horseback from Pike National Forest east of the property.

Access is a problem to this wildlife area tucked away on the southwestern slopes of Pikes Peak. The only way in is on foot or by horseback through Pike National Forest.

Fishing

None

Hunting

Bighorn sheep

Watchable Wildlife

Same as hunting

Camping and Facilities

Primitive camping, no facilities

General Restrictions

Public access is prohibited April 1–July 15.

Bighorn sheep prefer steep, rocky terrain.

33. Rosemont Reservoir SWA

Primary Use:	Trout fishing
Location:	Teller County, 20 miles southwest of Colorado Springs
Size:	20 acres
Elevation:	9,700 feet
Division of Wildlife:	Area office in Colorado Springs, 719-227-5200
Directions:	The best access is from Divide, on U.S. 24. Go 15 miles south on Highway 67 to Gold Camp Road and then 20 miles east (left) to the parking areas. Gold Camp Road is narrow and winding; some stretches narrow to one lane.

Rosemont is located halfway between Victor and Colorado Springs on the narrow, twisting Gold Camp Road. It is a water supply reservoir with a long list of NOs and a caretaker on the property.

Fishing

Take the trail from the parking lot to the reservoir to fish for stocked trout.

Hunting

Hunting is prohibited.

Watchable Wildlife

None

Camping and Facilities

Camping is prohibited. A portable toilet is located at the parking area.

General Restrictions

Everything is prohibited, including picnics and dogs.

34. Skaguay Reservoir SWA

From Victor (20 miles southwest of Colorado Springs), go ½ mile east on County Road 67 to County Road 86, then 1 mile south (right) to County Road 861, and then 6½ miles east (left) to the reservoir.

Skaguay Reservoir is a 174-acre body of water located in a mountain valley, 7 miles east of Victor. Camping is permitted in the upper parking area and in the small meadow by the boat ramp. Facilities include a concrete boat ramp, and toilets. Trout fishing is reported as fair to good.

35. Beaver Creek SWA

Primary Use:	Hunting, trout fishing
Location:	Fremont and Teller Counties, 15 miles northeast of Cañon City
Size:	2,740 acres
Elevation:	6,000–9,000 feet
Division of Wildlife:	Area office in Pueblo, 719-561-5300
Directions:	**South entrance:** From Cañon City, go 5 miles east on U.S. 50 to Highway 67, then north (left) almost 2 miles to County Road 123, then ½ mile east (right) to County Road 132, and then 12½ miles north (left) to the parking area.
	North entrance: From Victor, go ½ mile east on County Road 67, to County Road 86, then 1 mile south (right) to County Road 861, and then 6½ miles east (left) on County Road 441 to Skaguay Reservoir. A trail below the dam leads into the SWA.

Beaver Creek SWA straddles the creek for 7 miles below Skaguay Reservoir. Below the dam, the creek tumbles into a deep, narrow canyon where it twists and cascades through the canyon and emerges at Soda Springs Park. About halfway down the canyon, Beaver Creek is joined by East Beaver Creek. The BLM land surrounding the canyons is steep, rugged country. Access into the canyons is by foot or horseback and difficult either way.

On gentler terrain at the south end of the SWA, Beaver Creek slows to meander through open meadows and tall stands of cottonwoods. The creek banks are densely vegetated with box elders and willows. The hillsides are forested in long needle pine, Gambel's oak, and piñon pine.

Fishing

Beaver Creek is a wild-trout fishery dominated by a self-sustaining population of brown trout. Fishing is marginal in the lower, more accessible sections. Backpackers and hikers report excellent fishing for larger trout in the hard-to-reach areas of both canyons.

Hunting

This is prime habitat for wild turkeys, deer, and bighorn sheep. All big-game and turkey hunting is by limited license only. You may not hunt turkeys here or in the nearby Table Mountain State Trust Lands with an over-the-counter license. This is in Game Management Unit 59.

Watchable Wildlife

Same as hunting

Camping and Facilities

Overnight camping is prohibited, but overnight parking is permitted for backcountry users. There is a large parking area at the end of County Road 132. Also, there is parking under the cottonwood trees on both sides of the creek. All areas are well-marked with DOW signs.

General Restrictions

Fires are prohibited.

South Central Colorado

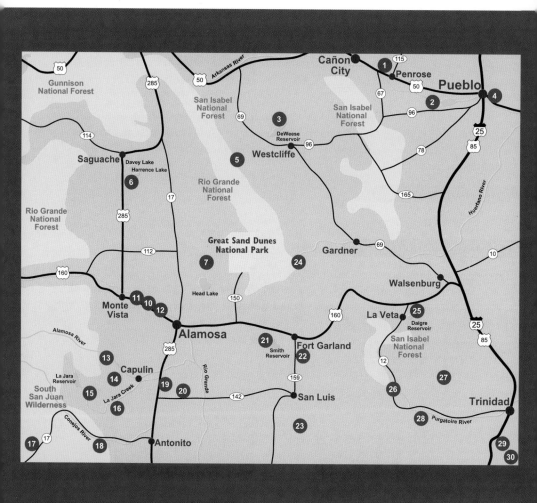

	Interstate Highway		Creek
	U.S. Highway		River
	State Highway		Lake
	City or Town		Wilderness Area
	State Wildlife Areas		National Park

See map on page 70 for Southwest Region in which 8 and 9 are located.

The south central region encompasses all of the San Luis Valley, from Salida south to New Mexico, and from Wolf Creek Pass east to Interstate 25. State Wildlife Areas are scattered throughout the region, offering 30 different locations to fish and hunt on public lands. The DOW is actively involved in wetlands and waterfowl habitat projects that continue to enhance waterfowl nesting and hunting opportunities in the San Luis Valley. And **Bosque del Oso**, one of the newest SWAs, has preserved 35,000 acres of prime wildlife habitat from development and provided big- and small-game hunters with quality hunting on a limited basis.

Anglers visiting the SWAs in this region will find plenty of fishing for a variety of cold-water and warm-water species. There's trout fishing in **Trujillo Meadows Reservoir**, located in the headwaters of the Rio de los Pinos near Cumbres Pass, excellent pike fishing in **Sanchez Reservoir**, and small streams in unlikely places that harbor remarkable populations of self-sustaining wild brown trout. Anglers may also try their luck for a state-record tench at **Home Lake SWA**.

Premium waterfowl, turkey, deer, elk, and small-game hunting awaits hunters in the south central region. Duck hunting in the Rockies just doesn't get any better than the San Luis Valley, and several SWAs offer hunters plenty of room to spread out. Turkey hunting is legendary at **Spanish Peaks**, **Lake Dorothey**, **James M. John**, and **Bosque del Oso**.

Wildlife Areas in South Central Colorado

1. Brush Hollow SWA

Primary Use:	Cold-water and warm-water fishing
Location:	Fremont County, 10 miles east of Cañon City
Size:	461 acres
Elevation:	5,600 feet
Division of Wildlife:	Area office in Colorado Springs, 719-227-5200
Directions:	From U.S. 50 at Penrose, go 2 miles north on Highway 115 to County Road 123, then 1¾ miles west (left) to the access road on the right, and then go 2 miles north (right) to the property.

Brush Hollow is a pretty good reservoir, for a switch hitter with a fluctuating water level. This popular fishing hole, located in the hills north of Penrose, is managed as both a warm-water and a cold-water fishery.

Fishing

Brush Hollow performs better than most reservoirs as both a cold-water and a warm-water fishery. The DOW stocks 10-inch catchable rainbow trout to keep everybody happy, but the best fishing here is for largemouth bass, walleye, bluegill, and channel catfish. Heavy aquatic vegetation makes fishing difficult from shore, but provides excellent habitat for the largemouth bass, and some grow to more than 5 pounds. The minimum size for largemouth, smallmouth, and spotted bass is 15 inches.

Hunting

Hunting is prohibited.

Watchable Wildlife

Waterfowl

Camping and Facilities

Camping is prohibited. Facilities include boat ramps, toilets, and picnic shelters.

General Restrictions

1. Boating is prohibited if it creates a white-water wake.
2. Fires are prohibited.

Fly-fishing for largemouth bass

2. Pueblo Reservoir SWA

Primary Use:	Warm-water fishing, upland game hunting, and bird watching
Location:	Pueblo County, 7 miles west of Pueblo at Pueblo Reservoir
Size:	4,000 acres
Elevation:	4,600 feet
Division of Wildlife:	Area office in Pueblo, 719-561-5300
Directions:	To reach the boat ramp, from the town of Pueblo West go 4 miles south on McCulloch Boulevard to Nichols Road and then approximately 1 mile south (left) to the gravel access road on the right. The access road is about 100 yards before the park entrance. To reach the bulk of the wildlife area located south of the reservoir, from Pueblo Dam go 7 miles west on Highway 96 to the access road on the right.

This large wildlife area straddles the upper end of Pueblo Reservoir and several miles of the Arkansas River. It is a quiet retreat from the fast-paced crowds at the adjacent Pueblo State Park. Visitors here can hike a nature trail; observe herons, cormorants, swallows, and raptors from an observation deck on a cliff overlooking the lake; hunt upland game and waterfowl; fish the river or the lake; and launch a fishing boat at a free ramp.

Fishing

Both the upper end of the reservoir and the river have excellent fishing for largemouth bass, smallmouth bass, wipers, walleye, catfish, and crappie.

A good concrete boat ramp is located on the north side of the lake. The ramp is restricted to fishing boats with a maximum 50hp motor. Jet skis, sailboats, sailboards, and water skiers are prohibited. To reach the boat ramp, follow the signs from the gravel access road that turns west 100 yards before the north entrance to the State Park. This road also provides fishing access to Turkey Creek Cove and other smaller coves on the north shore.

Fishing access to the south shore, including Mid-lake Shoals and Three Finger Coves, is from a gravel access road on Highway 96. All the access roads are well-marked with DOW signs.

Hunting

The property on the south side of the reservoir has hunting for scaled quail, waterfowl, deer, dove, and turkey. Duck hunting can be good at the potholes on the far-west end of the property and on the river. Follow the access road from Highway 96 to the end of the road. This road also provides access for upland game hunting. There are several coveys of scaled quail that live in the hills and draws on the south side. Also in this area, there is good hunting for cottontail rabbits and doves.

Watchable Wildlife

There are two excellent locations for viewing wildlife, one north of the river and one south. The north side has the Audubon Trail and the Bob Overton wildlife-viewing platform. To get there, go 5 miles west of Pueblo West on U.S. 50 to Swallows Road, and go 5 miles south (left) on this gravel road to the areas. The viewing platform is on a cliff overlooking the river and the heron rookery. At different times, visitors can expect to see bald eagles, cliff swallows, prairie falcons, great blue herons, cormorants, ducks, geese, and a host of songbirds.

The south side has the Conduit Nature Trail, an easy 3-mile hike through the hills. On the same access road, there is a parking area overlooking the river and a cottonwood forest. It is a great spot for watching a variety of birds.

Camping and Facilities

Camping is prohibited in the wildlife area, but campgrounds with all facilities are available at the State Park. There are toilets in most areas, a boat ramp on the north shore, hiking trails, a wildlife viewing platform, and good access roads to all areas.

General Restrictions

1. Discharging firearms is prohibited, except shotguns and bows while hunting.
2. Target practice is prohibited.
3. Fires are prohibited.
4. Field trials are prohibited, except in February and August.

3. DeWeese Reservoir SWA

Primary Use:	Trout fishing
Location:	Custer County, 5 miles north of Westcliffe and 20 miles southwest of Cañon City
Size:	780 acres
Elevation:	7,800 feet
Division of Wildlife:	Area office in Pueblo, 719-561-5300
Directions:	From Westcliffe, go 5 miles northwest on Highway 69 to Copper Gulch Road, then 2 miles north (right) to the reservoir.

This wildlife area is located in Wet Mountain Valley between the Sangre de Cristo Mountains and the DeWeese Plateau. The valley is relatively flat and treeless but the scenery isn't bad, if you block out the subdivisions. The lake's bare shorelines afford plenty of camping.

Fishing

The reservoir has fishing for trout and for smallmouth bass. Catchable-sized (10-inch) cutthroat and rainbow trout are stocked annually. Brown trout are stocked as fingerlings and grow up in the reservoir as wild trout. The stream above the reservoir is a seasonal fishery with a decent run of brown trout in fall. Ice fishing for trout is reported as excellent.

A thriving population of small smallmouth bass in the reservoir provides anglers with fast action and high catch rates. There is no size limit on the smallmouth.

Hunting

Hunting is permitted, but the area is small and there are houses in all directions. There is pretty good dove hunting in September.

Watchable Wildlife

Waterfowl

Camping and Facilities

Primitive campsites are located on the north and south sides near the dam. There are boat ramps and toilets.

4. Runyon/Fountain Lakes SWA

Primary Use:	City park
Location:	Pueblo County, in Pueblo
Size:	40 acres
Elevation:	4,000 feet
Division of Wildlife:	Area office in Pueblo, 719-561-5300
Directions:	From Interstate 25 at Exit 98A, go south on Santa Fe Drive to Runyon Field, and then east (left) on Runyon Field Road to the lakes.

Situated around a small lake beside the Arkansas River near downtown Pueblo, this parklike wildlife area is a nice facility for fishing and picnicking.

Fishing

Stocked year-round with 10-inch rainbow trout, the lakes also have warm-water fishing for bass and catfish.

Hunting

Hunting is prohibited.

Watchable Wildlife

None

Camping and Facilities

Camping is prohibited. Facilities include toilets, a nature trail, and a handicapped-fishing pier.

General Restrictions

1. Public access is prohibited from sunset to sunrise, except for fishing.
2. Boating is prohibited.
3. Ice fishing is prohibited.
4. Fires are prohibited.
5. All water contact activities are prohibited.

5. Middle Taylor Creek SWA

From the town of Westcliffe 20 miles southwest of Cañon City, go 8 miles west on Hermit Lakes Road to the property.

This 500-acre property is located at the base of the Sangre de Cristo Mountains. Although hunting is allowed on the property, the primary use is for big-game hunting camps. Primitive camping is unrestricted. There was a toilet here until vandals had their way with it.

6. Russell Lakes SWA

Primary Use:	Waterfowl hunting
Location:	Saguache County, San Luis Valley, 10 miles south of Saguache
Size:	800 acres
Elevation:	7,600 feet
Division of Wildlife:	Area office in Monte Vista, 719-587-6900
Directions:	From the small town of Saguache in the northwest corner of the valley, go 9 miles south on U.S. 285 to County Road R and then 1½ miles east (left) to the access roads on the right. The first access road dead-ends at the parking and camping area that serves Davey and Harrence Lakes. The second access road also leads to a parking and camping area. Another parking area is located on U.S. 285 about 1 mile south of County Road R. And another parking area is located on the south end of the property. To get there, go 2 miles south of County Road R on the highway and then 4 miles east (left) on County Road N to the access road.

Russell Lakes SWA is a large, flat section of wetlands located in the northwest corner of the San Luis Valley. A spring creek flows through the property, feeding a maze of wetlands, dikes, canals, and shallow lakes designed and built by the DOW to provide habitat for nesting waterfowl. The property is closed to all public access during the nesting season. One of the larger lakes on the property is a refuge for waterfowl, and remains closed during hunting season. Levees separating the flooded lowlands offer good walk-in access to remote corners of the property.

Fishing

None

Hunting

Russell Lakes is known for its duck hunting. A great variety of ducks nest on the property and stay in the area until the wetlands freeze over. The area also attracts a lot of migratory ducks and geese. Many hunters use the grillwork of levees and roads that separate the flooded wetlands to jump-shoot ducks. Other hunters prefer to hunt over decoys. Both methods are effective here. Jump shooters perform a service to all hunters by bumping ducks off the wetlands. The largest bodies of water are two lakes located within easy walking distance of the northwest parking/camping area. These lakes are good spots to set out a big spread of decoys.

Watchable Wildlife

A large variety of waterfowl and shorebirds may be viewed here after the property opens on July 15.

Camping and Facilities

Camping is prohibited, except in self-contained units in designated areas. There are no facilities.

General Restrictions

1. Public access is prohibited February 15–July 15 to protect nesting waterfowl.
2. Public access is prohibited, except as posted.
3. Parking is prohibited, except in designated areas.
4. Field trials are prohibited, except in February, March, August, and September.

7. San Luis Lakes SWA

Primary Use:	Waterfowl hunting
Location:	Alamosa County, San Luis Valley, 15 miles northeast of Alamosa
Size:	2,000 acres
Elevation:	7,700 feet
Division of Wildlife:	Area office in Monte Vista, 719-587-6900
Directions:	From Alamosa, go 13 miles north on Highway 17 to Road 6N (Sand Dunes Monument Road), and then 8 miles east (right) to the entrance to San Luis Lakes State Park. The SWA sits on the north side of the park. Hunters do not need a parks pass to access the wildlife area during hunting seasons.

This wildlife area sits on the northern boundary of San Luis Lakes State Park, within eyeshot of the Great Sand Dunes. The property features a combination of wetlands, ponds, and shallow lakes similar in design to **Russell Lakes SWA** (see p. 225). The wetlands attract a variety of ducks, geese, cranes, and shorebirds.

Fishing

San Luis Lake is stocked with 10-inch rainbow trout. Head Lake is full of carp.

Hunting

The northern tip of San Luis Lake is within the SWA and it is legal to hunt north of the buoy line. The best waterfowl hunting is found at Head Lake and on wetlands located on the northern end of the property. In most years, hunting for ducks and Canada geese is good until the lakes freeze.

Watchable Wildlife

In addition to ducks and geese, there are plenty of opportunities to view sandhill cranes and shorebirds.

Camping and Facilities

Camping is prohibited at the SWA, but is available at the State Park. There are no facilities at the SWA.

General Restrictions

1. Boats are prohibited north of the buoy line.
2. Public access is prohibited north of the buoy line and the east-west fence line February 15–July 15 to protect nesting waterfowl.

8. Coller SWA

Primary Use:	Trout fishing
Location:	Mineral and Rio Grande Counties, Rio Grande, 5 miles north of South Fork
Size:	733 acres
Elevation:	8,200 feet
Division of Wildlife:	Area office in Monte Vista, 719-587-6900
Directions:	From U.S. 160 in South Fork, go 5 miles north on Highway 149 to the south end of the property. There are access roads and parking areas for several miles along the river. The areas are well-marked.

Stretching out for 5 miles beside the Rio Grande, this wildlife area provides easy access to the river. At most of the access points, there are multiple parking areas near the river, and picnic spots shaded by tall cottonwood trees. This stretch of the river flows beneath the cliffs of the Rio Grande Palisades. This SWA, like the rest of the Rio Grande, receives heavy fishing pressure during tourist season.

Fishing

The Rio Grande has long been known as a good brown trout fishery, with browns totaling about 90 percent of the trout population. The other 10 percent are wild rainbow trout trying to hold on against whirling disease. All rainbow trout must be returned to the water immediately. Anglers are asked to play trout to the net quickly and release them carefully back into the water, with a minimum amount of handling.

Through this stretch, the river is wide and runs relatively straight. There are long riffles scattered with a few large boulders. The best trout-holding water is found near the banks. This is choice water for fishing with dry flies.

Dry-fly fishing turns on in June, with heavy hatches of caddis and stoneflies, and again in July, with the emergence of the giant green drake mayfly. Anglers do well at other times fishing nymphs, wet flies, and streamers. Dry flies suggested for the Rio Grande include Elk-hair Caddis, Royal Humpy, Green Drake Mayfly, Blue-winged Olive, and the Stimulator.

Hunting

The wildlife area itself has a limited amount of land for hunting elk and deer, but it provides public access to the surrounding Rio Grande National Forest.

Watchable Wildlife

Waterfowl and raptors

Camping and Facilities

Camping is prohibited. Facilities include toilets and picnic tables.

General Restrictions

Overnight parking is prohibited.

9. Beaver Creek Reservoir SWA

Primary Use:	Trout and kokanee salmon fishing
Location:	Rio Grande County, 8 miles southwest of South Fork
Size:	2,000 acres
Elevation:	9,000 feet
Division of Wildlife:	Area office in Salida, 719-530-5520
Directions:	From South Fork, go 2 miles southwest on U.S. 160 to Forest Service Road 360, and then 6 miles south (left) to the reservoir.

Beaver Creek Reservoir SWA is the most heavily used wildlife area in the San Luis Valley, but not by wildlife. Access from South Fork is easy on a paved road, and tourists flock here in summer.

Fishing

Although there is a fair population of self-sustaining brown trout in the reservoir, it's hatchery rainbows that keep the anglers busy. Kokanee salmon are also stocked, and boat anglers pursue them by trolling flashy arrays of metal and colored plastic, called pop gear. Amazing fighters, the salmon often drag the entire array into the air behind them when they leap. Ice fishing for trout and salmon is reported as good to excellent.

Hunting

Hunting is prohibited.

Watchable Wildlife

Waterfowl

Camping and Facilities

Camping is available at nearby Forest Service campgrounds. Facilities include boat ramps, restrooms, drinking water, and picnic tables.

General Restrictions

1. Kokanee snagging is permitted October 1–December 31.
2. Boating is prohibited if it creates a white-water wake.
3. Discharging firearms or bows is prohibited.
4. Open fires are prohibited on the ice.

10. Rio Grande SWA

Primary Use:	Waterfowl hunting
Location:	Rio Grande County, San Luis Valley, 3 miles east of Monte Vista
Size:	935 acres
Elevation:	7,600 feet
Division of Wildlife:	Area office in Monte Vista, 719-587-6900
Directions:	There are six parking areas for the wildlife area. To reach the west parking areas, go 3 miles east of Monte Vista on Sherman Avenue to the parking areas located at **Home Lake SWA** (see p. 232). To reach the east parking areas, go 6 miles east of Monte Vista on U.S. 160/285 to County Road 6E and then 2 miles north (left) to the river. There are parking areas on both sides of the river.

Straddling 2 miles of prime bottomland on the Rio Grande, this wildlife area encompasses a corridor of riparian habitat flanked by marshes, oxbow ponds, and fields of grain crops.

Fishing

There is marginal fishing for largemouth bass in the duck ponds, and a few northern pike in the river.

Hunting

Duck hunting here can be either awesome or awful, depending on the weather, the amount of water in the valley, and the amount of hunting pressure. Bad weather, low water, and few hunters means better duck hunting. This wildlife area is located close to Monte Vista and receives heavy use. Nevertheless, this area is always worth checking out, because duck hunting here can be rewarding—even in the awful times.

Watchable Wildlife

Bald and golden eagles are sometimes seen here in winter. Waterfowl include blue herons, white-faced ibis, snowy egrets, black-crowned night herons, sandhill cranes, and a host of nesting ducks such as cinnamon teal.

Camping and Facilities

Camping is prohibited except in the parking areas that have toilets.

General Restrictions

1. Public access is prohibited February 15–July 15.
2. Fires are prohibited.

11. Home Lake SWA

Primary Use:	Trout fishing
Location:	Rio Grande County, Monte Vista
Size:	About 100 acres
Elevation:	8,000 feet
Division of Wildlife:	Area office in Monte Vista, 719-587-6900
Directions:	From Monte Vista, go 1½ miles east on Sherman Avenue to the lake.

This small lake located on the outskirts of Monte Vista holds the state record for tench, a carplike fish imported from Europe and first stocked in Colorado in 1894. Little is known about the hearty tench, but Home Lake has big ones. The record fish, caught in 1998, was 20 inches long and weighed 5 pounds, 6 ounces. The lake is rimmed by a wall of tall cottonwoods and suited for fishing from shore or small boats.

Fishing

Home Lake is managed as a put-and-take trout fishery. The DOW puts in 10-inch rainbows in April and May, and anglers take them out all summer.

Hunting

Hunting is prohibited.

Watchable Wildlife

Waterfowl

Camping and Facilities

None

General Restrictions

1. Boating is prohibited except craft propelled by hand, wind, or electric motor, or motorboats up to 10hp.
2. Public access is prohibited from sunset to sunrise, except for fishing.

12. Higel SWA

Primary Use:	Waterfowl hunting
Location:	Alamosa County, Rio Grande River, 7 miles east of Monte Vista
Size:	1,200 acres
Elevation:	8,000 feet
Division of Wildlife:	Area office in Monte Vista, 719-587-6900
Directions:	From Monte Vista, go 6 miles southeast on U.S. 160 to County Road 3S (just past the Texaco truck stop), and then 1½ miles east (left) to the DOW sign at the access road leading to the ranch. Drive north (left), following the road around the ranch house to the parking areas.

Textbook waterfowl habitat and a duck hunter's dream all in one location, Higel is one of those remarkable pieces of property that the DOW manages for quality waterfowl hunting. The wildlife area encompasses a considerable portion of prime wetlands beside the Rio Grande. The landscape is a boggy network of shallow seasonal ponds, oxbows, wet meadows, and marshes rimmed with thick patches of cattails and bulrushes.

Higel SWA is part of the Colorado Wetlands Initiative program, which includes participation from private landowners, municipalities, state and federal governments, and nongovernmental organizations. The partners include The Nature Conservancy, Ducks Unlimited, and Partners for Fish and Wildlife.

Fishing

None

Hunting

Waterfowl hunting would be good here even it weren't so close to the Monte Vista National Wildlife Refuge. Special regulations prevent overuse.

1. Permits are required and are free of charge to a maximum of 25 hunters per day.
2. From September 1 to September 30, and November 11 to the end of waterfowl season, permits may be obtained by calling 719-587-6923 or in person at the DOW Monte Vista Service Center.
3. From October 1 to November 10, permits must be obtained by calling the number above. Earliest reservations for any date may be made 14 days in advance, but not fewer than 2 days before the day requested.
4. Public access is prohibited from September 1 to February 14, except for Saturdays, Sundays, Wednesdays, and legal holidays.

In addition to outstanding opportunities for waterfowl hunting, Higel also has hunting for elk. It doesn't seem likely, but a herd of 80–100 elk frequent this stretch of the river. All big-game hunting is by limited licenses issued in drawing. This is in Game Management Unit 79.

Watchable Wildlife

The extensive marshlands on the property attract several species of waterfowl, including sandhill cranes, black-necked stilt, black terns, cinnamon teal, and other ducks.

Camping and Facilities

None

General Restrictions

Public access is prohibited February 15–July 15 to protect nesting waterfowl.

Bighorn sheep, Terrace Reservoir SWA

13. Terrace Reservoir SWA

Primary Use:	Wildlife viewing
Location:	Conejos County, Alamosa River, 30 miles southwest of Alamosa
Size:	About 500 acres
Elevation:	9,000 feet
Division of Wildlife:	Area office in Monte Vista, 719-587-6900
Directions:	From Monte Vista, go 12 miles south on Highway 15 to Forest Service Road 250, then 9 miles southwest to the reservoir.

Here lies the prettiest dead body of water in Colorado.

Fishing

The lake is virtually void of fish because of heavy metals from mines leaching into the river.

Hunting

None

Watchable Wildlife

Bighorn sheep

Camping and Facilities

None

14. Hot Creek SWA

Primary Use:	Big-game hunting
Location:	Conejos County, San Luis Valley, 20 miles south of Monte Vista
Size:	3,500 acres
Elevation:	8,000 feet
Division of Wildlife:	Area office in Monte Vista, 719-587-6900
Directions:	From Alamosa, go 28 miles south on U.S. 285 to Highway 15 at La Jara, then 10 miles west (right) to County Road X at Centro. Look for DOW signs at the junction. Then go 5 miles west (left) to the DOW property sign and the access road on the left. Follow this road southwest over the hill to the parking lot and beyond.

Hot Creek Canyon is surprising at first sight. The lush wetlands at the bottom of this narrow valley seem strangely out of place in the dry and treeless landscape. There are beaver ponds rimmed with willows, and marshes choked with cattails. The terrain ranges from rolling hills, ridges, and small canyons, to broad mountain meadows and pine forests at higher elevations.

This wildlife area and the State Trust Lands nearby are critical wintering areas for elk, deer, and other game.

Fishing

Hot Creek has no sport fishing, but it harbors two endangered native species, the Rio Grande sucker and the Rio Grande chub.

Hunting

Elk, deer, bighorn sheep, mountain lion, black bear, and antelope hunting are by limited license. There is additional hunting to the west on the 32,000-acre La Jara Reservoir State Trust Land. There is a limited amount of duck hunting on the beaver ponds. These areas are in Game Management Unit 81.

Watchable Wildlife

Same as hunting

Camping and Facilities

None

General Restrictions

1. Snowmobiles are prohibited.
2. All vehicles are prohibited December 1–April 30.

15. La Jara Reservoir SWA

Primary Use:	Big-game hunting
Location:	Conejos County, San Luis Valley, 30 miles southwest of Alamosa
Size:	635 acres
Elevation:	9,700 feet
Division of Wildlife:	Area office in Monte Vista, 719-587-6900
Directions:	From Alamosa, go 28 miles south on U.S. 285 to Highway 15 at La Jara, then 10 miles west (right) to County Road X at Centro. Look for DOW signs at the junction. Then go 10 miles west (left) to the reservoir. Watch out for fast-moving logging trucks on all roads in this area!

La Jara Reservoir sits in a high meadow at the headwaters of La Jara Creek. The meadow is used as summer pasture for cattle. There are no fish in the reservoir.

Fishing

A population of native Rio Grande cutthroat trout inhabits Jim Creek, a small stream that flows into the reservoir from the west.

Hunting

Elk and deer are found throughout the area. Also in the area are antelope, bighorn sheep, black bear, mountain lion, and small game. There are more than 32,000 acres to hunt in the adjacent La Jara Reservoir State Trust Land.

Watchable Wildlife

Same as hunting

Camping and Facilities

Camping is allowed in designated areas. Facilities include modern toilets and parking areas.

General Restrictions

Vehicles are prohibited, except on established and designated roadways.

16. La Jara SWA

Primary Use:	Big-game hunting, trout fishing
Location:	Conejos County, 30 miles south of Monte Vista
Size:	3,320 acres
Elevation:	8,400–9,000 feet
Division of Wildlife:	Area office in Monte Vista, 719-587-6900
Directions:	From Monte Vista, go 20 miles south on Highway 15 to Capulin and then about 9 miles south (left) on County Road 8 to the entrance at the northern boundary of the property.

Set off by itself in the southwest corner of the San Luis Valley, this wildlife area is one of those special, out-of-the-way places. La Jara Creek is the major artery in a network of creeks that have carved deep canyons where the flat floor of the valley rises to the foothills. Riparian woodlands with cottonwoods, willows, alders, and other deciduous shrubs and tall grass meadows flank the meandering creek. Piñon and juniper dot the slopes of the canyon walls.

A primitive road leads up the canyon, crossing the stream several times before reaching the end of the canyon. A high-clearance or four-wheel-drive vehicle is recommended to ford the stream. A parking area and campsite are conveniently located before the first stream crossing for those unwilling to drive through the creek.

Fishing

This wildlife area has one of the best "out-of-the-way" trout streams in Colorado. La Jara Creek supports a healthy and robust population of wild brown trout that share the stream with a few brook trout. The browns are small on average, but trout up to 20 inches long are not rare. La Jara is an obliging little creek. It welcomes fly fishers with its long pools, gravelly riffles, dark runs sweeping under the cutbanks on outside bends, and stretches of pocket water strewn with boulders.

Hunting

The diversity of habitat in the canyons and surrounding foothills supports elk, deer, bighorn sheep, black bears, mountain lions, antelope, and a host of small game. Hunting is excellent for cottontail rabbits.

Big-game hunting on this property and the adjacent Vicente Canyon and La Jara Reservoir State Trust Lands is reported to be better in the later hunting seasons, when harsh weather forces the animals from their summer range at higher elevations. This area is in Game Management Unit 81.

Watchable Wildlife

Same as hunting

Camping and Facilities

Primitive camping is available at intervals along the access road. Please use existing sites and fire rings, and pack out all trash. There are no facilities.

General Restrictions

1. Vehicles are prohibited December 1–April 30.
2. Snowmobiles are prohibited.

Velvet-antlered mule deer

17. Trujillo Meadows SWA

Primary Use: Trout fishing

Location: Conejos County, Cumbres Pass, 30 miles southwest of Antonito

Size: 950 acres (the lake's high-water mark is the boundary)

Elevation: 10,000 feet

Division of Wildlife: Area office in Monte Vista, 719-587-6900

Directions: From Antonito on U.S. 285, go 36 miles west on Highway 17 to Forest Service Road 118 at the top of Cumbres Pass (elevation 10,022 feet), and then 4 miles northwest (right) to the reservoir.

Trujillo Meadows Reservoir rests in a valley nestled by rolling mountains near the headwaters of the Rio de los Pinos. It's easy to see why this wildlife area is so popular with anglers, hikers, and tourists. It offers easy access to good fishing, nice facilities, long views, and meadows filled with wildflowers.

Fishing

The reservoir is managed as a put-and-grow trout fishery, stocked periodically with fingerling rainbow, brown, and brook trout. The trout have a fair-to-good growth rate, reaching 15 inches in about three years. The lake has a maximum depth of 35 feet. This entire region is very popular with tourists.

The reservoir is situated on the Rio de los Pinos, and a trail leads up the river from the parking area. Fishing in the stream is for brook and brown trout for 3 miles below the waterfall, where the stream enters the South San Juan Wilderness. Above the waterfall lives a population of native Rio Grande cutthroat trout. Fishing is by flies and lures only, and all cutthroats must be returned to the water immediately.

Hunting

None

Watchable Wildlife

Waterfowl

Camping and Facilities

Camping is prohibited at the SWA but there is Forest Service campground adjacent to the reservoir. Facilities at the reservoir include a boat ramp and toilets.

General Restrictions

Boating is prohibited if it creates a white-water wake.

18. Conejos River SWA

Primary Use:	Trout fishing
Location:	Conejos County, Conejos River, west of Antonito
Size:	Unknown
Elevation:	8,000 feet
Division of Wildlife:	Area office in Monte Vista, 719-587-6900
Directions:	From Antonito on U.S. 285, go 15 miles west on Highway 17 and look for DOW signs on the south (left) side of the road. Starting at the Conejos Ranch, parking areas are spaced intermittently along Highway 17 for the next 16 miles.

This wildlife area consists of a group of fishing easements scattered along a 16-mile stretch of the Conejos River. The easements provide several points of public access to the river. The Conejos River is a beautiful place to cast a fly. Giant blue spruce and ponderosa pines mingle with stately cottonwoods by the river, and rock outcroppings and mesas loom high in the background. The Conejos is typical of a classic freestone mountain stream, with broad quick riffles spilling into pools, and deep runs sweeping through outside bends.

Fishing

The Conejos River is a fine wild-trout fishery. The population of self-sustaining brown trout averages 80 pounds of trout per surface acre, and range in size from fingerlings to more than 20 inches. The browns are wary, but will rise to dry flies if not spooked by clumsy anglers. There is a significant hatch of yellow stoneflies in spring, and a profusion of caddisfly hatches throughout the summer.

Hunting

Hunting is prohibited.

Watchable Wildlife

Ouzels (dippers), kingfishers, and many other species of birds and wildlife are common in southern Colorado.

Camping and Facilities

None

General Restrictions

Public access is prohibited, except for fishing.

19. Conejos County Ponds SWA

This wildlife area consists of shallow ponds and wetlands located behind the county maintenance barns on Highway 136 east of La Jara, 28 miles south of Alamosa on U.S. 285. The area is managed as a habitat for nesting waterfowl. It is closed to public access February 15–July 15.

20. Sego Springs SWA

Primary Use:	Waterfowl and dove hunting
Location:	Conejos County, San Luis Valley, 20 miles south of Alamosa
Size:	640 acres
Elevation:	7,500 feet
Division of Wildlife:	Area office in Monte Vista, 719-587-6900
Directions:	From Alamosa, go 20 miles south on U.S. 285 to Highway 142 at Romeo, then 6¼ miles east (left), through Manassa, to the unmarked dirt road on the left, and then ½ mile north to the property. Follow the two-track dirt road northwest over the hill to the parking area for the ponds.

This secretive little wildlife area is just far enough out of the way to make it a special place to hunt ducks and mourning doves. The property has two spring-fed ponds situated at the edge of the cottonwood trees on the North Branch of the Conejos River.

Fishing

None

Hunting

Sego Springs is an excellent location for hunting waterfowl and mourning doves.

Watchable Wildlife

Ducks

Camping and Facilities

Primitive camping, no facilities

General Restrictions

1. Public access is prohibited February 15–July 15 to protect nesting waterfowl.
2. Fires are prohibited.
3. Field trials are prohibited, except in August and September.

21. Smith Reservoir SWA

Primary Use:	Trout fishing and waterfowl hunting
Location:	Costilla County, San Luis Valley, 20 miles east of Alamosa
Size:	700 acres
Elevation:	7,500 feet
Division of Wildlife:	Area office in Monte Vista, 719-587-6900
Directions:	From Alamosa, go 20 miles east on U.S. 160 to Airport Road (just before Blanca), then 4 miles south (right) to the reservoir.

Smith is an irrigation reservoir serving the farmlands in the southeast corner of the San Luis Valley. Although subject to extreme water fluctuations, the reservoir has good facilities and a well-earned reputation for growing big trout.

Fishing

Smith Reservoir is managed as a put-and-take rainbow fishery, stocked with 10-inch hatchery trout. The lake is rich in nutrients and the trout grow quickly. When they are able to hold over for a winter or two, they get big. There is a nice concrete boat ramp on the property, but it is unusable when the water level is low. Fishing is prohibited from November 1 through the last day of waterfowl season, except within 200 yards of the dam.

Hunting

Waterfowl hunting is usually good for local ducks and geese, including the ones that nest on the east shore, during the first and second split seasons. The shallow shorelines are suitable for setting out decoys, unless low water exposes too much mud. At times the waterline might be 30 yards from high-water mark.

Watchable Wildlife

Waterfowl and white pelicans

Camping and Facilities

Primitive camping is allowed in most areas. Facilities include toilets, a boat ramp, and a trailer dump station.

General Restrictions

1. Public access is prohibited on the north and east shores February 15–July 15 to protect nesting waterfowl.
2. Vehicles are prohibited within 50 feet of the water.

22. Mountain Home Reservoir SWA

Primary Use: Trout fishing

Location: Costilla County, San Luis Valley, 5 miles southeast of Fort Garland

Size: 1,100 acres

Elevation: 8,000 feet

Division of Wildlife: Area office in Monte Vista, 719-587-6900

Directions: From Fort Garland (26 miles east of Alamosa), go 2½ miles east on U.S. 160 to the Forbes/Trinchera Ranch Road, then 2 miles south (right) to Ice House Road, and then 1 mile west (right) to the north side of the lake. Access to the south side is 1 mile south of Ice House Road.

Mountain Home Reservoir is an irrigation reservoir located in the foothills of the Sangre de Cristo Mountains. The lake stretches from wide shallows at the inlet, to a deep and narrow channel cradled between two knobby hills at the dam.

Fishing

Mountain Home Reservoir is managed as a put-and-take trout fishery, stocked with 10-inch trout. There is a problem here with northern pike catching the half-witted hatchery trout before the anglers can. Anglers who prefer catching trout are encouraged to eat all the pike they catch. Many of the pike are large, some measuring 3 feet long, but are hard to catch. They didn't get big by being dumb.

Hunting

Hunting is prohibited.

Watchable Wildlife

Waterfowl

Camping and Facilities

Primitive campsites are located in the hills around the lake.
Facilities include boat ramps and modern toilets.

General Restrictions

Waterskiing is prohibited.

23. Sanchez Reservoir SWA

Primary Use:	Warm-water fishing
Location:	Costilla County, San Luis Valley, 35 miles southeast of Alamosa
Size:	Approximately 400 acres of water
Elevation:	8,000 feet
Division of Wildlife:	Area office in Monte Vista, 719-587-6900
Directions:	From the small town of San Luis on Highway 159 in the southeast corner of the valley, at the Phillips 66 station go 3 miles southeast on County Road P.6 to County Road 21, then 5¼ miles south (right) to the access road. DOW signs mark the turns.

Tucked away in the southeast corner of the San Luis Valley, Sanchez Reservoir is a medium-sized irrigation reservoir situated between the Sangre de Cristo Mountains and San Pedro Mesa. Sanchez offers its visitors great views, a feeling of solitude, and some of the best fly-fishing for northern pike in the state. The nearby town of San Luis is the oldest town in Colorado.

Fishing

Sanchez Reservoir was once famous for high catch rates of big yellow perch, and fisherman flocked here to catch them through the ice in winter. The big perch eventually toppled in the wake of angling pressure, but now are making a comeback. Although the reservoir is stocked regularly with walleye, the best fishing is for northern pike. Large areas of shallow, reedy water provide an ideal environment for the lake's thriving population, and pike up to 20 pounds have been caught here. The inlet is good for pike in early spring.

Hunting

Hunting is prohibited.

Watchable Wildlife

Waterfowl and coyotes

Camping and Facilities

Primitive camping is available in designated areas.
Facilities include toilets and a boat ramp.

General Restrictions

1. Public access is prohibited, except for fishing.
2. Waterskiing is prohibited.
3. Camping is prohibited in the boat ramp parking area.

Coyotes are common throughout Colorado.

24. Huerfano SWA

Primary Use:	Trout fishing and hunting
Location:	Huerfano County, 14 miles west of Gardner
Size:	544 acres
Elevation:	7,600 feet
Division of Wildlife:	Area office in Pueblo, 719-561-5300
Directions:	From Walsenburg, go 25 miles northwest on Highway 69 to Gardner, and then 14 miles west (left) on County Road 550, which becomes 580, to the property.

The Huerfano River is a happy little stream teeming with brown trout. Situated in an out-of-the-way glacial valley on the eastern slope of the Sangre de Cristo Mountains, this narrow wildlife area has 3 miles of fishing on the Huerfano and several nice campsites.

Fishing

There are about 1,300 fish per mile according to the most recent DOW electro-fishing survey, and nearly 100 percent of them are brown trout that range in size up to 14 inches. Fly fishing is made difficult in spots by thick growths of willows and alders on the banks.

Hunting

Deer, turkey, and small game

Watchable Wildlife

Same as hunting

Camping and Facilities

Camping is permitted, and there are toilets at the parking areas.

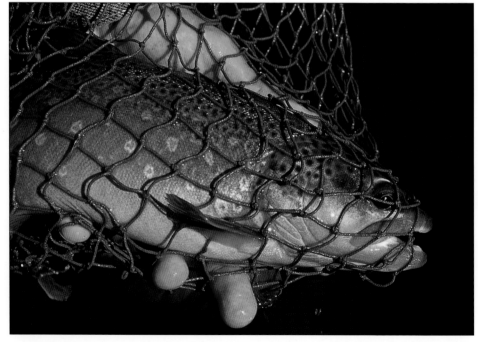

Stable and self-sustaining populations of wild brown trout exist in many out-pf-the-way streams in Colorado. Brown trout have the reputation of being more difficult to catch than rainbow trout, but this misconception is vanishing as anglers learn more about this excellent sport fish.

25. Wahatoya SWA

Primary Use:	Trout fishing
Location:	Huerfano County, La Veta
Size:	200 acres
Elevation:	7,000 feet
Division of Wildlife:	Area office in Pueblo, 719-561-5300
Directions:	From La Veta (14 miles southwest of Walsenburg), go 1 mile east on Bear Creek Road.

Wahatoya SWA consists of two lakes located on the outskirts of La Veta. Both are stocked with hatchery rainbows, and one is known for producing large brown trout.

Fishing

Daigre Reservoir is legendary for a 30-inch brown trout that came from its waters. Both Daigre and Wahatoya Reservoirs receive annual stockings of 10-inch rainbows. The fishing is best at ice-out.

Hunting

Hunting is prohibited.

Watchable Wildlife

Waterfowl

Camping and Facilities

Camping is prohibited. Facilities include a toilet.

General Restrictions

1. Fishing is by artificial flies and lures only.
2. Boating is prohibited, except by craft propelled by hand or wind.
3. Ice fishing is prohibited.
4. Fires are prohibited.

26. North Lake SWA

Primary Use:	Trout fishing
Location:	Las Animas County, 35 miles west of Trinidad
Size:	840 acres
Elevation:	8,700 feet
Division of Wildlife:	Area office in Pueblo, 719-561-5300
Directions:	From Trinidad, go 35 miles west on Highway 12 toward Cucharas Pass, to the lake.

The wildlife area has great views of the Sangre de Cristo Mountains and is a fine place to fish for stocked trout. Good turkey hunting lies to the west in the San Isabel National Forest. North Lake receives heavy use in summer.

Fishing

The lake has approximately 100 surface acres and is stocked with catchable rainbows. The lake was also stocked with fingerling splake that have grown to about 15 inches. Fishing in North Lake is restricted to artificial flies and lures only.

Hunting

There is hunting for deer, elk, bighorn sheep, and turkeys on the property and in the neighboring San Isabel National Forest. An access road leads into the forest from the lake along the North Fork of the Purgatoire River. This is in Game Management Unit 85.

Watchable Wildlife

Same as hunting

Camping and Facilities

Camping is prohibited on the property, but campsites are available in the National Forest. Facilities include a boat ramp and toilets. There is parking at the lake and on the river.

General Restrictions

1. Boating is prohibited, except by craft propelled by hand, wind, or electric motor.
2. Fires are prohibited.

27. Spanish Peaks SWA

Primary Use: Big-game and turkey hunting

Location: Las Animas County, 20 miles northwest of Trinidad

Size: 6,450 acres

Elevation: 7,000–8,000 feet

Division of Wildlife: Area office in Pueblo, 719-561-5300

Directions: There are four individual parcels of land in the wildlife area.

Dochter Tract: From Aguilar (at Interstate 25 Exit 30 or 34), go 18 miles southwest on the Apishapa Road, following the signs to the property. From Trinidad, go approximately 15 miles west on Highway 12 to County Road 41.7 (Sarcillo Canyon Road), and then 20 miles north (right) to the property.

Sakariason Tract: From Trinidad, go about 8 miles west on Highway 12 to Cokedale, then 18 miles north (right) on Reilly Canyon Road, through Boncarbo, to the property. All turns are well-marked with DOW signs.

Oberosler and Beebe Tracts: These tracts are adjacent to, and accessed from, the Sakariason tract.

The forest service road that runs between the Dochter and Sakariason tracts is a rough four-wheel-drive road when dry, and closed when wet.

This impressive wildlife area spreads across the Park Plateau south of the Spanish Peaks. It encompasses 5 square miles of the best habitat a Merriam's turkey or a mule deer could ask for. Heavily timbered ridges separating lush meadows carve the landscape. Gambel oak and other deciduous shrubs cover the slopes. Old-growth ponderosa pines tower over the creeks.

Fishing

None

Hunting

This wildlife area is one of the best places on the Front Range to hunt turkeys with an unlimited (over-the-counter) license in spring. Turkey hunting in fall is by limited license only. The wildlife area and the surrounding San Isabel National Forest are popular places for deer and elk archery hunting. This is in Game Management Unit 85.

Watchable Wildlife

Same as hunting

Camping and Facilities

Camping is allowed only in designated campgrounds. Facilities include vault toilets and drinking water.

General Restrictions

1. Public access is prohibited, except in designated areas.
2. Public access is from established parking areas only.
3. Public access beyond the parking areas is by foot or horseback only.
4. Fires are prohibited, except in camping areas.

Merriam's turkeys forage for grasshoppers and other insects in open meadows.

28. Bosque del Oso SWA

Primary Use:	Habitat preservation and big-game hunting
Location:	Las Animas County, 25 miles west of Trinidad
Size:	30,000 acres
Elevation:	7,200–8,800 feet
Division of Wildlife:	Area office in Pueblo, 719-561-5300
Directions:	From Trinidad, go 20 miles west on Highway 12 to Weston. Just before you enter town look for the DOW signs on the south (left) side of the highway. Turn south on the access road that leads to six parking areas, including the Oso Malo (Bad Bear) camping area. Another access road west of Weston heads south into the property, and leads to the Apache camping area.

Hunting and wildlife viewing opportunities seem endless at this expansive wildlife area draped across the southern foothills of the Sangre de Cristo Mountains. The property lies in the Ute Hills, south of the Purgatoire River, just north of New Mexico. The landscape features rounded 8,000-foot mountains sculpted by a network of numerous creeks and dry canyons separated by high ridges.

The ecosystem on Bosque del Oso (Forest of the Bear) is a blending of different habitats. In the low areas, there are creek bottoms filled with cottonwood forests, deciduous shrubs, and wet meadows. As the terrain rises, the habitat transforms to hay fields rimmed with patches of Gambel's oak bordering rocky hillsides studded with piñon and juniper. At higher elevations, the scenery changes to forests of aspen, pine, and fir, and fast creeks shaded by stately ponderosas.

Bosque del Oso is home to a spectacular array of wildlife including black bears, mountain lions, mule deer, raptors, songbirds, small mammals, wild turkeys, and the second-largest elk herd in Colorado. Acquiring this valuable and highly sought-after piece of real estate for the public required the combined efforts of the Rocky Mountain Elk Foundation, the DOW, Great Outdoors Colorado, and many private citizens.

Fishing

The South Fork of the Purgatoire River flows through the eastern side of the property to its confluence with the Middle Fork at Weston. The South Fork is a small, freestone stream with a self-sustaining population of brown trout. The best fishing is in the upper portion of the stream, where access is by foot or horseback only. There are good hatches of caddis, stoneflies, and mayflies. The average-size trout is 12 inches long.

1. Fishing is prohibited on the South Fork from the day after Labor Day until the first day of the Memorial Day weekend.
2. Fishing is catch-and-release by artificial flies and lures only.
3. All fish must be released immediately upon catch.

Hunting

Bosque del Oso SWA is managed for preservation of habitat for wildlife and quality hunting; all other uses are secondary. Big-game and turkey hunting are by limited license only. It takes years of collecting preference points to draw an elk license for this area, because bull elk here grow to record-book proportions. This is in Game Management Unit 851.

You could not design a better habitat for wild turkeys, or a better place to hunt them. There are creek bottoms with mature cottonwoods for roosting, scrub oak and other deciduous shrubs for mast, broad meadows for strutting, and hay fields jumping with grasshoppers for lunch.

Watchable Wildlife

The diversity of habitat within the wildlife area attracts a lot of birds. Raptors are especially numerous and include bald eagles, golden eagles, peregrine falcons, prairie falcons, Cooper's hawks, red-tailed hawks, sharp-shinned hawks, northern goshawks, and turkey vultures. More than 30 species of songbirds can be seen here at various times of the year.

Camping and Facilities

Camping is prohibited outside of the Oso Malo and Apache Canyon camping areas, except for hunters during hunting seasons. Backpacking is otherwise prohibited. Facilities include toilets and fire pits.

General Restrictions

1. Public access is prohibited December 1–March 31, except for licensed big-game hunters and one nonhunting companion.
2. Discharging firearms or bows is prohibited, except while hunting.
3. Campfires are prohibited, except in the fire containment structures provided at the camping areas.
4. Parking is prohibited, except in designated parking areas.

29. James M. John SWA

Primary Use: Big-game and turkey hunting

Location: Las Animas County, Raton Mesa, 10 miles southeast of Trinidad

Size: 8,200 acres

Elevation: 7,500–10,000 feet

Division of Wildlife: Area office in Pueblo, 719-561-5300

Directions: The only access to the property is from the parking area located at **Lake Dorothey SWA** (see p. 258), and you get there via Raton, New Mexico. From Interstate 25 at Exit 452 in Raton, go 7 miles northeast on Highway 72, following the signs to Sugarite State Park. Drive through the park (there is no fee for passing through the park) to the Lake Dorothey SWA parking area. Follow the trail around Lake Dorothey, and then continue northwest on the trail for 3 miles to the top of the mesas.

Access to this wildlife area sitting on top of Raton and Fishers Peak mesas is difficult. However, a little shoe leather is a small price to pay for admission into such a remarkable place. The climb to the top of the mesa is steep and the trails are narrow, but once on top the going gets easier. The habitat varies from grassy subalpine meadows on the mesa, to creek drainages heavily timbered in fir and aspen.

James M. John, a former mayor of Trinidad and state senator, acquired this property in 1900 for grazing cattle. His great-grandson, David Vandermuelen, conveyed the property to Colorado for use as a State Wildlife Area in 1993.

Fishing

None

Hunting

This area and the adjacent Lake Dorothey SWA are known for their outstanding turkey hunting in spring and fall. Hunting for turkeys and big-game species is by limited license only. Other wildlife found on the property include black bears, mountain lions, blue grouse, bobcats, rabbits, and squirrels. This is in Game Management Unit 140.

Watchable Wildlife

Same as hunting

Camping and Facilities

Camping is permitted on the mesas, except within 100 feet of any stream. There are no facilities.

General Restrictions

1. Access is restricted to foot or horseback.
2. Public access is prohibited December 1–April 1.

30. Lake Dorothey SWA

Primary Use:	Deer and turkey hunting
Location:	Las Animas County, 12 miles southeast of Trinidad
Size:	4,804 acres
Elevation:	7,000 feet
Division of Wildlife:	Area office in Pueblo, 719-561-5300
Directions:	From Interstate 25 at Exit 452 in Raton, go 7 miles northeast on Highway 72 following the signs to Sugarite State Park. Drive through the park (there is no fee for passing through the park) to the Lake Dorothey SWA parking area. Follow the hiking trail ½ mile north to the lake.

This rugged tract of heavily timbered land sits at the base of Raton Mesa, just south of the **James M. John SWA** (see p. 257). There are three deep draws separated by long ridges extending out from the mesa here. The mesa and steep-sided canyons are suited for a host of wildlife, but they are ideal for turkeys.

Fishing

Lake Dorothey is managed as a put-and-take trout fishery, stocked with 10-inch rainbows, cutthroats, and splake. Fishing is restricted to artificial flies and lures only.

Hunting

There are plenty of wild turkeys roaming these hills. More limited turkey licenses are awarded here than in any other limited area in Colorado—75 each for the spring and fall seasons. However, that doesn't mean it's easy to draw a license. It takes several preference points to draw for a spring hunt.

Elk and deer hunting are by archery only. Deer hunting is by limited license only. Don't go south of the SWA or you'll be in New Mexico. This is in Game Management Unit 140.

Watchable Wildlife

Same as hunting

Camping and Facilities

Camping is allowed with restrictions, as listed below.
There is a toilet at the parking area.

General Restrictions

1. Camping is prohibited within 200 yards of the lake or 100 feet of any stream, except in designated areas.
2. Discharging firearms is prohibited, except shotguns or bows while hunting.
3. Public access is by foot or horseback only from the parking area.

A longbeard Merriam's turkey struts in spring.

Northeast Colorado

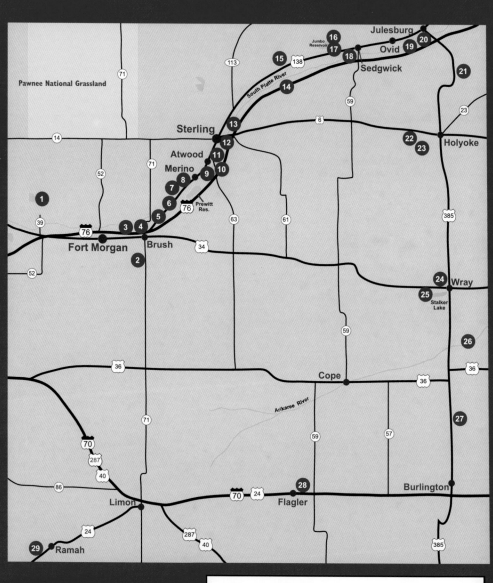

Pawnee National Grassland

Jumbo Reservoir

Julesburg

Ovid

Sedgwick

South Platte River

Sterling

Atwood

Merino

Prewitt Res.

Fort Morgan

Brush

Holyoke

Wray

Stalker Lake

Cope

Arikaree River

Burlington

Limon

Flagler

Ramah

	Interstate Highway		Creek
	U.S. Highway		River
	State Highway		Lake
●	City or Town		Wilderness Area
1	State Wildlife Areas		National Park

T he venerable South Platte River, and the corridor of cottonwood riparian habitat that it creates, stretch across the dry plains of northeast Colorado like a leaky garden hose lying across a dead lawn. This riparian habitat and irrigated farmland support a myriad of wildlife species.

White-tailed deer, mule deer, Rio Grande turkeys, bobwhite quail, pheasant, Canada geese, and many species of ducks are found at all 20 of the State Wildlife Areas located on the South Platte. In addition, there are many predators and hundreds of nongame species that depend on the riparian habitat.

One of the biggest problems facing the DOW at the SWAs on the South Platte is overuse. Due to their close proximity to the Front Range, they're being loved to death. Overcrowding during upland game and waterfowl seasons, and otherwise heavy use year-round, has forced the DOW to limit public access at many of the areas. These limits and closures are necessary to protect the wildlife and to provide a quality hunting experience.

Wildlife Areas in Northeast Colorado

1. Jackson Lake SWA

Primary Use:	Warm-water fishing and waterfowl hunting
Location:	Morgan County, Jackson Reservoir, 20 miles northeast of Fort Morgan
Size:	394 acres
Elevation:	4,445 feet
Division of Wildlife:	Area office in Brush, 970-842-6300
Directions:	From Interstate 76 at the Highway 39 exit (Exit 66), go 7½ miles north on Highway 39 to Highway 144, then 1 mile east (right) to County Road 5, then 4 miles north (left) to County Road CC, then 1 mile west (left) to the access road and sign.

This wildlife area lies across the northern shore of Jackson Reservoir, but is not part of Jackson Lake State Park. The area has two gravel parking areas with access to fishing in the lake, and waterfowl hunting in the ponds located between the lake and a large irrigation ditch. The Weldon Valley State Trust Land northwest of the SWA has 5,600 acres for hunting deer, antelope, doves, and waterfowl.

Fishing

Jackson Reservoir has fair fishing for warm-water species such as walleye and wipers, and is stocked with catchable-sized rainbow trout in early spring.

Hunting

Waterfowl, dove, and pheasant

Watchable Wildlife

Same as hunting

Camping and Facilities

Camping is prohibited at the SWA. A toilet is located at the parking area.

General Restrictions

1. Fires are prohibited.
2. Fishing is prohibited from November 1 to the last day of the regular waterfowl season, except fishing from the dam is permitted until November 30.
3. Ice fishing is allowed only in designated areas, as posted, from November 1 to the last day of the regular waterfowl season.
4. Hunting is prohibited from the frozen surface of the lake.
5. Discharging firearms or bows is prohibited, except while hunting.
6. Target practice is prohibited, except when authorized by an area wildlife manager.

2. Brush Prairie Ponds SWA

Primary Use:	Waterfowl hunting
Location:	Morgan County, 3 miles south of Brush
Size:	1,600 acres
Elevation:	4,271 feet
Division of Wildlife:	Area office in Brush, 970-842-6300
Directions:	From Brush, go south on Clayton Street to the check station and kiosk located in the parking lot at Brush Memorial Park. The entrance to the hunting areas is 2½ miles south of the park on Clayton Street.

This wildlife area is a patch of flooded prairie south of Brush that is leased from the city, and managed by the DOW for quality waterfowl hunting. The property consists of a cluster of small ponds and wetlands divided into eight hunting areas. The ponds are shallow, often freezing as early as mid-November.

Quality waterfowl hunting is the traditional style of hunting over decoys and calling birds into close range. Sky busting is not allowed on the property. Walking around the ponds and jump shooting, and shooting at birds working another hunter's decoy spread, are regarded as poor hunting etiquette.

Fishing

Fishing is prohibited.

Hunting

Waterfowl

Watchable Wildlife

Waterfowl and shorebirds

Camping and Facilities

Camping is prohibited. There are no facilities, except duck blinds.

General Restrictions

1. The restrictions are too numerous and complicated to list here. All users are advised to read the regulations posted on the kiosk at the check station.
2. All hunters must check in and out of the check station.
3. Hunting areas may be reserved from the opening of the first waterfowl season to the end of November. Call 1-800-846-9453.
4. Reservations are not available from December 1 through the last day of waterfowl season. Hunting is available on a first-come, first-served basis.

5. From the opening of the first waterfowl season through November 30, only migratory bird hunting is allowed. Hunting is allowed only on Saturdays, Sundays, and Wednesdays, Columbus Day, Veteran's Day, and Thanksgiving Day.

6. From February 1 until the opening of the first waterfowl season, only wildlife observation is permitted, with access limited to areas posted.

7. Hunters must use designated ponds, and there is a maximum of four hunters per pond.

A black Lab delivers a green-winged teal to her master.

3. Dodd Bridge SWA

Primary Use:	Small-game and waterfowl hunting
Location:	Morgan County, South Platte River, 6 miles northeast of Fort Morgan
Size:	900 acres
Elevation:	4,200 feet
Division of Wildlife:	Area office in Brush, 970-842-6300
Directions:	From Fort Morgan, go 4 miles east on Interstate 76 to the Dodd Bridge Road exit, and then 2 miles north (left) to the parking area at the bridge. To reach the north parking area, go over the bridge and then 1 mile east (right) on County Road T.9.

Dodd Bridge is the most used and abused of all State Wildlife Areas located on the South Platte. Straddling 4 miles of the river near Fort Morgan, it is the closest public hunting area to the Front Range via Interstate 76. The habitat is typical South Platte riparian, consisting of tall cottonwoods, willows, deciduous shrubs, and prairie grasses.

Fishing

None

Hunting

Expect big crowds on weekends and the opening days of pheasant and waterfowl seasons. Waterfowl hunting is better on weekdays in late December and January.

Watchable Wildlife

Same as hunting, plus wild turkeys and white-tailed deer

Camping and Facilities

No overnight camping, no facilities

General Restrictions

1. Public access prohibited 9 p.m.–3 a.m., except by permit.
2. Discharging firearms or bows is prohibited, except while hunting.
3. Small-game and waterfowl hunting is prohibited the opening weekend of the regular plains rifle season.
4. Target practice is prohibited, except when authorized by an area wildlife manager.
5. Fires are prohibited.

Curley, the golden retriever, loves his job.

4. Brush SWA

Primary Use:	Hunting
Location:	Morgan County, South Platte River, 2 miles north of Brush
Size:	588 acres
Elevation:	4,200 feet
Division of Wildlife:	Area office in Brush, 970-842-6300
Directions:	From Brush, go 2½ miles north on Highway 71, then bear left on County Road 28 for 1 mile to the south parking area. Another parking area is located on the north side of the river on County Roads T.9 and 27.

Typical of all of the State Wildlife Areas on the South Platte, Brush offers hunting in riparian habitat for a variety of small-game species.

Fishing

Largemouth bass, smallmouth bass, and bluegills on Chartier Ponds

Hunting

Deer, turkey, waterfowl, quail, and pheasant. The property north of the river is better for pheasant and quail hunting in part because of heavy cover of switchgrass in the fields. To hunt pheasant in tall grass effectively, hunters need either a good hunting dog or to hunt using a combination of pushers and blockers. The DOW clears swaths in the switchgrass to aid hunters. Turkey and deer hunting is by limited license only. This is in Game Management Unit 96.

Watchable Wildlife

Same as hunting

Camping and Facilities

None

General Restrictions

1. On Chartier Ponds, smallmouth and largemouth bass must be 15 inches or longer.
2. Discharging firearms or bows is prohibited, except while hunting.
3. Public access prohibited 9 p.m.–3 a.m. daily, except with night hunting permit.
4. Target practice must be authorized by an area wildlife manager.
5. Small-game and waterfowl hunting is prohibited the opening weekend of the regular plains rifle deer season.

5. Cottonwood SWA

Primary Use:	Hunting
Location:	Morgan County, South Platte River, 5 miles northeast of Brush
Size:	884 acres
Elevation:	4,100 feet
Division of Wildlife:	Area office in Brush, 970-842-6300
Directions:	From Brush, go 5 miles north on Highway 71 to the South Platte River. A parking area is located on the right side of the road just before the bridge. To reach the main parking area, continue across the bridge to Snyder, then go 2 miles northeast (right) on County Road W.7 to the property sign. A third parking area is located at the southeast corner of the property on County Road 33.

This wildlife area features 4 miles of typical South Platte riparian habitat augmented with fields of switchgrass and cultivated food plots, to improve habitat for wildlife and provide hunting opportunities.

Fishing

None

Hunting

Waterfowl, pheasant, quail, deer, and turkeys may be hunted on the property. Deer and turkey hunting is by limited license only in Game Management Unit 96. The parking area north of the river is the best access point for pheasant and quail hunting.

Watchable Wildlife

Same as hunting

Camping and Facilities

None

General Restrictions

1. Discharging firearms or bows is prohibited, except while hunting.
2. Target practice prohibited, except when authorized by an area wildlife manager.
3. Fires are prohibited.

Pheasant are the most sought-after game birds on the plains.

6. Elliott SWA

Primary Use:	Waterfowl hunting
Location:	Morgan County, South Platte River, 10 miles northeast of Brush
Size:	2,576 total acres in all tracts
Elevation:	4,100 feet
Division of Wildlife:	Area office in Brush, 970-842-6300
Directions:	**North Tract:** From Snyder, go 5 miles northeast on County Road W.7 to the sign and parking area.
	Union Tract: From Brush, go 6 miles north on Highway 71 to the town of Snyder, then 6 miles northeast (right) on County Road W.7 to the sign and parking area on the right side.
	Elliott Tract: From Snyder, go 6 miles northeast (past the Union Tract) on County Road W.7 to the sign and parking area on the right.

Elliott has it all. There are sloughs, ponds, the river, and extensive wetland improvements sponsored by Ducks Unlimited, to provide nesting habitat for waterfowl and excellent hunting opportunities. In addition to the wetlands, the property encompasses nearly 2,000 acres of river bottom with cottonwood forests, and side fields of switchgrass studded with deciduous shrubs. The wildlife area is divided into three separate tracts of land, each with its own set of regulations.

Fishing

None

Hunting

North Tract is the latest addition. It has 440 acres of lowlands that offer excellent duck hunting when there is enough water. The lowlands rely on seep water from the North Sterling Canal, and the DOW has no control over the flow. The North Tract is divided into two zones, east and west. Hunting is by reservation only. See the regulations below.

Union Tract is another reservation-only duck hunting hot spot. The long slough in the middle of the field east of the parking area consistently produces limits of ducks. The DOW has installed two pit blinds, one on each end of the slough.

Elliott Tract, the largest, is the site of a recent wetland improvement project. Dikes, canals, and islands provide nesting habitat for ducks and geese. Reservations are not required to hunt waterfowl. Deer and turkey hunting is good here, and by limited license only. This is in Game Management Unit 96.

Watchable Wildlife

The many sloughs on the property afford photographers and birdwatchers plenty of opportunities to view waterfowl. In spring, wood ducks nest by the river in man-made boxes, and green-winged teal and mallards haunt the sloughs. Rio Grande turkeys are here year-round. Be careful to observe and obey seasonal closures at the property.

Camping and Facilities

None

General Restrictions

All Tracts:

1. Discharging firearms or bows is prohibited, except while hunting.

2. Fires are prohibited.

3. Target practice is prohibited, except when authorized by an area wildlife manager.

4. Small-game and waterfowl hunting is prohibited the opening weekend of the regular plains rifle season.

Union Tract:

1. Closed, except for limited waterfowl hunting on specific dates.

2. Public access is prohibited, except for waterfowl hunting on specific dates and from designated blinds.

3. Waterfowl hunting is permitted on a first-come, first-served basis, and is limited to the two designated blinds during the September teal season, and the first split waterfowl season.

4. Blind reservations for the remainder of the waterfowl season are decided by a lottery drawing on October 13. Reservation dates and instructions for entering the drawing are published in the Waterfowl Hunting Brochure under "Elliott SWA" in the Restricted Hunting Areas section.

North Tract:

1. Public use is prohibited from September 1 through the last day of the regular waterfowl season, except for limited hunting on specific days.

2. All hunting is by reservation only.

3. Call 1-800-846-9453, 8 a.m.–5 p.m., Monday–Friday for reservations. Reservations will not be accepted more than 14 or fewer than 2 days before the hunting date. Reservations accepted only for Saturdays, Sundays, Wednesdays, and holidays. Hunters may reserve either the west or the east unit. Only two hunting parties of four hunters each are allowed on the property.

4. Hunters must park in the designated area. Only one parking space per party.

5. No excavation of or hunting from pit blinds or other permanent structures. No nails or spikes in trees.

6. Dogs are allowed only as an aid to hunting. Field trials and dog training are not permitted.

7. Messex SWA

Primary Use:	Hunting
Location:	Logan and Washington counties, South Platte River, 2 miles northeast of Prewitt Reservoir
Size:	680 acres
Elevation:	4,100 feet
Division of Wildlife:	Area office in Brush, 970-842-6300
Directions:	From Interstate 76 at the Merino exit (exit 102), go 2 miles north to Highway 6, then 1¾ miles east (right) to County Road R, then 1½ miles north (left) to County Road 59, and then ½ mile west (left) to parking areas located at the bridge.
	To reach the Skaggs portion, go 2 miles west from the parking areas on County Road 59 to County Road P.5, then ½ mile north (right) to an unmarked gravel road on the north side of the railroad tracks, and then 1¼ miles northeast (right) to the parking area.

Like pieces in a jigsaw puzzle, Messex is composed of three separate tracts of land interspersed among private property, lying along either side of the South Platte. The tracts are fenced and marked with boundary signs. Each tract has a parking area.

Fishing

None

Hunting

Messex SWA has better-than-average deer hunting and especially good turkey hunting for hunters who draw a limited license for Game Management Unit 96. Deer hunters must have the landowner's permission to hunt on the Skaggs lease. The landowner's phone number is posted in the parking area. Duck hunting can be good on this stretch of river, in part because of its close proximity to Prewitt Reservoir. The reservoir often houses thousands of ducks and geese in December and January. The South Platte River at Messex is braided with sandbars and sloughs and is well-suited for waterfowl hunting.

Watchable Wildlife

Same as hunting

Camping and Facilities

None

General Restrictions

1. Fires are prohibited.
2. Discharging firearms or bows is prohibited, except while hunting.
3. Target practice is prohibited, except when authorized by an area wildlife manager.
4. Small-game and waterfowl hunting is prohibited the opening weekend of the regular plains rifle season.

8. Prewitt Reservoir SWA

Primary Use:	Warm-water fishing, waterfowl and dove hunting
Location:	Washington County, 20 miles northeast of Brush
Size:	2,924 acres
Elevation:	4,100 feet
Division of Wildlife:	Area office in Brush, 970-842-6300
Directions:	From Interstate 76 at the Merino exit (Exit 102), go 1 mile north to U.S. 6, then 3½ miles northeast (right) to the entrance and follow signs to the boat ramp. There is parking below the dam for fishing the dam or hunting the sloughs to the east.

Prewitt is a shallow irrigation reservoir fed by canal from the South Platte River. The water level fluctuates greatly from agricultural demands. During periods of low water it may be impossible to launch a boat from a trailer. The reservoir is visible from the rest area on Interstate 76 near mile marker 106.

Fishing

Bank fishing for catfish, wipers, and saugeye is a popular activity at Prewitt. The mile-long dam has a walking path along the top that gives anglers access to the deepest part of the reservoir.

Caution! Stay off the concrete face of the dam. The concrete at the water's edge is extremely slick and treacherous. If you slip into the water, it is impossible to climb back out without help. Fishermen are advised to carry a rope and wear a life vest.

Hunting

The sloughs, marshes, and riparian habitat below the dam are good for dove and waterfowl hunting. From the parking area below the dam, head east ¼ mile on the path that leads to a long slough that has two makeshift duck blinds. You must arrive early and be ready for a foot race to secure one of these blinds on the weekend. It is common to see duck hunters, loaded down with waders, bags of decoys, and shotguns, scrambling for the slough in the dark. Hunting during the middle of the week is less frantic. Crowding is a problem on the opening of dove season, too. Goose hunting is permitted from behind a firing line on the upper (southwestern) portion of the reservoir, as posted.

Watchable Wildlife

Prewitt Reservoir is a good place to view thousands of ducks and geese in winter. Occasionally, a huge flock of snow geese will roost on the reservoir, flying out in early morning to feed in cornfields.

Camping and Facilities

Primitive camping is allowed on the south side of the reservoir. There are plenty of shaded campsites, modern toilets, and a boat ramp.

General Restrictions

1. Annual or daily use permits are required. Annual permits are available during business hours at any DOW office. Daily permits are available at the entrance to the reservoir.
2. Fishing is restricted to the shores of the reservoir October 1–31.
3. Fishing is prohibited from November 1 to the last day of waterfowl season, but fishing from the dam is allowed until November 30.
4. Hunting from floating devices is prohibited.
5. Craft propelled by hand may be used to set out decoys and retrieve downed waterfowl.
6. Boating is prohibited if it creates a white-water wake.
7. Sailing and windsurfing are prohibited, except during July and August.
8. Glass beverage containers are prohibited.

9. Atwood SWA

Primary Use:	Hunting
Location:	Logan County, South Platte River, 3 miles southwest of Atwood
Size:	180 acres
Elevation:	3,980 feet
Division of Wildlife:	Area office in Brush, 970-842-6300
Directions:	From Atwood, go 3 miles southwest on U.S. 6, then ½ mile south (left) on County Road 29.5 to the parking area.

Although Atwood is one of the smaller properties, with only ½ mile of the river, waterfowl hunting can be as good here as in the larger areas. There are rows of switchgrass and food plots for upland game on the south side of the property. Parking areas are located on both sides of the river.

Fishing

None

Hunting

Waterfowl, deer, and turkeys

Watchable Wildlife

Same as hunting

Camping and Facilities

None

General Restrictions

1. Fires are prohibited.
2. Discharging firearms or bows is prohibited, except while hunting.
3. Target practice must be authorized by an area wildlife manager.
4. Small-game and waterfowl hunting are prohibited the opening weekend of the regular plains rifle season.

10. Overland Trail SWA

Primary Use:	Hunting
Location:	Logan County, South Platte River at Atwood
Size:	192 acres
Elevation:	3,980 feet
Division of Wildlife:	Area office in Brush, 970-842-6300
Directions:	From Interstate 76 at the Atwood exit (Exit 115), go 2½ miles north on Highway 63 to County Road 16, then ½ mile east (right) to the sign and access road on the left.

This recent addition to the list of State Wildlife Areas on the South Platte is managed for quality hunting for all species. Reservations are required for any access to the property during hunting seasons. This wildlife area contains a fine stretch of typical South Platte riparian habitat.

Fishing

None

Hunting

Waterfowl, deer, turkey, quail, dove, and small game can be hunted here. Deer and turkey hunting is by limited license. This is in Game Management Unit 96.

Watchable Wildlife

Same as hunting. Access is by reservation only during hunting seasons.
See the restrictions below regarding wildlife viewing.

Camping and Facilities

No overnight camping, no facilities

General Restrictions

1. All access and hunting is by reservation only. Call 1-800-846-9453 for reservations and information.
2. Turkey hunting reservations are made through the Brush office, 970-842-6300.
3. Reservations will not be accepted more than 14 or fewer than two days prior to the hunting date.
4. Access is limited to four groups of vehicles with a maximum number of four people per group.
5. June 1–August 31, access is limited to wildlife observation only and only on Saturdays, Sundays, and Wednesdays. No reservations are required during this period.

6. September 1–May 31, hunting is permitted only Saturdays, Sundays, Wednesdays, legal holidays, and the opening days of plains rifle and late rifle deer seasons.

7. Small-game and waterfowl hunting are prohibited the opening weekend of rifle deer season.

8. Discharging firearms or bows is prohibited, except while hunting.

9. Field trials and dog training are prohibited.

10. Fires are prohibited.

11. Dune Ridge SWA

Primary Use:	Hunting
Location:	Logan County, South Platte River, 5 miles southeast of Sterling
Size:	400 acres
Elevation:	4,000 feet
Division of Wildlife:	Area office in Brush, 970-842-6300
Directions:	From Interstate 76 at the Sterling exit, go ½ mile west (left) on Highway 14 to County Road 370, then 5 miles southwest (left) to the parking areas.

Although typical of all the wildlife areas on the South Platte, Dune Ridge has undergone significant improvements to habitat in the fields adjacent to the river. Food plots, switchgrass, and shrub rows provide food and cover for pheasant, quail, turkeys, and deer.

Fishing

None

Hunting

Waterfowl, deer, turkey, pheasant, and quail are found on the property.
This is in Game Management Unit 96.

Watchable Wildlife

Same as hunting

Camping and Facilities

None

General Restrictions

1. Discharging firearms or bows is prohibited, except while hunting.
2. Fires are prohibited.
3. Target practice must be authorized by area wildlife manager.
4. Small-game and waterfowl hunting are prohibited the opening weekend of the regular plains rifle season.

12. Knudson SWA

Primary Use:	Hunting
Location:	Logan County, South Platte River near Sterling
Size:	581 acres
Elevation:	3,900 feet
Division of Wildlife:	Area office in Brush, 970-842-6300
Directions:	From Interstate 76 at the Sterling exit (Exit 125), go north ½ mile to County Road 370, and then ½ mile southwest (left) to the property.

Being close to town is not always a bad thing. Knudson SWA has all the attributes of other wildlife areas on the South Platte River.

Fishing

None

Hunting

Deer hunters must watch for and obey the signs about deer closures on portions of this property. These portions are leases, and the landowner's permission is required to hunt deer. Other hunters don't need permission. Deer and turkey hunting is by limited license only. This is in Game Management Unit 96.

Watchable Wildlife

Same as hunting

Camping and Facilities

None

General Restrictions

1. Fires are prohibited.
2. Discharging firearms or bows is prohibited, except while hunting.

13. Bravo SWA

Primary Use:	Hunting
Location:	Logan County, South Platte River, 2 miles northeast of Sterling
Size:	1,081 acres
Elevation:	3,890 feet
Division of Wildlife:	Area office in Brush, 970-842-6300
Directions:	From Interstate 76 at the Sterling exit (Exit 125) , go ½ mile west on Highway 14 to County Road 370, then 2 miles northeast (right) to the first parking area on the left. The second parking area is 2 miles farther on CR 370 and on the left.
	Additional parking areas are on the north side of the river. From Sterling, go north on U.S. 138 to County Roads 36 and 38, and then south (right) to the parking areas. The parking area for Ford Bridge STL is located on County Road 40.

Stretching east along the South Platte, from just outside Sterling to County Road 40, Bravo SWA and the adjoining 280-acre Ford Bridge State Trust Land straddle more than 6 miles of river bottom.

Fishing

None

Hunting

Mule deer, white-tailed deer, waterfowl, turkey, quail, dove, rabbits, and squirrels may be hunted here. Waterfowl hunting can be spotty from year to year, depending on from which direction the ducks fly out to feed from North Sterling Reservoir. At times, they trade back and forth over the wildlife area on their way to and from the reservoir.

Deer and turkey hunting are by limited license only, and it takes several preference points to draw a license for either. Big mule deer and white-tailed deer are not unusual on Bravo. Quail hunting is good here some years. Dove hunting is reliable. Bravo and Ford Bridge STL are in Game Management Unit 91.

Deer hunters should take note that Ford Bridge STL is closed to deer hunting with rifles, and closed to all use May 31–September 1.

Watchable Wildlife

Same as hunting

Camping and Facilities

None

General Restrictions

1. Discharging firearms or bows is prohibited, except while hunting.
2. Fires are prohibited.
3. Field trials are prohibited except February 1–March 31, and August 1–September 30.
4. Target practice must be authorized by area wildlife manager.
5. Small-game and waterfowl hunting are prohibited the opening weekend of the regular plains rifle deer season.

Rio Grande jakes (juvenile males) often band together.

14. Tamarack Ranch SWA

Primary Use:	Hunting
Location:	Logan County, South Platte River, 25 miles northeast of Sterling
Size:	10,500 acres
Elevation:	3,700 feet
Division of Wildlife:	Area office in Brush, 970-842-6300
Directions:	From Sterling, go 25 miles northeast on Interstate 76 to the Crook exit (Exit 149), and then ½ mile north (left) to the check station.

This sprawling strip of land straddling the river near Crook sets the standard for public hunting opportunities on the South Platte. Tamarack Ranch is in a category by itself, encompassing 15 miles of the South Platte River, hundreds of acres of riparian habitat, food plots tailored for a variety of wildlife, and a management plan that guarantees all users a quality outdoor experience.

Fishing

There is marginal fishing for largemouth bass and sunfish in the Tamarack Ranch and Pronger ponds. The size limit for largemouth and smallmouth bass is 15 inches.

Hunting

You name it and it's good here—deer, turkey, waterfowl, pheasant, quail, rabbit, and squirrels. White-tailed and mule deer frequent the property, and trophy bucks are not out of the question. Spring turkey hunters have the entire place to themselves, enjoying the only hunting season open outside of fall and winter. Deer and turkey hunting are by limited license only in Game Management Unit 91.

Waterfowl hunting varies from year to year, depending on weather conditions and other factors known only to the ducks. The first split duck season in October is usually good hunting for mallards, teal, and wood ducks that nest on the river. There is a growing population of wood ducks on the sloughs and backwater areas.

Opening day of pheasant and quail season is the busiest day of the year at Tamarack, with hunters queued up at the check station well before daylight, in hopes of securing an area to hunt. Reservations are available for opening day, weekends, and holidays by calling 1-800-846-9453. Please see "General Restrictions" below for additional information.

Hunters check in and out of a check station for assigned hunting areas. The property is sectioned into 33 river hunting zones spaced about ½ mile apart, and eight meadow hunting zones featuring shrub rows and food plots.

Watchable Wildlife

There's great bird-watching on the sloughs for nesting wood ducks. In spring, the colorful drakes are in full mating plumage. Look for DOW-installed nesting boxes on the sloughs.

Camping and Facilities

Overnight camping is prohibited, except in the established camping area at the check station. Facilities at the check station include a toilet and drinking water.

General Restrictions

1. All users must check in and out of the check station.
2. Hunting reservations are available by calling 1-800-846-9453. The first date available for reservations is normally November 1 and the last date is the last day of duck season.
3. Reservations are not accepted more than 14 or fewer than 2 days in advance of the hunting date.
4. Reservations are for licensed hunters only, and the reservation holder must be present the day of the hunt. Call the same number to cancel reservations.
5. Discharging firearms or bows is prohibited, except while hunting.
6. Target practice is prohibited, except when authorized by an area wildlife manager.
7. Small-game and waterfowl hunting is prohibited the opening weekend of the regular plains rifle season.
8. Field trials are prohibited, except February 1–March 31 and August 1–September 30.
9. Fires are prohibited, except in the camping area at the check station.

15. Duck Creek SWA

Primary Use:	Hunting
Location:	Logan County, 30 miles northeast of Sterling
Size:	1,121 acres
Elevation:	3,700 feet
Division of Wildlife:	Area office in Brush, 970-842-6300
Directions:	From Interstate 76 at the Crook exit (Exit 149), go 3½ miles north on Highway 55 to the parking are on the right. Additional parking areas for the property are located on County Road 83.

Ironically, seldom are there any ducks at Duck Creek. This property lies away from the South Platte River, on the north side of the town of Crook. The terrain is relatively flat and treeless, like most of the High Plains, and rarely is there much water in the creek.

Fishing

None

Hunting

Pheasant, dove, and waterfowl. Despite the lack of water, Duck Creek has good potential for hunting geese over decoys owing to its proximity to **Jumbo** (see p. 285) and Sterling Reservoirs; these reservoirs usually house thousands of geese each winter. There are several good locations on the eastern portion of the property for setting out goose decoys.

Watchable Wildlife

Same as hunting

Camping and Facilities

None

General Restrictions

1. Public access is prohibited, except as posted.
2. Discharging firearms or bows is prohibited, except while hunting.
3. Target practice is prohibited, except when authorized by an area wildlife manager.
4. Fires are prohibited.

16. Jumbo Reservoir SWA

Primary Use:	Warm-water fishing and waterfowl hunting
Location:	Logan and Sedgwick Counties, 35 miles northeast of Sterling
Size:	1,703 acres
Elevation:	3,700 feet
Division of Wildlife:	Area office in Brush, 970-842-6300
Directions:	From Interstate 76 at the Red Lion exit (Exit 155), go 3 miles north (left) to U.S. 138, then 1 mile northeast (right) to County Road 95, then 2 miles north (left) to the reservoir.

The fishing in Jumbo Reservoir goes up and down like a yo-yo. When the reservoir is flush with water for a few years, the fishing gets good. Then a drought hits and the fishing goes down the drain—or down the canal in this case—as farmers empty the reservoir to irrigate their crops. Check with the DOW office in Brush for current information.

Fishing

Rainbow trout are stocked in early spring as the water level rises in the reservoir. Fishing for warm-water species is questionable following massive draw-downs of water during dry years.

Hunting

Jumbo Reservoir is a goose refuge and closed to all goose hunting. Duck hunting success around the reservoir depends on the water level. The northwest side of the property has the best pheasant and dove hunting.

Watchable Wildlife

Same as hunting, plus bald eagles, shorebirds, waterfowl, pheasant, and doves

Camping and Facilities

Primitive camping, drinking water, toilets, boat ramps, and picnic shelters are at the reservoir.

General Restrictions

1. Annual or daily use permits are required. Permits are available at all DOW offices.
2. October 1–31, fishing is restricted to the reservoir's shores.
3. November 1–30, fishing is allowed only on the south dams.
4. Fishing is prohibited from December 1 through the last day of waterfowl season.
5. Fishing is prohibited within 50 feet of the outlet structure.
6. Boating is prohibited from October 1 to the last day of waterfowl season.
7. Hunting is prohibited from floating devices.
8. Hand-propelled craft may be used for setting out decoys and retrieving downed waterfowl.
9. Hunting is prohibited from the frozen surface of the reservoir.

17. Red Lion SWA

Primary Use:	Waterfowl hunting and warm-water fishing
Location:	Logan County, 35 miles northeast of Sterling
Size:	1,300 acres
Elevation:	3,700 feet
Division of Wildlife:	Area office in Brush, 970-842-6300
Directions:	From Interstate 76 at the Red Lion Road exit (Exit 155), go 2 miles north to U.S. 138, then 1 mile northeast (right) to County Road 95, then ¼ mile north (left) to the three parking areas located on the west side of the property. Additional parking areas are located to the east, on County Road 97.

This wildlife area sits directly below **Jumbo Reservoir**, and includes Jumbo Annex Reservoir, Red Lion Ponds, and the wetlands in between.

Fishing

Jumbo Annex Reservoir has fishing for largemouth bass, smallmouth bass, and crappie from the shore only.

Hunting

Red Lion Ponds consists of two big ponds located within sight of Highway 138. At times, these can be duck hunting hot spots. Each pond is big enough for two parties of hunters. Ducks, trading back and forth from Jumbo Reservoir, often fly over the ponds. Jumbo Annex Reservoir is open to waterfowl hunting only as posted.

Dove hunting is good around the reservoirs, and pheasant and quail hunting can be good in the neighboring fields. Deer hunting is allowed. This is in Game Management Unit 90.

Watchable Wildlife

Bald eagles, shorebirds, and a great variety of waterfowl

Camping and Facilities

Overnight camping is prohibited. There are no facilities on the Red Lion property but camping and toilets are located at nearby Jumbo Reservoir.

General Restrictions

1. Public access is prohibited, except as posted.
2. Fishing is prohibited on Jumbo Annex Reservoir, except January 1–September 30, when bank and ice fishing is permitted in designated areas.
3. Boating is prohibited, except for hand-propelled craft used to set out and pick up decoys, and to retrieve downed waterfowl.
4. Discharging firearms or bows is prohibited, except while hunting.
5. Target practice is prohibited, except when authorized by an area wildlife manager.
6. Fires are prohibited.

Sedgwick Bar SWA (see p. 288)

18. Sedgwick Bar SWA

Primary Use:	Hunting
Location:	Sedgwick County, South Platte River, 40 miles northeast of Sterling
Size:	885 acres
Elevation:	3,569 feet
Division of Wildlife:	Area office in Brush, 970-842-6300
Directions:	From Interstate 76 at the Highway 59 exit (Exit 165), go north on Highway 59 to parking areas located on both sides of the river at the bridge. Another parking area is located 2 miles northeast of Sedgwick on U.S. 138 and 1 mile south (right) on an unmarked access road.

Brush-choked islands, long sandbars, and backwater sloughs weave a basket full of waterfowl and small-game hunting opportunities on this braided stretch of the South Platte.

Fishing

None

Hunting

Better-than-average hunting for waterfowl, quail, turkeys, and deer awaits hunters willing to hike in on the south side of the river. Deer and turkey hunting is by limited license only. This is in Game Management Unit 92.

Watchable Wildlife

Same as hunting

Camping and Facilities

None

General Restrictions

1. Discharging firearms or bows is prohibited, except while hunting.
2. Target practice is prohibited, except when authorized by an area wildlife manager.
3. Small-game and waterfowl hunting is prohibited the opening weekend of the regular plains rifle season.
4. Fires are prohibited.

19. Julesburg SWA

Primary Use:	Hunting
Location:	Sedgwick County, South Platte River between Ovid and Julesburg
Size:	1,100 acres
Elevation:	3,500 feet
Division of Wildlife:	Area office in Brush, 970-842-6300
Directions:	From Interstate 76 at the Ovid exit (Exit 172), go 1 mile north on County Road 29 to County Road 28 and turn right. There are four individual tracts located between Road 29 and U.S. 385 at Julesburg. Parking areas for each tract are marked with DOW signs.

In addition to quality hunting, this wildlife area and the adjacent **Pony Express SWA** (see p. 291) share an interesting chapter in the history of the West.

A band of Cheyenne Dog Soldiers attacked a stagecoach and a wagon train near here on January 7, 1865. A small troop of U.S. Cavalry set out from a nearby fort in pursuit of the Dog Soldiers, but soon found themselves surrounded, and had to fight their way back to the fort. The Indians then proceeded to Julesburg, looting the town and burning the buildings.

The town of Julesburg was named after Jules Beni, a shady character fired from the stage line for theft. Afterwards, Beni fought several gun battles with Jack Slade, a supervisor with the stage line. Slade eventually killed Beni in a gunfight and cut off both his ears, nailing one to a fence post and using the other as a watch fob.

Fishing

None

Hunting

This wildlife area has good hunting for deer, ducks, turkeys, bobwhite quail, and doves. All of Julesburg SWA is within the goose-resting area and is closed to goose hunting. This is in Game Management Unit 92.

Watchable Wildlife

Same as hunting

Camping and Facilities

None

General Restrictions

1. Fires are prohibited.
2. Discharging firearms or bows is prohibited, except while hunting.
3. Target practice is prohibited, except when authorized by area wildlife manager.
4. Small-game and waterfowl hunting is prohibited the opening weekend of the regular plains rifle season.

20. Pony Express SWA

Primary Use:	Hunting
Location:	Sedgwick County, South Platte River between Ovid and Julesburg
Size:	1,101 acres
Elevation:	3,500 feet
Division of Wildlife:	Area office in Brush, 970-842-6300
Directions:	From Interstate 76 at the Julesburg exit (Exit 180), go ½ mile north on U.S. 385 to County Road 28, then 1½ miles west (left) to the access road, then turn right to the parking area. To reach the other parking area on the north side of the river, from downtown Julesburg go 1 mile west on U.S. 138 to County Road 39, and then 1 mile south (left) to the river.

In 1860, Pony Express riders thundered through here on pounding hooves, and daring pioneers whooped and hollered as they plummeted their wagons down a treacherous cliff called Devil's Dive. Nowadays, the easygoing pace of rural life on the high plains seems a little dull when compared to those rip-roaring times. The café in Ovid has paintings hanging in the dining area, depicting exciting scenes from those days.

Fishing

None

Hunting

All the typical species are here. Deer and turkey hunting is by limited license only in Game Management Unit 92. Johnson Pond and the entire river area from Ovid to Julesburg are closed to goose hunting.

Watchable Wildlife

Same as hunting

Camping and Facilities

None

General Restrictions

1. Closed to goose hunting.
2. Target practice prohibited, except when authorized by an area wildlife manager.
3. Discharging firearms or bows is prohibited, except while hunting.
4. Small-game and waterfowl hunting is prohibited the opening weekend of the regular plains rifle season.
5. Field trials are prohibited, except February 1–March 31 and August 1–September 30.
6. Fires are prohibited.

Monument commemorating Pony Express riders

21. Sand Draw SWA

Primary Use:	Youth/mentor hunting area
Location:	Sedgwick County, 8 miles south of Julesburg
Size:	200 acres
Elevation:	3,700 feet
Division of Wildlife:	Area office in Brush, 970-842-6300
Directions:	From Interstate 76 at the Julesburg exit (Exit 180), go 8 miles south on U.S. 385 to County Road 16, go east (left) to County Road 49, then south (right) 1 mile to the parking area.

This unique little wildlife area is like a divot in the plains, a coppice of habitat for wildlife, sitting amidst an ocean of plowed earth. Rows of trees flank fields of corn, switchgrass, and sorghum. Thick hedgerows rim the property, providing excellent cover for pheasant and rabbits. Dove hunting is outstanding when the pond holds water in September. Here is a good place to teach youngsters to hunt.

Fishing

None

Hunting

Youth/mentor hunting for deer, doves, and pheasants.
This is in Game Management Unit 93.

Watchable Wildlife

Same as hunting

Camping and Facilities

None

General Restrictions

1. Hunting is prohibited, except by youths ages 15 and under and their mentors. Each youth may be accompanied by only one mentor. Mentors must be 18 years old or older, and must comply with hunter education requirements.
2. Discharging firearms or bows is prohibited, except while hunting.
3. Target practice is prohibited, except when authorized by an area wildlife manager.
4. Fires are prohibited.

22. Frenchman Creek SWA

Primary Use: Hunting

Location: Phillips County, 5 miles west of Holyoke

Size: 69 acres

Elevation: 3,800 feet

Division of Wildlife: Area office in Brush, 970-842-6300

Directions: From Holyoke on U.S. 385, go 5 miles west on U.S. 6 and then ½ mile south (left) on County Road 29 to the parking area. Another parking area is located on the opposite end of the property, on County Road 27.

This wildlife area is a narrow strip of land on the prairie with a wide draw and a seasonal pond. Habitat improvements include food plots and shrubbery cover for pheasant. Expect lots of hunters here on opening days of dove and pheasant seasons.

Fishing

None

Hunting

This property is noted for good dove hunting, especially in years when the pond has water in it. Pheasant hunting is best on opening day, or after heavy snows.

Watchable Wildlife

Same as hunting

Camping and Facilities

None

General Restrictions

1. Target practice prohibited, except when authorized by an area wildlife manager.
2. Discharging firearms or bows is prohibited, except while hunting.

23. Holyoke SWA

Primary Use:	Hunting
Location:	Phillips County, 5 miles southwest of Holyoke
Size:	80 acres
Elevation:	3,800 feet
Division of Wildlife:	Area office in Brush, 970-842-6300
Directions:	From Holyoke, go 4 miles south on U.S. 385 and then 4 miles west (right) on County Road 14 to the parking area.

The tall grass that blankets this small patch of prairie affords marginal hunting for pheasant and deer. The only feature here is a wide, shallow draw carved into the otherwise flat landscape.

Fishing

None

Hunting

Pheasant, deer, and rabbit

Watchable Wildlife

Same as hunting

Camping and Facilities

None

General Restrictions

1. Discharging firearms or bows is prohibited, except while hunting.
2. Target practice is prohibited, except when authorized by an area wildlife manager.

24. Stalker Lake SWA

Primary Use:	Fishing and picnicking
Location:	Yuma County, 3 miles west of Wray
Size:	66 acres
Elevation:	3,500 feet
Division of Wildlife:	Area office in Brush, 970-842-6300
Directions:	From Wray on U.S. 385, go 2 miles west on Highway 34 to County Road FF, then ½ mile north (right) to the access road, then ½ mile west (left) to the lake.

The fish hatchery is just over the hill from this small lake near Wray. There is a parklike atmosphere with shady picnic spots and a playground.

Fishing

Stalker Lake held the state record for largemouth bass until recently. The lake, Colorado records notwithstanding, is a fine place for getting youngsters hooked on fishing.

Hunting

None

Watchable Wildlife

None

Camping and Facilities

Camping is prohibited. Facilities include a boat ramp, toilet, picnic shelters, and a playground.

General Restrictions

1. Boating is prohibited, except for crafts propelled by hand, wind, or electric motor.
2. Discharging firearms or bows is prohibited, except while hunting.
3. Target practice prohibited, except when authorized by an area wildlife manager.
4. Hunting is prohibited, except with shotguns and bows.
5. Fires are prohibited.

Bluegill

25. Sandsage SWA

Primary Use:	Hunting
Location:	Yuma County, 5 miles west of Wray
Size:	300 acres
Elevation:	3,500 feet
Division of Wildlife:	Area office in Brush, 970-842-6300
Directions:	From Wray, go 4½ miles west on U.S. 34 to County Road 35, then ½ mile west (left) to County Road CC, and then ½ mile south (left) to the property.

Don't come here looking for sand and sage. All you'll find is a grove of cottonwoods, a flowing creek, fields of food plots for wildlife, a wide draw overgrown with brush, and more cover for small game than you can shake a shotgun at.

Fishing

None

Hunting

The parking areas are filled with Front Range hunters on the opening day of pheasant season. A better time to hunt pheasant and quail is after a heavy snow. Deer hunting is by limited license only. This is in Game Management Unit 101.

Watchable Wildlife

Same as hunting

Camping and Facilities

None

General Restrictions

1. Hunting by shotgun, archery, or muzzle-loader only.
2. Discharging firearms or bows is prohibited, except while hunting.
3. Target practice is prohibited, except when authorized by an area wildlife manager.
4. Fires are prohibited.

26. Simmons Ranch SWA

Primary Use:	Hunting
Location:	Yuma County, Arikaree River, 11 miles southeast of Wray
Size:	2,170 acres
Elevation:	3,600 feet None
Division of Wildlife:	Area office in Brush, 970-842-6300
Directions:	From Wray, go 5 miles south on Highway 385 to County Road 30, turn east (left) and follow the paved road through a series of well-marked turns toward Beecher Island. At County Road 22 (½ mile north of Beecher Island), go 1 mile east (left) to the first parking area, and 2 more miles to the second parking area.

The DOW scored a major coup for hunters and wildlife watchers with the perpetual easement of this large tract of land situated at the confluence of the Arikaree River and Black Wolf Creek, near the Kansas state line.

The Arikaree River is considered the last remaining free-flowing High Plains river in Colorado. It is critical habitat for a diverse community of wildlife, including overlapping populations of eastern and western bird species, and several globally-imperiled species. The plains riparian ecosystem is a mixture of cottonwood forests, shrubland, wet meadows, and other wetlands. The watershed's higher terrain consists of rolling sandsage hills, shortgrass prairie, and finger canyons.

Although the property is still under development, the parking areas are completed and the property is open for limited use.

Fishing

None

Hunting

Deer and turkey hunting are by limited license only in Game Management Unit 102, which includes Sandy Bluffs State Trust Land and the entire Arikaree River drainage, from the town of Cope to the Kansas border.

Sandy Bluffs STL, located 8½ miles due north of Idalia on County Road DD, opens an additional 3,200 acres of the Arikaree to hunters September 1–February 28.

Watchable Wildlife

The Arikaree River drainage is a favorite with birdwatchers. The area is known as a melting pot for eastern and western species. Birds found here include rare curve-billed thrashers and Cassin's sparrows.

Camping and Facilities

Camping is prohibited and there are no facilities. The closest camping is located at Beecher Island Memorial Park, upriver from the SWA.

General Restrictions

1. Property is closed to all use June 1–September 1.
2. Turkey hunting is prohibited in the fall.
3. Spring turkey licenses are available only through the limited-license drawing.
4. Access is by foot only from designated parking areas. There is no access from county roads.
5. Target practice is prohibited, except when authorized by an area wildlife manager.

27. South Republican SWA
(Bonny Reservoir)

Primary Use:	Warm-water fishing and hunting
Location:	Yuma County, South Republican River, 21 miles north of Burlington
Size:	13,140 acres
Elevation:	3,600 feet
Division of Wildlife:	Area office in Colorado Springs, 719-227-5200
Directions:	From Burlington, go 21 miles north on U.S. 385 to County Road 2 on the south side of the South Republican River, or to County Road 3 on the north side. Turn east (right) on either road to reach the reservoir. Turn west (left) on County Road 3 to reach additional river-bottom hunting areas. To reach Hale Ponds, from the south end of the dam go 2 miles east on County Road 3.5 to Road LL, then ½ mile north (left) to Road 4, and then 4½ miles east (right) to the access road.

There is a lot more here than the most popular reservoir on the plains. South Republican SWA is big, beautiful, and poised for a variety of uses other than fishing and waterskiing. Few visitors to the reservoir ever venture below the dam to discover the fishing, camping, hunting, and wildlife observation available at Hale Ponds (pictured above).

Bonny Reservoir State Recreation Area surrounds the eastern portion of the reservoir and requires a state park permit to enter. Facilities include a bait shop, campsites, boat ramps, toilets, trailer dump stations, drinking water, and picnic areas.

Fishing

Bonny Reservoir is noted as a somewhat reliable producer of good fishing for walleye, crappie, wipers, white bass, and catfish. However, as go the rains on the plains, so goes the fishing. In dry years the reservoir is drawn down for irrigation, and fishing suffers.

Walleyes are by far the most sought-after fish at Bonny Reservoir. Walleye enthusiasts come from far and near to drag nightcrawlers across the reservoir's sandy, snag-free bottom. The northeast shoreline is a favorite spot.

What the walleye fanatics are missing is good fishing for channel catfish, white bass, wipers, largemouth bass, and northern pike. The inlet bay is good for catfish in summer and the dam is good for crappie in spring. White bass and wipers are pelagic, more often found in open water.

Hale Ponds has fishing for largemouth bass, crappie, channel catfish, and bluegills.

Hunting

Turkey hunters flock to Bonny in spring, if they draw a limited license for Game Management Units 103 and 109. A large, highly visible population of Rio Grande turkeys roams the woodlands above and below the reservoir, often venturing out onto the surrounding sage hills.

Waterfowl hunting here is some of the best that the eastern plains have to offer. The reservoir and the wetlands by the river provide plenty of opportunities for hunting geese and a variety of ducks. Porter Ponds and Hopper Ponds are part of a chain of small ponds, marshes, and wetlands on the south side of the river above the reservoir. Access to the parking area is via the service road on County Road 2.

North Bay, and the area in front of the dam, are closed to waterfowl hunting from the first Monday in November through the last day in February. The large tract of land below the dam has good walk-in access for pheasant and quail hunting.

Watchable Wildlife

Bobcats, owls, turkeys, American white pelicans, waterfowl, and shorebirds top a long list of wildlife that can be seen around the reservoir and in the riparian habitat beside the river.

Camping and Facilities

Free camping is available at Hale Ponds, and facilities include toilets and picnic shelters. Campsites and full facilities are available in the state park (fee required) at Bonny Reservoir.

General Restrictions

1. Waterfowl hunting is prohibited, as posted by the DOW.
2. Parking for waterfowl hunting is allowed only in designated areas.
3. Boating is prohibited from one-half hour after sunset to one-half hour before sunrise March 15–April 15.
4. Seining minnows is prohibited in the South Republican River in Kit Carson and Yuma Counties. This is to protect species of small fish like orangethroat darters, stonerollers, and other prairie minnows.
5. Field trials are prohibited, except February 1–March 31 and August 1–September 30.

28. Flagler Reservoir SWA

Primary Use:	Warm-water fishing and waterskiing
Location:	Kit Carson County, 5 miles east of Flagler on the north side of Interstate 70
Size:	400 acres
Elevation:	5,000 feet
Division of Wildlife:	Area office in Brush, 970-842-6300
Directions:	From Flagler, go 5 miles east on County Road U to the reservoir.

For people living in eastern Colorado, Flagler Reservoir provides water recreation and a place to cool off under the large cottonwoods that shade the campgrounds.

Fishing

You never know what you might catch in Flagler Reservoir. Through the years it has received plantings of yellow perch, crappies, largemouth bass, channel catfish, northern pike, and tiger muskies.

Hunting

Youth/mentor hunting for deer, small game, and waterfowl

Watchable Wildlife

Same as hunting

Camping and Facilities

Camping is allowed in established areas. Facilities include a concrete boat ramp and toilets.

General Restrictions

1. Boating is prohibited during waterfowl seasons, except craft propelled by hand, wind, or electric motors.
2. Boating is prohibited if it creates a white-water wake. Waterskiing is permitted Sundays and Mondays June 1–August 31.
3. Hunting is prohibited, except for youths and their mentors. See the Small-game Hunting Brochure (available free where hunting licenses are sold) for youth/mentor hunting regulations and seasons.

29. Ramah Reservoir SWA

Primary Use:	Warm-water fishing
Location:	El Paso County, 30 miles southwest of Limon
Size:	245 acres
Elevation:	6,200 feet
Division of Wildlife:	Area office in Colorado Springs, 719-227-5200
Directions:	From the town of Ramah, go 4 miles west on U.S. 24 to the access road. Follow the access road to the left around the western end of the reservoir to the north side and the boat ramp.

This medium-sized reservoir is located on Big Sandy Creek between the towns of Ramah and Calhan on U.S. 24. Access to the property is limited to the north side of the reservoir. The southwest corner of the reservoir is private, as posted.

Fishing

There can be good fishing for catfish and carp, and fair fishing for largemouth bass and northern pike, when the reservoir has water in it.

Hunting

Dove and waterfowl

Watchable Wildlife

Same as hunting

Camping and Facilities

None

General Restrictions

1. Discharge of firearms is prohibited, except shotguns and bows while hunting.
2. Boating prohibited from November 1 through the last day of migratory waterfowl season, except for craft propelled by hand, wind, or electric motor.
3. Water contact activities are prohibited.
4. Fires are prohibited.

Opposite: *Flies for largemouth bass are colorful and gaudy.*

Southeast Colorado

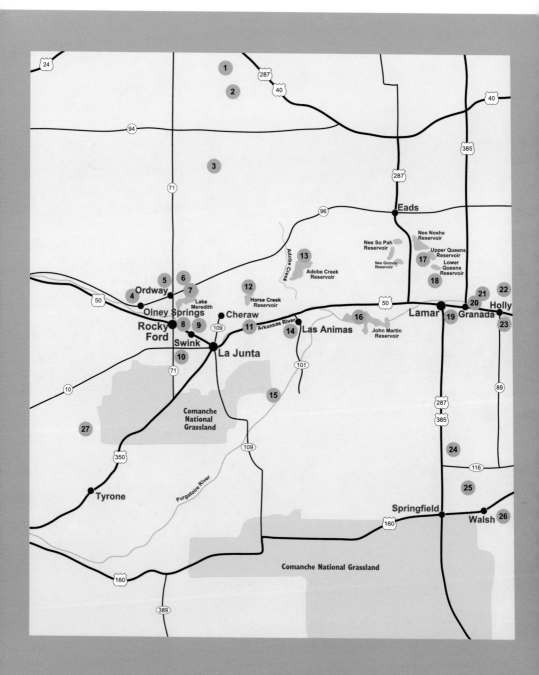

The southeast region encompasses all the land in Colorado east of Interstate 25 and south of Interstate 70. This vast area of the High Plains is completely within the Arkansas River watershed, and water from the river is the lifeblood of the region. The Arkansas River is the main artery in an elaborate system of canals and reservoirs that feed water to crops that otherwise would not grow on the arid plains. Although these reservoirs are used primarily for irrigation and are subject to drastic fluctuations in water level, they have the best warm-water fishing in Colorado. Walleye, saugeye, crappie, largemouth bass, catfish, and wipers top the list of game fish that flourish in these big dishes of water sitting on the High Plains. The majority of the 27 State Wildlife Areas in the southeast region are located at these reservoirs.

Waterfowl hunting is legendary in southeastern Colorado. The river, canals, and many reservoirs attract thousands of migrating ducks and geese to the area. **Queens State Wildlife Area** (see p. 328) is one of the only places in Colorado where goose hunters can hunt from pit blinds located on public land. Each year the DOW installs as many as 80 blinds in the corn and wheat fields located between Nee Noshe and Upper Queens Reservoirs. Late-season duck hunters at **John Martin Reservoir SWA** (see p. 326) often find exceptional big-water hunting for diving ducks like common goldeneyes.

Wildlife Areas in Southeast Colorado

—⑦—	**Interstate Highway**	~~~	**Creek**
—㊿—	**U.S. Highway**	~~~	**River**
—㉛⑧—	**State Highway**		**Lake**
●	**City or Town**		**Wilderness Area**
❶	**State Wildlife Areas**		**National Park**

1. Kinney Lake SWA

To reach the property from U.S. 287 at Hugo (14 miles southeast of Limon), go 12 miles south on County Road 109 to County Road 2J and then 1 mile east (left) to the access road on the left.

Kinney Lake is a 10-acre pond sitting in a shallow draw on the shortgrass prairie south of Hugo, in Lincoln County. A grove of large cottonwoods below the earthen dam provides shade for camping and picnicking. There is fishing for bluegill and bullhead catfish. Catchable-sized rainbow trout are stocked in early spring. There are 320 acres on the property for hunting deer, antelope, small game, and waterfowl. Dove hunting can be very good. Facilities include a boat ramp and an antique toilet. Boating is prohibited on Kinney Lake, except for craft propelled by hand, wind, or electric motor.

2. Hugo SWA

From U.S. 287 at Hugo (14 miles southeast of Limon), go 14 miles south on County Road 109 and then 2½ miles east (left) on County Road 2G to the property.

Camping is allowed and there are two toilets. The access road runs south through the property to the parking areas.

This 2,000-acre wildlife area lies in another wide draw, 2 miles south of **Kinney Lake SWA** (see above). There are three small ponds with a few trees around them, but the landscape overall is typical shortgrass prairie—flat and treeless. The wildlife area is used primarily for hunting doves, ducks, turkeys, deer, and antelope. Turkeys may be hunted with an unlimited license in Game Management Unit 113.

3. Karval Reservoir SWA

Primary Use:	Fishing and hunting
Location:	Lincoln County, 30 miles south of Hugo
Size:	235 acres
Elevation:	5,100 feet
Division of Wildlife:	Area office in Lamar, 719-336-6600
Directions:	From Hugo (14 miles southeast of Limon), go 30 miles south on County Road 109 to the entrance sign and access road on the west (right) side of the road.

Karval Reservoir sits behind a big earthen dam blocking a deep ravine in the shortgrass prairie south of Hugo. The seasonal creek in the ravine is part of the headwaters of Adobe Creek. There are few trees and little shade on the property.

Fishing

Crappie, catfish, bluegill, largemouth bass, and stocked rainbow trout

Hunting

Deer, dove, waterfowl, scaled quail, and rabbit. This is in Game Management Unit 120.

Watchable Wildlife

Same as hunting

Camping and Facilities

Primitive camping is available near the shoreline. Facilities include picnic tables, shade shelters, and a toilet that is closed in winter.

General Restrictions

1. Boating is prohibited, except for craft propelled by hand, wind, or electric motor.
2. Fires are prohibited.

Channel catfish are found throughout Colorado in ponds and reservoirs at lower elevations. They are easily distinguished from bullhead catfish by the deep fork in their tail. These scrappy fighters bite best at night and make excellent table fare.

4. Olney Springs SWA

Primary Use:	Fishing and picnicking
Location:	Crowley County, 2 miles northwest of Olney Springs
Size:	8 acres
Elevation:	4,330 feet
Division of Wildlife:	Area office in Lamar, 719-336-6600
Directions:	From Olney Springs on Highway 96, go 2 miles north on County Road 7 to the access road on the left.

Located near the big canal just north of downtown Olney Springs, this wildlife area is a fine place to sit back and watch a kid match wits with a bluegill, or to set out a tight line for catfish. Local fishermen tell of catching 10-pound channel catfish. The big cottonwood trees that surround the small lakes furnish plenty of shade.

Catfish, bluegill, and largemouth bass

None

None

Camping is permitted. A toilet is located at the parking area.

Discharge of firearms is prohibited.

5. Ordway Reservoir SWA

From Ordway at the intersection of Highways 96 and 71, go 2 miles north on Highway 71.

Half of the banks are lined with concrete at this 12-acre reservoir located in the hills north of Ordway. The other half is a typical dirt bank, with cottonwood trees, shrubs, and weeds. Ordway Reservoir's primary use is fishing for catchable rainbows stocked early in spring. For some real fun, try tangling with one of the reservoir's big carp. The place is loaded with them. Camping is allowed and there are two aging toilets located at the parking area.

6. Lake Henry SWA

From Ordway at the intersection of Highways 96 and 71, go 2 miles east on Highway 96 to County Road 20, and then 1½ miles north (left) to the reservoir.

Lake Henry is a big, nondescript dish of shallow water covering 1,000 acres of the prairie northeast of Ordway. Lake Henry has a reputation for big wipers, but the lake is too shallow to support much of any species except catfish and carp. Catfish, crappie, wipers, and largemouth bass are stocked periodically. Primitive camping is allowed around the shoreline; facilities include toilets and a gravel boat ramp.

7. **Meredith Reservoir SWA**

Primary Use:	Warm-water fishing and waterfowl hunting
Location:	Crowley County, 10 miles north of Rocky Ford
Size:	3,220 acres
Elevation:	4,100 feet
Division of Wildlife:	Area office in Lamar, 719-336-6600
Directions:	From Ordway (intersection of Highways 96 and 71), go 3 miles east on Highway 96 and then 1 mile south on County Road 21 to the boat ramp.

This wildlife area consists of the reservoir, a parcel of land located on the north shore at the boat ramp, and a strip of land circling the entire lake 50 feet above the high water mark. All other land around the reservoir is private property. Meredith is known for its fishing, hunting, waterskiing, sail boarding, bird watching, and other recreational opportunities.

Fishing

Meredith Reservoir is typical of the bigger reservoirs, with a mixture of saugeye, wiper, catfish, bluegill, crappie, and tiger muskie. Crappie fishing is good near the outlet.

Hunting

Waterfowl hunting can be quite good at Meredith, and hunting is permitted from boats prior to the boating closure on November 1. The shallow, cattail-rimmed bay just east of the boat ramp is a good location for hunting from shore. A waterfowl firing line encircling the lake is in effect from November 1 to the last day of the regular waterfowl season. The firing line is marked by signs.

Note to waterfowl hunters: Waterfowl hunting and pass shooting on private property near the reservoir is available by paying a trespass fee at the Junction Café in Ordway.

Watchable Wildlife

Same as hunting

Camping and Facilities

Primitive camping is allowed on the north shore near the boat ramp, and there is a toilet at the parking area.

General Restrictions

Public access to the reservoir is prohibited (except to retrieve downed waterfowl) from November 1 through the last day of migratory waterfowl season.

Saugeye is a walleye/sauger hybrid that looks and tastes like a walleye, but is easier to catch and fights harder than either of its parents. Biologists favor the saugeye because it doesn't migrate downstream out of reservoirs when water is released for irrigation.

8. Rocky Ford SWA

Primary Use:	Hunting
Location:	Otero County, Arkansas River at Rocky Ford
Size:	1,200 acres
Elevation:	4,000 feet
Division of Wildlife:	Area office in Lamar, 719-336-6600
Directions:	From the town of Rocky Ford on U.S. 50, go 2 miles northeast on Highway 266, cross over the river bridge, and turn right on County Road 805. The Rocky Ford tract is ½ mile in and the McClelland tract is 1 mile farther. Both are on the south side of the road.

This wildlife area consists of two tracts of bottomland on the Arkansas River just east of town. The Rocky Ford tract has 550 acres and the McClelland tract has 662. The habitat at both tracts is a mixture of cottonwood trees, willows, alders, open fields, and parched hillsides. The Rocky Ford tract has the most trees and also features a small pond. Most of the farmland on the property is cultivated with food plots and cover vegetation to enhance wildlife and hunting opportunities.

Fishing

None

Hunting

Hunting here is better for ducks and doves than it is for pheasant and quail. Deer and turkey hunting are by limited license only. Duck hunting can be good on the river and the small ponds found on both tracts. The McClelland tract contains about 1 mile of the winding river, and very few trees.

Watchable Wildlife

Same as hunting

Camping and Facilities

Camping is allowed at both tracts. A restroom is located at the Rocky Ford tract.

General Restrictions

Fires are prohibited.

9. Holbrook Reservoir SWA

Primary Use:	Recreation, warm-water fishing
Location:	Otero County, 5 miles northeast of Rocky Ford
Size:	670 acres
Elevation:	4,000 feet
Division of Wildlife:	Area office in Lamar, 719-336-6600
Directions:	From the town of Swink on U.S. 50, go 3 miles north on County Road 24.5, and then 1 mile east (right) on Road FF to the reservoir.

This 500-acre reservoir located in the farming country northeast of Rocky Ford is a popular spot for waterskiing and jetskiing. There are shady campsites under large cottonwood trees, modern restrooms, a concrete boat ramp, and a handicap-fishing pier.

Fishing

Holbrook is managed for the typical mixture of warm-water species—saugeye, wipers, crappie, and channel catfish. Night fishing for catfish can be good.

Hunting

Duck hunting over decoy spreads can be good on the shallow and reedy north shoreline. The fields north of the reservoir have upland hunting for pheasant, quail, and doves.

Watchable Wildlife

Same as hunting

Camping and Facilities

Primitive camping is allowed in established camping areas.
Facilities include a boat ramp and toilets.

Wipers are the sterile offspring produced by crossing white bass and stripers. Some say that the name comes from this powerful hybrid's ability to wipe out fishing tackle. Wipers can be caught at many SWAs located in Regions 6, 7, and 8.

10. Timpas Creek SWA

Primary Use: Small-game hunting

Location: Otero County, 6 miles south of Rocky Ford

Size: 141 acres

Elevation: 4,000 feet

Division of Wildlife: Area office in Lamar, 719-336-6600

Directions: From Rocky Ford on U.S. 50, go 4 miles south on Highway 71 to Highway 10, then 2 miles east (left) to County Road 21, then 1 mile south (right) to County Road Z, and west toward the county landfill.

Timpas Creek SWA has a small lake for warm-water fishing and about 100 acres for hunting small game.

Fishing

Otero Pond has fishing for bass and catfish.

Hunting

Hunting opportunities exist for rabbits, squirrels, pheasant, quail, doves, and waterfowl.

Watchable Wildlife

Same as hunting

Camping and Facilities

Primitive camping, no facilities

General Restrictions

Fires are prohibited.

11. Oxbow SWA

Primary Use:	Hunting
Location:	Otero County, 9 miles east of La Junta
Size:	405 acres
Elevation:	4,000 feet
Division of Wildlife:	Area office in Lamar, 719-336-6600
Directions:	From La Junta, go 9 miles east on U.S. 50 to County Road 36 and ½ mile north (left) to the parking area.

The Arkansas River skirts the north and east boundaries of this property in a series of wide bends. The wildlife area is bounded on the south by U.S. 50 and on the west by Bent's Old Fort National Historical Site. Although relatively small, this property provides public hunting opportunities in an area that is mostly private property. The habitat is a combination of prime riparian and grassy meadows.

Fishing

None

Hunting

In addition to outstanding hunting opportunities for deer and turkey, this area has hunting for bobwhite quail and mourning doves. Deer and turkey hunting are by limited license only. This is in Game Management Unit 125.

Watchable Wildlife

Rio Grande turkey

Camping and Facilities

Camping is prohibited. There are no facilities.

General Restrictions

Access is by foot only from the parking lot.

12. Horse Creek Reservoir SWA
(Timber Lake)

Primary Use:	Fishing
Location:	Otero County, 15 miles north of La Junta
Size:	2,603 acres
Elevation:	4,100 feet
Division of Wildlife:	Area office in Lamar, 719-336-6600
Directions:	From La Junta on U.S. 50, take Highway 109 north 8 miles to the town of Cheraw, then County Road JJ.5 east (right) 2 miles to County Road 33 and north (left) 7 miles to the reservoir.

Timber Lake is a good place to get away from it all. Out here on this remote parcel of prairie there are few roads, few houses, few people, and all the wide-open spaces that the eyes can hold. Although the fishing can be slow, Timber Lake has a way of calling you back.

Caution! Roads to the reservoir turn to gumbo after a rain. Even four-wheel drive will not prevent you from sliding off the road.

Fishing

Fishing is best in spring for the reservoir's channel catfish, wiper, and saugeye. Timber Lake is an irrigation reservoir and the water level is subject to extreme fluctuation. Sometimes the reservoir is dry. Check with the DOW office in Lamar for information about current water levels. Trotlines and jug fishing are allowed.

Hunting

The land around the reservoir is private property, and hunting is by landowner permission only. Waterfowl hunters might find it worth the effort to obtain permission, as the lake consistently harbors good numbers of ducks and geese in December and January.

Watchable Wildlife

Antelope, shorebirds, and waterfowl

Camping and Facilities

There are several good campsites, a restroom, and a concrete boat ramp located on the north shore.

General Restrictions

Public access is limited to fishing or boating only.

13. Adobe Creek Reservoir SWA
(Blue Lake)

Primary Use:	Warm-water fishing and waterfowl hunting
Location:	Bent and Kiowa Counties, 10 miles north of Las Animas
Size:	5,000 acres
Elevation:	4,128 feet
Division of Wildlife:	Area office in Lamar, 719-336-6600
Directions:	From Las Animas on U.S. 50, go 11 miles north on County Road 10 to the reservoir.

Typical of all Eastern Plains reservoirs, Adobe Creek is a nearly featureless saucer of water sitting on the open prairie. Trees are scarce, with only a few patches of cottonwoods growing on the north and west shores. Miles of unbroken sandy shorelines rim the 5,000-acre reservoir, and the bottom of the lake has little in the way of underwater structures that attract fish. This means that fish can be difficult to locate, especially pelagic species like wipers that roam widely in open water.

Adobe Creek is the primary reservoir on the Fort Lyon Ditch and is usually filled with water in the spring. May and June are the best months for catching crappie, wiper, and saugeye, when they move into the shallows to feed on gizzard shad.

Fishing

Although best known for its 15-inch crappie, the reservoir also offers excellent fishing for white bass—some say it's the best lake in Colorado for large ones. Also present are good numbers of channel catfish and blue catfish. Saugeye and wiper populations are less stable because of fluctuations in the water level.

Fishing Tip: In summer, look for schools of wipers feeding furiously at sunrise and sunset in the shallows on the windy side of the lake.

Hunting

There is good dove hunting at the reservoir, and good antelope hunting on the 14,000-acre Blue Lake State Trust Lands adjoining the south boundary of the SWA. Waterfowl hunting is marginal most of the season, but can be fair for local ducks during the early season. Waterfowl hunting is limited to the area outside the firing line as marked by signs. This is in Game Management Unit 125.

Watchable Wildlife

Least terns and piping plovers nest on the island in the center of the lake. The terns are an endangered species and the plovers are listed as threatened. The island is closed to access during nesting in April and May.

Camping and Facilities

Primitive camping is available on the east, south, and west sides of the reservoir. Parking areas, modern restrooms, and two concrete boat ramps are located on the east shore. There also is a low-water boat ramp located west of the main boat ramps.

General Restrictions

Public access to the reservoir is prohibited from November 1 through the last day of waterfowl season, except to retrieve downed waterfowl.

Crappies are among the most sought-after fish on the plains, and most of the reservoirs in the southeast region have good populations. Crappies are structure fish and are usually found around submerged trees and rocky drop-offs. Crappie fishing peaks in early spring when they congregate in shallow water to spawn and feed.

14. Purgatoire River SWA

Primary Use:	Hunting
Location:	Bent County, 2 miles south of Las Animas on the north side of the Purgatoire River
Size:	960 acres
Elevation:	4,000 feet
Division of Wildlife:	Area office in Lamar, 719-336-6600
Directions:	From Las Animas on U.S. 50, go 1 mile south on Highway 101 to County Road 10, and then 1 mile southwest to the property.

Situated in the bottomlands along the Purgatoire River south of Las Animas, this wildlife area opens a fair parcel of land for public hunting. A pond and a grove of mature cottonwood trees on the north end of the property are excellent for dove hunting.

Fishing

None

Hunting

Dove, turkey, bobwhite quail, scaled quail, and deer are found here in limited numbers. Quail hunting is pretty good at the beginning of quail season, but the coveys move across the river onto private land after they have been shot at a few times. You may still hunt turkeys here with an unlimited license.

Watchable Wildlife

Same as hunting

Camping and Facilities

None

General Restrictions

Access is by foot only from the parking areas.

Rio Grande turkeys are widely distributed in the Arkansas valley.

15. Setchfield SWA

Primary Use:	Hunting
Location:	Bent County, 20 miles south of Las Animas
Size:	2,438 acres
Elevation:	4,800 feet
Division of Wildlife:	Area office in Lamar, 719-336-6600
Directions:	From Las Animas on U.S. 50, go 16 miles south on Highway 101 to County Road P, then 1 mile west (right) to County Road 11, and then 6 miles south (left) on Road 11, which becomes County Road 10 at the wildlife area.

Prairie grasses, sagebrush, and cactus dominate the landscape in this wide and mostly dry valley. Muddy Creek trickles a ribbon of water through the property, except during droughts. This remote location is the least visited of all the wildlife areas. Dust devils rise from the valley floor and dance about on hot summer days. Similar public lands in the area may be found at Higbee Canyon State Trust Lands about 15 miles west.

Fishing

None

Hunting

Marginal hunting for scaled quail and bobwhite quail

Watchable Wildlife

Raptors

Camping and Facilities

None

General Restrictions

Fires are prohibited.

16. John Martin Reservoir SWA

Primary Use:	Warm-water fishing
Location:	Bent County, Arkansas River, 16 miles east of Las Animas
Size:	22,325 acres
Elevation:	3,850 feet
Division of Wildlife:	Area office in Lamar, 719-336-6600
Directions:	From Las Animas, go 16 miles east on U.S. 50 to County Road 24 at Hasty and then 2 miles south (right) to the dam and the main boat ramp. To reach the popular fishing spots on the south shore and the railroad trestle over Rule Creek Cove, drive over the dam and follow the unimproved roads west along the shoreline. *Note:* Please stay on established roads. Much of the scaled quail habitat on the south side of the reservoir has been damaged by off-road vehicles.

To reach the County Road 19 boat ramp, from Las Animas go 10 miles east on U.S. 50 to County Road 19 and then 1 mile south (right) to the concrete ramp, parking lot, and toilet.

The upper lake and inlet are accessed from county roads on both the north and south sides of the reservoir.

John Martin Reservoir is the largest body of water on the plains, covering more than 5,000 surface acres of water at full pool. The reservoir and the surrounding wildlife area are a focal point of fishing, hunting, bird watching, and recreation in southeastern Colorado. Although John Martin is soon to become Colorado's newest state park, the park boundaries will enclose only the eastern half of the reservoir. The remainder of the reservoir, the inlet, the river, and adjacent lands will remain a State Wildlife Area, where hunting is allowed and entrance is free. It appears that the small boat ramp located on County Road 19 will remain open for fishing boats and not require a Parks Pass.

Fishing

This is a remarkable fishery known for its outstanding crappie and largemouth bass fishing. It has good fishing for saugeyes and wipers, and is one of the top lakes in Colorado for channel and blue catfish. Crappie and saugeye fishing peaks in late spring when the fish migrate to shallow water to feed on gizzard shad in the flooded tamarack trees. Good fishing for wipers usually begins in May and can last all summer. Dawn and dusk are the best times to find schools of wipers feeding in shallow flats or chasing schools of shad to the surface. Catfishing gets good in April and stays good all summer.

Fishing tip: The DOW has installed habitat structures for crappie and other fish in several locations around the lake. These structures are marked with orange/white structure buoys.

Hunting

This expansive body of water attracts great numbers of migratory ducks later in the hunting season. Hunting steadily improves November–January. Late season arrivals include diving ducks like goldeneyes and buffleheads. Divers are big-water ducks and best hunted from boat blinds.

For scaled quail, hunt the grassy lands south of the reservoir. There is hunting for deer, small game, and dove. This is in Game Management Unit 146.

Watchable Wildlife

Piping plover, least tern, bald eagles, and American white pelicans

Camping and Facilities

Campsites are available at the Lake Hasty Campground below the dam. Call 1-877-444-6777 for reservations. There are two concrete boat ramps and modern restrooms located on the north side of the dam. A smaller boat ramp is located 2½ miles farther west on the north shore and is accessed by County Road 19 from U.S. 50.

General Restrictions

1. Public access is prohibited as posted from November 1 through the last day of waterfowl season, except to retrieve downed birds.
2. Field trials are prohibited, except February 1–March 31 and August 1–September 30.
3. Hunting is prohibited on U.S. Corps of Engineers property.
4. Public access to the south shore may be prohibited May–October for plover and tern nesting.

17. Queens SWA

Primary Use:	Warm-water fishing and waterfowl hunting
Location:	Kiowa County, 20 miles north of Lamar
Size:	4,426 acres
Elevation:	3,800 feet
Division of Wildlife:	Area office in Lamar, 719-336-6600
Directions:	From Eads, go 15 miles south on U.S. 287 to County Road E, then 1 mile east (left) to Nee Noshe, Upper Queens, and Lower Queens Reservoirs, and 2 miles to the hunter's check station. To reach the public ramp at Nee Gronda, turn west on County Road C. From Lamar, go 18 miles west and north on U.S. 287 to the property.

The Great Plains Reservoirs, Nee Noshe, Nee Gronda, Nee So Pah, and Upper and Lower Queens, are a chain of irrigation reservoirs fed by a canal from the Arkansas River. These sparkling pools of blue water sit on the prairie north of Lamar and are the crown jewels of Queens State Wildlife Area. The reservoirs, their wooded shorelines, and the surrounding prairie and farmlands are excellent habitat for a variety of wildlife.

Fishing

Sometimes fantastic and sometimes dreadfully slow, the fishing in these big dishes of water can be puzzling. Fishing normally peaks in May and June when schools of saugeyes and wipers congregate in the shallows to feed on gizzard shad, and when largemouth bass and crappie move into shallow water in the flooded tamarack trees. Sometimes good fishing lasts all summer and peaks again in October.

All of the reservoirs have a mixture of saugeye, wiper, crappie, largemouth bass, white bass, and catfish.

Hunting

Waterfowl hunting can be outstanding on and around these reservoirs. Migratory ducks and geese use the reservoirs as resting areas, flying out to feed in the grain fields and returning to roost. Some ducks and geese remain here all winter, depending on the availability of food. Hunting from boats is allowed on Upper and Lower Queens.

Goose hunting pits at the wildlife area are available on a first-come, first-served basis. Check-in time is 5 a.m.–6 a.m. at the check station. The pits, which are dug and maintained by the DOW, are located in the corn and wheat fields south of Nee Noshe and west of Upper Queens.

This area is known to have good dove hunting, too.

Watchable Wildlife

All of these reservoirs offer excellent opportunities for watching shorebirds, snow geese, and a variety of ducks. Mud Lake (the shallow lake between Nee Gronda and Nee Noshe Reservoirs) is especially good for viewing the endangered least tern and the threatened piping plover.

Camping and Facilities

At Nee Noshe, there are plenty of primitive campsites around the shoreline. Toilets are located near the boat ramps. The north boat ramp has been improved and a new toilet was installed. This ramp receives a lot less use than the south ramp.

At Nee Gronda, the public boat ramp located on the southeast side of the reservoir is unimproved and launching a boat can be difficult, especially when the water level is low. There is a concrete ramp, campsites with electricity, showers, and a small store located on the north shore at Cottonwood Park Marina. Follow the signs from U.S. 287.

General Restrictions

1. Boating is prohibited in the channel between Upper and Lower Queens Reservoirs in a manner that creates a white-water wake.
2. On Upper Queens (including the channel), Nee Noshe, and Nee Gronda Reservoirs:
   a. All hunters must check in and out at the check station when it is open.
   b. Public access is prohibited as posted from November 1 through the last day of the migratory waterfowl season, except to retrieve downed waterfowl.
3. On Lower Queens Reservoir:
   a. Boating is prohibited in a manner that creates a white-water wake, from the opening of migratory waterfowl season through December 1.
   b. All hunters must check in and check out when the check station is open.
   c. Public access is prohibited as posted from December 1 through the last day of the migratory waterfowl season, except to retrieve downed waterfowl.

18. Thurston Reservoir SWA

Primary Use:	Fishing, hunting, and bird watching
Location:	Prowers County, 8 miles north of Lamar
Size:	173 acres
Elevation:	4,000 feet
Division of Wildlife:	Area office in Lamar, 719-336-6600
Directions:	From Lamar U.S. 50, go 8 miles north on Highway 196 to County Road TT, then 1 mile west (left) to County Road 7, and then ½ mile north (right) to the reservoir.

What this shallow reservoir lacks in fishing and hunting, it makes up for in excellent bird-watching. It is a popular spot for viewing migrating sandhill cranes.

Fishing

Fishing is reported as marginal for catfish, wipers, saugeye, and tiger muskies.

Hunting

Waterfowl

Watchable Wildlife

Sandhill cranes, shorebirds, and waterfowl

Camping and Facilities

Camping is prohibited. Facilities include a concrete boat ramp and toilets.

General Restrictions

Boating is prohibited in a manner that creates a white-water wake, from November 1 through the last day of the migratory waterfowl season.

19. Mike Higbee SWA

Primary Use:	Archery and rifle ranges
Location:	Prowers County, 5 miles east of Lamar
Size:	876 acres
Elevation:	3,400 feet
Division of Wildlife:	Area office in Lamar, 719-336-6600
Directions:	From Lamar, go 4 miles east on U.S. 50 to the signs at the access road on the right.

This property is located in the dry hills east of Lamar and south of the Arkansas River. DOW maintenance barns are located here. There is a small pond on the property that is a good place to take kids fishing. The abundant bluegill and bullheads are willing players and will keep the kids entertained. An archery range is located on the west side of the property and a rifle range is on the east side.

Fishing

Sunfish and bullhead catfish

Hunting

Doves and cottontail rabbits

Watchable Wildlife

Same as hunting

Camping and Facilities

None

20. X-Y Ranch SWA

Primary Use:	Hunting
Location:	Prowers County, Arkansas River, 1 mile east of Granada
Size:	3,672 acres
Elevation:	3,400 feet
Division of Wildlife:	Area office in Lamar, 719-336-6600
Directions:	**Parking Area 1:** From Granada on U.S. 50, go north on U.S. 385 to the edge of town and turn east (right) on the dirt road beside Wolf Creek Canal. Follow the drainage canal about 1½ miles to the parking area.

Parking Area 2: From Granada, go north on U.S. 385 to the edge of town and turn east (right) on the dirt road beside Wolf Creek Canal. Follow the canal about 1½ miles, and turn east (right) on the two-track road. Follow the two-track about 1 mile to the parking area located under the power lines.

Parking Area 3: From Granada, go ½ block north and turn east (right) on the first road north of the railroad and go 1½ miles to the parking area.

Parking Area 4: From Granada, go 3½ miles east on U.S. 50 to County Road 28 and then north (left) 1 mile to the parking area.

Parking Area 5: From Granada, go 3½ miles east on U.S. 50 to County Road 28, then south (right) less than ½ mile to the south side of the railroad, and then 1 mile east (left) to the parking area.

A recent addition to wildlife areas on the Arkansas River, X-Y Ranch opens nearly 4,000 acres for hunting in an area where public access is difficult to come by. The property will be under development for several years with tree plantings and wetland projects, spearheaded by Ducks Unlimited.

Fishing

None

Hunting

Hunting opportunities on the ranch include waterfowl, small game, and deer. This is in Game Management Unit 127 north of the Arkansas River, and Game Management Unit 132 south of the river.

Watchable Wildlife

Same as hunting

Camping and Facilities

None

General Restrictions

1. Closed to the public one hour after sunset until one hour before sunrise.
2. Motor vehicles restricted to access roads. Parking is in designated areas only.

21. Deadman SWA

From Granada, go 2½ miles north on U.S. 385 to County Road JJ, then 2½ miles east (right) to County Road 27, and south (right) ½ mile to the parking area.

Deadman SWA is a 500-acre parcel of land lying on the north side the Arkansas River, 3 miles northeast of Granada. There is fair hunting for waterfowl and marginal hunting for small game on Buffalo Canal.

22. Red Dog SWA

From Holly on U.S. 50, go 3 miles north on County Road 35 to County Road JJ and then 2 miles east (right) to the intersection of County Roads JJ and 37. Park at the intersection.

The DOW acquired this flat, treeless 500-acre tract of shortgrass prairie 5 miles northeast of Holly for water rights to offset evaporation in the High Plains reservoirs. Pheasant hunting can be good here some years.

23. Arkansas River SWA

Primary Use:	Hunting
Location:	Prowers County, Arkansas River, 4 miles east of Holly
Size:	98 acres
Elevation:	3,400 feet
Division of Wildlife:	Area office in Lamar, 719-336-6600
Directions:	From Holly, go 4 miles east on U.S. 50 to County Road 39, then 1 mile south (right) across the railroad tracks, past the ranch house, over the irrigation canal, and then west (right) ½ mile on the two-track road to the parking areas.

This property is targeted for disposal as an SWA because of its poor access and small size. Nevertheless, it contains a short stretch of the river and has potential as a good out-of-the-way duck hunting spot.

Fishing

Catfish in the Arkansas River

Hunting

Duck hunting on the river is the primary use, although there are a few pheasant and quail here.

Watchable Wildlife

Same as hunting

Camping and Facilities

Camping is allowed. There are no facilities.

General Restrictions

Seining is prohibited.

Two Buttes Reservoir SWA

Primary Use:	Recreation, fishing, and hunting
Location:	Prowers and Baca Counties, 40 miles southeast of Lamar
Size:	6,793 acres
Elevation:	4,400 feet
Division of Wildlife:	Area office in Lamar, 719-336-6600
Directions:	From Lamar go 37 miles south on U.S. 287 to County Road B.5, then 3 miles east (Left) to the reservoir. Or from Springfield, go 18 miles north on U.S. 287 to County Road B.5, then 3 miles east (right) to the reservoir.

Two Buttes Reservoir sits in a narrow canyon just south of the landmark buttes. The buttes are the tallest things on the prairie and can be seen for miles. Two Buttes Reservoir is troubled by a split personality. Depending on the amount of local rainfall, it can be either a scenic canyon reservoir filled with sparkling blue water, or a hot and dry crack in the sun-baked prairie.

Fishing

The fishing depends entirely on the amount of rainfall, and the reservoir often is extremely low or even dry. When filled, is has a surface area of about 1,500 acres and a depth of 40 feet at the dam. When there is sufficient water, warm-water fish are stocked in the spring. Fishing is more consistent in the Black Hole Ponds located immediately below the dam. The ponds are deep plunge pools that also are ideal for swimming and diving, and there are several campsites in the tall cottonwood trees. Mosquitoes are ravenous in the Black Hole.

Hunting

There is a lot of land here for hunting deer, turkey, and quail. Duck hunting can be good when the reservoir holds enough water to flood the inlet bay. Deer and turkey hunting is by limited license only in Game Management Units 132 and 139.

Watchable Wildlife

Bald eagles and golden eagles are occasional visitors. Rattlesnakes, buzzards, mockingbirds, and herons are regulars.

Camping and Facilities

Primitive campsites, drinking water, toilets, boat ramps, picnic shelters, and an RV dump station are located on the north and south sides of the reservoir. And there is a rifle range for target practice. Bring your own shade; trees around the lake are short and sparse.

General Restrictions

Public access is prohibited November 1 through the end of the migratory waterfowl season, except to retrieve downed waterfowl.

25. Turk's Pond SWA

Primary Use:	Fishing
Location:	Baca County, 20 miles northeast of Springfield
Size:	200 acres
Elevation:	4,400 feet
Division of Wildlife:	Area office in Lamar, 719-336-6600
Directions:	From Springfield, go 2 miles north on U.S. 287 to County Road HH, then 14 miles east (right) to County Road 39, and then 3 miles north (left) to the access road.

Outstanding fishing attracts visitors to this remote corner of the plains. Turk's Pond tops the list for out-of-the-way bass fishing holes.

Fishing

Turk's Pond just might have the best largemouth bass fishing in Colorado. The weedy inlet, the rock-rubble dam, and the shallow shorelines all provide good habitat for bass. There also is good fishing for wipers, crappie, and catfish.

Hunting

Hunting is prohibited.

Watchable Wildlife

Waterfowl and shorebirds

Camping and Facilities

Overnight camping is prohibited. The nearest camping is 20 miles away at **Two Buttes SWA** (see p. 336). Facilities include a boat ramp, toilets, and picnic shelters.

General Restrictions

1. Closed to hunting (see the Waterfowl Regulations Brochure about closures).
2. Boating is prohibited, except for craft propelled by hand, wind, or electric motor.
3. Public access is prohibited on the reservoir from November 1 through the end of the migratory waterfowl season.

Anglers delight in the tail-walking antics of largemouth bass.

26. Burchfield SWA

Primary Use:	Hunting
Location:	Baca County, 30 miles east of Springfield
Size:	178 acres
Elevation:	4,000 feet
Division of Wildlife:	Area office in Lamar, 719-336-6600
Directions:	From the town of Walsh, located 20 miles east of Springfield on U.S. 160, go 11 miles east on County Road DD to the property.

This property sits in a patch of dense woods and underbrush surrounded by a sea of corn and wheat. Since it contains the only significant amount of cover within miles, it attracts a lot of wildlife. There was once a small lake here, but now there is only a small creek. There is a nice campsite on the hill behind the property sign.

Fishing

None

Hunting

White-tailed deer, mule deer, bobwhite quail, pheasant, and dove can be found here. This is in Game Management Unit 139.

Watchable Wildlife

Same as hunting

Camping and Facilities

Several primitive campsites are scattered around the perimeter.
There are no facilities.

27. Apishapa SWA

Primary Use:	Hunting
Location:	Las Animas County, 30 miles east of Walsenburg
Size:	8,000 acres
Elevation:	5,400 feet
Division of Wildlife:	Area office in Pueblo, 719-561-5300
Directions:	From Walsenburg, go 18½ miles east on Highway 10 to County Road 77, then 7 miles south (right) to County Road 90, then 11 miles east (left) to the property. There is access from the south on county roads running north from Highway 350 at Tyrone. All the turns from Tyrone to the property are well marked with DOW signs.

This remote wildlife area covers a vast expanse of weathered landscape on the High Plains east of Walsenburg. This is a land punished by time. The Apishapa River and its tributaries have been at work here for thousands of years, carving dramatic red-rock canyons into an otherwise flat landscape. Rock-rimmed, steep-sided, and deep, Apishapa Canyon is the main artery in a network of ravines, arroyos, gulches, and gullies.

The terrain at the top is gently rolling and sparsely studded with piñon and juniper, quite different from the bottom of the canyon where the river supports greener vegetation. Even in dry years, the Apishapa River is a source of water for wildlife.

Fishing

None

Hunting

Mule deer, pronghorn antelope, turkey, scaled quail, and bighorn sheep are all common in the area. Big-game and turkey hunting is by limited license in Game Management Units 133 and 134. You may not hunt turkeys here with an over-the-counter license. This area is in Bighorn Sheep Unit S38 and only two ram-only archery licenses are issued by drawing. Only Colorado residents may apply in the sheep drawing.

Additional public hunting is available on the adjacent 1,880-acre Apishapa North State Trust Lands. The parking lot for the STL is located in the northeast corner of the SWA. Access into the STL is by foot or horseback only.

Watchable Wildlife

Same as hunting

Camping and Facilities

There are no restrictions on camping, but please use established campsites. There are no facilities.

General Restrictions

Vehicles are not allowed off designated roads, or past parking lots when the ground is wet.

The open plains provide safety as well as habitat for the fleet-footed pronghorn (antelope), the fastest animal in North America.

Index

NOTE: Citations followed by the letter "p" denote photos; citations followed by the letter "m" denote maps.